PREPARATORY COURSE FOR THE ASWB BACHELORS LEVEL EXAM

Assessment

**Association for Advanced Training
in the Behavioral Sciences**
212 W. Ironwood Drive, Suite D #168 Coeur d'Alene, ID 83814
(800) 472-1931

© Association for Advanced Training in the Behavioral Sciences. All rights reserved. No part of these materials may be reproduced in any form, or by any means, mechanical or electronic, including photocopying, without the written permission of the publisher. To reproduce or adapt, in whole or in part, any portion of these materials is not only a violation of copyright law, but is unethical and unprofessional. As a condition of your acceptance of these materials, you agree not to reproduce or adapt them in any manner or license others to do so. The unauthorized resale of these materials is prohibited. The Association for Advanced Training in the Behavioral Sciences accepts the responsibility of protecting not only its own interests, but to protect the interests of its authors and to maintain and vigorously enforce all copyrights on its material. Your cooperation in complying with the copyright law is appreciated.

BACHELORS LEVEL

ASSESSMENT

Table of Contents

Chapter Introduction 1
Assessment in Practice with Clients 1
I. Overview of Assessment in Practice with Clients 2
II. Issues and Areas Explored in Assessment 7
    A. The Presenting Problem 7
    B. Unmet Needs 10
    C. History of the Problem 10
    D. Coping Effort and Coping Skills 14
    E. Other Issues Affecting Functioning 14
    F. Biophysical Functioning 15
    G. Emotional Functioning 19
    H. Cognitive/Perceptual Functioning 21
    I. Mental Disorders (Psychiatric Symptoms) 24
    J. Personality and Ego Functions 25
    K. Behavioral Functioning 27
    L. Social Functioning 28
    M. Environmental Systems 30
    N. Motivation, Resistance, and Ambivalence to Change 32
    O. The Need for External Resources 34
    P. Culture and Social Class 34

III. Assessment Methods and Techniques 37
    A. Client Interviews 37
    B. Obtaining Information From Collateral Sources 38
    C. Observation of Interactions 40
    D. Home Visits 40
    E. Clinical Tools for Understanding the Client and Her Situation . 41
    F. Behavioral Assessments 43
    G. Mental Status Exam 44
    H. Structured and Semistructured Diagnostic Interviews 48
    I. Psychological Testing 48

Assessment
Table of Contents

    J. Computer-Assisted Assessment 56
    K. Client-Focused Measures 56

IV. Assessment of Families and Children **58**
    A. Assessment of Risks in a Family 58
    B. Family System Assessment 58
    C. Assessment of Children 61

V. Social Histories and Social Assessment Reports **66**

VI. Diagnosis **68**

VII. DSM-5 Mental Disorders and Conditions **73**
    A. Neurodevelopmental Disorders 73
    B. Schizophrenia Spectrum and Other Psychotic Disorders 79
    C. Bipolar and Related Disorders 84
    D. Depressive Disorders 86
    E. Anxiety Disorders 91
    F. Obsessive-Compulsive and Related Disorders 95
    G. Trauma- and Stressor-Related Disorders 96
    H. Dissociative Disorders 99
    I. Somatic Symptom and Related Disorders 100
    J. Feeding and Eating Disorders 103
    K. Elimination Disorders 106
    L. Sleep-Wake Disorders 107
    M. Sexual Dysfunctions 108
    N. Gender Dysphoria 109
    O. Disruptive, Impulse-Control, and Conduct Disorders 110
    P. Substance-Related and Addictive Disorders 114
    Q. Neurocognitive Disorders 118
    R. Personality Disorders 121
    S. Paraphilic Disorders 128
    T. Other Conditions That May be a Focus of Clinical Attention 130

VIII. Understanding and Assessing Addictive Behaviors **134**
    A. Dependence, Tolerance, and Withdrawal 134
    B. Etiology and Risk Factors for Addiction 134
    C. Consequences of Drug Addiction 139
    D. Assessment of Substance Use Disorders 140
    E. Addiction and the Family System 142
    F. Relapse 143
    G. Effects of MDMA and Methamphetamine 144
    H. Blood Alcohol Level 144
    I. Behavioral Addiction 145

IX. Dynamics, Indicators, and Assessment of Abuse and Neglect **146**

    A. Child Abuse and Neglect 146
    B. Spousal/Partner Abuse 156
    C. Elder Abuse 159

X. Identifying the Needed Level of Care 161

XI. Organizing Assessment Data and Formulating the Problem 165

Assessment in Practice with Client Systems 169

XII. Initiating Macro Change – Understanding the Problem, Population, and Arena .. 171

Appendix I: Descriptions of Common Medical Disorders and Diseases 178

Appendix II: Psychoactive Drugs and Their Uses and Side-Effects 185

BACHELORS LEVEL

ASSESSMENT IN PRACTICE WITH CLIENTS

Chapter Introduction

NOTE: The use of pronouns is extensive in our study material. To avoid cumbersome phrasing and simplify your reading, we use primarily masculine pronouns in some chapters and primarily feminine pronouns in others.

The first major division of this chapter (including Sections I through XI) covers Assessment in Practice with Clients. Practice with Clients refers to social work activities involving frequent face-to-face interaction with client(s). Treatment goals are reached through personal contact and direct influence with clients. Examples of direct service activities include individual, family, and couples psychotherapy and counseling; group treatment; referral work; case management; and advocacy.

The second major division of this chapter (Section XII) covers Assessment in Practice with Client Systems. Practice with Client Systems includes social work activities undertaken to improve the effectiveness and efficiency of service provision and bring about changes in policies, programs, or budgets. Indirect practice activities are usually performed with a committee, coalition, or other group and do not involve personal contact with clients. Activities associated with indirect practice include policy development, program planning, program evaluation, administration, and intervention with communities.

Two levels of social work intervention – mezzo and micro – are forms of direct practice, while the third level – macro – is associated with indirect practice. At the mezzo and micro levels, interventions are used to benefit an individual, family, or small group. Mezzo practice typically takes place with small groups and families and emphasizes facilitating communication, providing education, and bringing people together. Micro practice is usually performed on a case-by-case basis or in a clinical setting and involves using technical skills to help resolve the psychosocial problems experienced by individuals, families, or small groups.

At the macro level, interventions are intended to benefit relatively large groups (i.e., a specific client population, residents of a community, or personnel at an agency). Macro practice activities are designed to improve either the quality of life for clients or communities or the quality of work-life for employees at an organization. In the latter case, the goal is to help employees provide the best possible services to clients or communities (Netting et al., 2004).

Finally, if a micro service worker discovers that the causal factors involved in a client's problem reside in the practices or policies of an organization or community, he may initiate an episode of macro change by helping to identify the systems that need to change and the type of change needed.

Assessment in Practice with Clients

I. Overview of Assessment in Practice with Clients

In direct practice, assessment is used to understand a client and her situation, identify her motivation and goals, and assess her capacity and opportunity to change. When conducting an assessment, you collect relevant data from a variety of sources about all dimensions of the client's problem and their interaction and then evaluate and integrate the data to develop an accurate description of the client, the systems that play a significant role in her problem, and the resources that need to be mobilized. You and the client then use this description to formulate the problem(s) to be worked on and the intervention plan.

1. The Multidimensional Nature of Assessment: Many client problems that present in a similar way differ with regard to the processes that produce or reinforce them, and, therefore, an important goal of assessment is developing an understanding of the various factors that are causing and maintaining a client's problem. Most social workers adopt a **biopsychosocial approach** to assessment. This approach offers a multidimensional framework that reminds social workers to consider and examine the full range of possible causes and explanations of a client's functioning and to integrate information and theory from the biophysical, psychological, and social dimensions of human behavior. In addition, when working to identify potential causal factors, social workers consider precipitants (activating situations) to the problem, predisposing and risk factors for the problem, and factors that are maintaining the problem.

A unique aspect of assessment in social work is its focus on areas where a client and her environment intersect and how each one influences the other. In other words, social workers seek to understand their clients' situations from a **person-in-environment framework**, a structure that views the client as part of an environmental system and emphasizes the reciprocal (back and forth) relationships and other influences between the client and her physical and social environment (Barker, 2003). Understanding this enables the social worker to focus the intervention on finding an appropriate match between the client and her environment.

2. The Phases of Assessment:

a. Data Collection: Assessment begins with data collection when you interview the client to gather detailed information from her about the presenting problem, concern, or request. Data collection initiates a mutual effort with the client to identify the problem(s) to be addressed during intervention. This process starts when you ask the client to tell you why she has come in. Your job is then to listen to the client's unique report, ask questions to get information that will help clarify the cause and context of her problem, and observe her nonverbal communications (affect, speech, behavior, etc.). Other useful information may be obtained by comparing what the client reports to what you observe and to information you've received from a referral source.

In addition to interviewing the client to learn her view of her problem and situation, you also gather factual information from other involved people and sometimes from other sources such as relevant life records. You also seek to identify perceptions and beliefs about the situation held by the client and significant people. These people may include the client's family members, teachers, employers, and the referring agency or person (court, school, spouse, etc.).

It's important to avoid jumping to conclusions about the nature or causes of the client's problem at this time because you still need to test your initial impressions by completing a thorough assessment.

b. Organizing and Studying the Data: The second phase of assessment involves organizing and studying the raw data you've collected in an effort to understand the client's situation and establish a basis for intervention planning. You combine this raw data with your professional knowledge base to develop hypotheses about the nature and causes of the client's problem and what can be done to resolve it. Because you may need to modify your hypotheses if new information emerges, anything you say at this time to a client about your view of her problem or situation should be stated in tentative terms.

After studying the data to identify significant problem areas, you then evaluate relevant aspects of the client's functioning. This process should include identifying the client's personal strengths and deficiencies and those in her environment.

3. The "Presenting Problem": The "presenting problem" consists of the perceived symptoms and overt issues or difficulties that, according to the client, constitute the problem for which she has sought help. The presenting problem (or presenting concern or request) includes any statements made by the client concerning her reason for coming in. Examples can include, "I have trouble forming relationships with men," "I'm so depressed I can't stand it anymore," "My husband and I can't stop fighting," or "I can't afford to feed my family anymore." The presenting problem may also include statements from other individuals, such as the client's family members, who recognize that the client needs help.

4. Questions Explored in a Problem Assessment: Problem assessment involves exploring a wide range of factors that may be relevant to a client's presenting problem, concern, or request including those on the list that appears below (Hepworth et al., 2006). These factors comprise a **problem system** – i.e., the client, other people, and elements in the environment that interact to produce and/or maintain the client's problem situation. You don't need to explore all of these factors with every client. Instead, this list reflects the questions that are important to consider when accumulating data for a **biopsychosocial history** in order to ensure that you don't overlook a significant factor when exploring and attempting to understand a client's problem.

- What are the client's problems and concerns as she perceives them?
- Are there any current or impending legal mandates relevant to the situation?
- Are there any serious health or safety issues that need attention?
- What are the specific signs and symptoms of the problem? A client may present with a variety of indicators suggesting an emotional, behavioral, or social-functioning problem or underlying mental or physical disorder. A "sign" is an objective manifestation of the problem or disorder. It is something observed by you rather than reported by the client.

A "symptom" is a subjective manifestation of the problem or disorder. It is something reported by the client rather than only observed by you.

- What individuals and/or systems are involved in the problem? Examples of systems with which clients commonly engage in transactions include the family, extended family, or kinship network; the social network (e.g., friends, neighbors, coworkers, religious leaders and associates, club members, and cultural groups); public institutions (e.g., educational, employment, heath care, social service, law enforcement, recreational); personal service providers (e.g., doctor, lawyer, landlord); and a religious or spiritual belief system. (The term "kinship" refers to a group of people connected by the same bloodline who usually also share similar behaviors, values, and talents.)

- How do relevant participants (individuals and/or systems) interact to cause and maintain the problem? What unmet needs and wants are involved in the problem?

- How severe is the problem?

- What is the duration of the problem?

- Where do the problematic behaviors occur? When do the problematic behaviors occur? What is the frequency of the problematic behaviors?

- What are the consequences of the problem?

- What are the client's emotional reactions to the problem?

- What meanings does the client ascribe to the problem?

- What developmental stage or life transition is involved in the problem?

- Have other issues (e.g., alcohol abuse, physical abuse) affected the functioning of the client or family members?

- How has the client attempted to cope with the problem and what are the required skills to resolve the problem?

- What are the client's skills, strengths, and resources?

- How do cultural, societal, and social class factors affect the problem?

- What support systems exist or need to be created for the client?

- What external resources are needed by the client?

5. Guidelines for Conducting a Competent Assessment:

a. Follow the Principles of Relevance and Salience: When collecting information for an assessment, you should narrow your focus by emphasizing information that is relevant to the client's problem, concern, or request (including its context and causes) and the type of help you can offer the client. Generally, the amount and type of data you collect will depend on such factors as the client herself, the nature of her problem, concern, or request, the treatment setting, your theoretical orientation, the services required, and, if you work at an agency, the mission of your agency.

Additionally, because most clients are limited to a specific number of sessions under managed care, it's usually impossible to obtain a full history of a client. Therefore, you should focus your attention on elements that are affecting the problem situation in either positive or negative ways. Some of these elements may be obvious (e.g., financial problems due to unemployment) and others may be more subtle (e.g., parents who don't spend adequate time with their child).

b. Address Top Priorities First: While the issues you should focus on during assessment depend largely on the client and the setting, the following three issues should receive priority attention during *any* assessment:

- *Any potentially serious health or safety concerns that require attention.*

- *What the client sees as her primary problem or concern* (i.e., "start where the client is").

- *Any current or upcoming legal mandates.* The fact that a client has been mandated to receive services or is facing other legal concerns will influence the nature of the assessment and how the client presents herself. Therefore, this issue should be addressed at the beginning of your assessment.

c. Gather Information From a Variety of Sources: The data you use in formulating an assessment should be derived from a variety of relevant sources. These sources may include background sheets and other forms that clients fill out; interviews with clients; direct observation of nonverbal behavior; direct observation of interactions between family members, marital partners, etc.; collateral information; psychological tests or assessment instruments; and your personal experiences based on your direct interactions with the clients (e.g., how you react to a client may provide you insight about how others react to her). Because each of these sources has limitations, you should use at least two sources whenever possible in order to increase the accuracy of the inferences you draw from the data you collect.

d. Recognize the Uniqueness of the Client: Assessment in social work is an individualized process that requires you to recognize the uniqueness of each client and situation. Although you may apply a particular theory (e.g., psychodynamic) to help you derive hypotheses about your client, you should not use these impressions by themselves to draw final conclusions about her.

e. Adopt a Strengths Perspective: You must avoid focusing exclusively on a client's problems, deficiencies, or pathology. Using a **strengths perspective** reminds you to identify the client's skills and internal and environmental strengths and resources and to think about how they can be used to help the client resolve her difficulties.

f. Be Aware of Factors That Can Affect a Client's Responses: Assessment interviews are guided, in part, by a client's responses to your questions. These responses, however, may be unreliable for a variety of reasons including, for example, a temporary state (e.g., the client has had a stressful day) or conscious or unconscious faking (see below). Your gender, race, age, and skill level may also affect a client's responses. Moreover, questions about sensitive topics such as substance use, child abuse, spousal abuse, or sexual behavior may elicit different responses depending on the circumstances of the assessment and who is interviewing the client. In addition, if rapport is not sufficiently developed, there is a greater likelihood that information obtained from the client will be inaccurate or incomplete.

The terms "**malingering**" and "**defensiveness**" are used in this context to refer to conscious and deliberate efforts by clients to falsify the information they share and, thereby, mislead you. These efforts may involve only minor exaggerations of problems or capabilities or complete fabrications of nonexistent difficulties or achievements.

Malingering: In this context, malingering ("faking bad") refers to a conscious effort by the client to present herself as being worse off than is really the case. Clients who "fake bad" during assessments are usually motivated by a specific external incentive for wanting to come off as more disturbed or less able than they actually are. Some clients are concerned about not getting the help they would like and overstate or falsify symptoms in order to convince you that they need assistance. Others malinger in order to receive disability payments, unemployment insurance, or medication; others do so because they are seeking damages in personal injury cases.

Defensiveness: In this context, defensiveness ("faking good") refers to a conscious effort by a client to convince you that she is better off than is really the case. Motivations for "faking good" vary depending on the setting in which the client is being evaluated. For example, some clients hide the extent of their difficulties because they want to be released from a hospital; others want to be told, or to have others such as family members or employers be told, that they don't have any significant problems. Parents in a custody battle may "fake good" in order to make a favorable impression on you.

g. View Assessment as Both a Product and a Process: Your initial judgment concerning a client's case will often change during the course of intervention when new information emerges, the client's goals or situation change, and/or the client makes progress toward attaining her goals. Thus, as a "product," a formal assessment takes place at the beginning of the helping process when you formulate a working definition of the problem based on how you and the client understand things at that point. Then, as a "process," assessment continues throughout the helping process. In the intervention and monitoring phase of helping, for example, the client may share new information or may respond in a particular way to an intervention, and this could shed new light on her problem or personality. When relevant, you should use this information to reshape the assessment and, as necessary, to reformulate the interventions.

6. Independent and Clinical Team Assessments:

a. Independent Assessment: In some settings, including private practice, a social worker makes an independent assessment. Even with an independent assessment, however, the worker may consult with colleagues or professionals from other disciplines, particularly when the client's case situation is complicated. When a social worker performs an independent assessment, assessment is generally completed in one to three sessions.

b. Clinical Team Approach: In other settings (e.g., schools, mental health clinics, medical hospitals), the social worker is a member of a clinical team that makes an assessment. The other team members may include a psychologist, a psychiatrist, a physician, and, often, professionals from other disciplines as well. Team members have specific roles in the assessment process based on their professional expertise. The social worker's role is to compile a **social history** of the client (see also Section V in this chapter). Usually, when a clinical team approach is used, the client's case is more complicated, and assessment by the various professionals may take several weeks.

II. Issues and Areas Explored in Assessment

In this section, we review key issues and areas that usually require attention in a comprehensive assessment, including (a) problem analysis (Parts A-E of the section); (b) assessment of the client's biophysical, emotional, cognitive/perceptual, behavioral, and social functioning (Parts F-L); and (c) assessment of the client's environment (Part M). Examining relevant aspects of a client's biopsychosocial functioning and environment is important for gaining an accurate understanding of the problem as well as for identifying the client's strengths.

Finally, this section also addresses assessment of the client's initial level of motivation, resistance, and ambivalence to change and how to perform competent assessments of culturally diverse clients and clients living in poverty.

A. The Presenting Problem

As noted in Section I, the **presenting problem** (or concern or request) consists of the perceived symptoms and overt issues or difficulties that, according to the client, constitute the problem for which she has sought help. Of course, the presenting problem may not be the actual problem or the problem that needs attention. A client's presenting problem may be a distortion of the actual problem or a matter that she feels safer disclosing. Moreover, most human problems are the result of underlying factors, and, therefore, many clients (and their family) misunderstand the problem or don't understand it fully.

For these reasons, focusing on the presenting problem is important primarily at the beginning of assessment when you ask the client why she came in. In particular, discovering the presenting problem can be important for one or more of the following reasons (Morrison, 1995):

- Because the presenting problem represents the issues and feelings that are uppermost in the client's mind, it can tell you what areas you should explore first.

- Knowing what led the client to come in for help can reveal a range of other useful data, including how distressed she is about the problem, whether she has come in voluntarily or been pressured by others, how motivated she is to work on her problem, and what her expectations for treatment are.

- A client's initial disclosures to you, even if they reflect a distortion or incomplete understanding of the problem, usually provide valuable clues concerning what the actual problem is. Your job is to use your professional knowledge and skill to make sense of the information that emerges when the client initially describes her problem.

In addition, even a client's assertion that nothing is wrong can provide valuable data, including information about her level of motivation, insight into herself and others, and willingness to cooperate with you. Her assertion may indicate a misunderstanding of the interview's purpose, resistance, or, sometimes, mental illness.

1. Interview Skills for Eliciting the Presenting Problem:

a. "Start Where the Client Is": To **start where the client is**, you focus on the client's priorities, including her emotional state and here-and-now concerns (what she considers important or what she wants to talk about).

- Generally, you should allow a client to speak freely about the concerns that are uppermost in her mind, with little prompting or interruption from you, until you believe you have a basic outline of her primary concerns. Typically, you will allow a client to speak freely for up to 10 or 15 minutes.

- If the client is emotionally upset, you should focus first on reducing her distress or other negative feelings: (a) Respond empathically to her feelings and communicate your understanding and acceptance. (b) Use a reflective opening, which can be effective for conveying that you intend to address her feelings openly and will listen to and accept whatever she has to say. For example, you might say, "Sometimes, it can be difficult to get started" or "You seem upset today."

- Although you may help the client clarify certain issues at this time, you must remain aware of *her* primary concerns as well as her readiness to share information. You should frame your questions in a way that allows the client to choose what information to share and when to share it (see open-ended questions, below). Do not rush the client or pressure her to self-disclose.

- Because you're still building trust, do not dismiss or challenge the client's definition of her problem at this time. Emphasize what she considers to be the most immediate problem or concern, even if your view of her situation is different. Efforts to alter a client's view of her problem are appropriate only after rapport has developed.

b. Make Statements That Allow Client to Choose Her Own Direction: Some clients need encouragement before they begin sharing their problem. An appropriate way of providing this encouragement is to say something brief and neutral that allows the client to choose how to get started (e.g., "You came in to see me about something today" or "Why have you come to see me?") (Sheafor & Horejsi, 2003). Avoid statements that could come off as superficial or ungenuine (e.g., "I'm so happy you've come to see me"); that give the impression that you, rather than the client, will be the primary problem-solver in the helping relationship (e.g., "How can I help you?"); or that convey to the client that you view her as deficient in some way (e.g., avoid using the word "problem," as in, "Tell me about your problem") (Zastrow, 2003).

c. Ask Open-Ended Questions: Unless you need to elicit specific data, you should use open-ended questions when initially exploring the problem (e.g., "Tell me some more about your husband"). **Open-ended questions** allow the client to present her own view of the problem, leave her free to express what she thinks is most important, and encourage expanded expression. Therefore, they tend to elicit more, and more elaborate, information than closed-ended questions and are more effective for revealing areas that warrant fuller exploration.

Closed-ended questions (e.g., "When was your most recent physical exam?"), by contrast, elicit responses that include either factual information or a simple "yes" or "no." They are useful for eliciting specific information required to more fully understand factors involved in the client's problems (such as data the client has omitted) and are used primarily in the latter portion of an interview to obtain this data.

d. Seek Clarification: You should ask the client to clarify any descriptive terms (e.g., "depressed," "confused," "fed up"), vague terms, words with multiple meanings, or metaphors or other figures of speech she uses when describing her problem. (A **metaphor** is an analogy or implied comparison used to describe a person or thing in a nonliteral way, as in, "My marriage is like World War III.")

e. Ask the Client About Other Concerns: Most clients, when initially telling their story, describe only those concerns that are uppermost in their mind. Therefore, after the client has had a chance to describe her problem, you should ask her directly whether there are other reasons that brought her in, beyond those she has shared. This reduces the danger that you will overlook important areas when collecting information for an in-depth assessment.

f. Verify Your Understanding of the Presenting Problem: An effective way of making sure you understand a client's presenting problem is to summarize the issues she has expressed and then invite her to either confirm or disconfirm your understanding. If multiple clients, such as family members, have presented different views of the problem, you should try to incorporate each person's understanding of the issue so that you can help the clients find common ground.

2. Additional Tools for Eliciting the Presenting Problem:

a. Problem Checklists or Vignettes: A **problem checklist** consists of a list of problems and concerns commonly reported by a group of clients served by an agency. If a client has difficulty identifying or articulating her concerns, you can present her with a checklist and ask her to identify which statements best reflect her concerns. A checklist can also be useful for structuring an interview when a client is easily distracted. In some cases, you may assign completion of the checklist as homework between the first and second interview.

If you work in a practice situation in which you need to collect information that's difficult to elicit by asking specific questions, you can prepare vignettes (brief stories) and use them as tools for initiating exploration. Having a client respond to a vignette is an indirect (projective) way of gathering information that elicits her feelings and beliefs.

b. The "Problem Search": The **problem search** is an agreement between you and a client to spend up to three sessions exploring her situation in more depth (focusing on two or three concerns you've identified) in order to determine whether a problem exists and, if so, whether it should be addressed. The client delays making a decision about her need for service until after these meetings, and the two of you agree that, if these meetings aren't useful, you won't continue to meet.

3. Factors That May Affect What the Client Initially Discloses:
Although it's important to pay close attention to what the client says as she describes her problem, you must also be aware of factors that may affect what she initially discloses about the problem:

- A client may test your competency and trustworthiness before disclosing the real problem or sharing complete information about a problem. If the client is a member of a minority group, this behavior may stem from her experiences with discrimination.

- A voluntary client may exaggerate the complexity, seriousness, and/or urgency of her presenting problem.

- An involuntary client may withhold information and/or minimize the presenting problem. In other cases, an involuntary client may not perceive herself as having a problem or may describe pressure from the referral source as the problem. When this occurs, you can try engaging the client in an exploration of her life situation (see also The Problem Search, above). This exercise may identify areas of dissatisfaction on the part of the client. If the client ends up acknowledging a problem, then you can proceed with problem exploration in a normal manner.

B. Unmet Needs

Many client problems involve unmet needs resulting from a poor fit between those needs and resources in the environment. Sometimes resources are available, but the client is unable to acquire or use them for some reason. In other situations, the resources don't exist or they exist but are unresponsive to the client's needs. Some clients have unmet needs related to basic necessities, such as a need for food, shelter, health care, or safety. You must take steps quickly to assist a client to meet her **basic needs** because basic needs must be at least partially met for adaptive physical and mental functioning. Other client needs are related to factors that, if present, would increase the client's sense of personal fulfillment and well-being. These needs can be described as "wants" on the part of the client, and examples include having more self-confidence and having less family discord.

When exploring a client's needs, keep the following in mind:

- Needs are often related to a person's developmental stage and the tasks and transitions associated with it; therefore, it is critical to take into account a client's developmental stage when attempting to identify her needs.

- The client may describe some obvious needs when telling you about her problem. Presenting problems, however, often reveal only surface needs. Careful exploration and empathic tuning-in are usually required to identify less obvious unmet needs and wants or ones that the client is not aware of.

- Often, a client's unmet needs or wants can be translated into goals when you and she plan intervention. Before translating a need or want into a goal, however, you must assess whether what the client desires is realistic given her capacity and the opportunities in her social environment.

C. History of the Problem

Obtaining a detailed history of the problem can clarify its magnitude and the factors contributing to it, as well as the client's current level of functioning and motivation for seeking help at this time. It can also suggest appropriate interventions.

Components of the problem history include the onset, progression, and severity of the problem; its precipitants, environmental antecedents, and consequences; the factors maintaining it; its effects on the client's adaptive functioning; the client's ideas about its causes; and what the client has done to try to resolve it, including what has worked and what hasn't worked. When seeking information about factors causing and/or maintaining the problem, it's important to identify what *combination* of factors has contributed to it (e.g., a client's chronic anxiety may be influenced by physical factors, marital discord, and high stress at work). This breadth of understanding will prevent you from overlooking important targets for change when developing the intervention plan.

1. Onset, Progression, and Severity of the Problem: When exploring the onset, progression, and severity of the problem, you should generally ask the following questions:

- When did the problem or symptom begin? Under what circumstances? Was there a specific precipitating cause, such as a significant change in the client's life? A **precipitating cause** is an event or change that seems to have resulted in the problem. It is often the "last straw" that leads a client to seek a social worker's help.

- If the client has reported multiple problems or symptoms, which one appeared first? For example, did depression begin before the client started drinking heavily or the other way around?

- How often does the problem or symptom occur?

- Is the problem or symptom chronic or does it come and go?

- If the problem or symptom is episodic, how often does it occur? How long does it last?

- How intense is the problem or symptom? Has it become increasingly more intense? Does its intensity vary? Under what circumstances does it vary?

2. Stressors Affecting the Problem: A current or recent psychosocial stressor may have precipitated the client's problem. In other cases, a current or recent stressor may be exacerbating a pre-existing problem or symptom. To understand the role played by psychosocial stressors, you should explore the following questions:

- What psychosocial stressors are affecting the client? Are these also affecting her family?

- What is the duration and severity of the stressor? Is the stressor ongoing or has it been removed?

- How does the client think the stressor may have affected the course of her problem?

- What coping skills and strategies (adaptive and maladaptive) has the client used in her efforts to cope with the stressor and its consequences?

- What resources does the client have and what resources does the client need in order to cope with the stressor?

Holmes and Rahe (1967) have developed a scale for assessing the severity of psychosocial stressors. Their scale, called the **Life Events Scale** or the **Social Readjustment Scale**, includes over 40 life changes. Listed in order from most to least serious or debilitating, the first 10 changes on the scale are: death of spouse or child, divorce, marital separation, imprisonment, death of a close family member, personal injury or illness, marriage, dismissal from work, marital reconciliation, and retirement.

3. Antecedents and Consequences of the Problem: Analyzing the antecedents and consequences of the problem (or problematic behavior) allows you to describe it in specific terms, including identifying the participants involved and the roles they play and the factors that motivate dysfunctional behavior for the client and are appropriate targets of intervention.

(**Antecedents** are events that precede, or come before, a behavior and are thought to influence it.)

This area emphasizes both internal (e.g., cognitive) and environmental events producing and maintaining the problem (or problematic behavior). In terms of the client's social environment, for example, you should explore how relevant participants (individuals and/or systems) interact to cause and maintain the problem. Important antecedents and consequences usually include the circumstances associated with a problematic behavior, how each participant affects and is affected by the others, and what participants say and do before, during, and after the behavior occurs. In exploring these factors, you may use an approach called the **ABC model**, in which A = antecedent, B = behavior, and C = consequences.

4. Degree of Impairment in Adaptive Functioning: Exploring how and how much the problem has affected the client's adaptive functioning can provide a reliable index of problem severity. This is partly because this data is more objective than what the client says when describing her problem, especially when you also incorporate information from collateral sources and your own observations. To understand the degree of impairment in the client's adaptive functioning, you would explore the following questions:

- Has the problem affected the client's family members and their day-to-day functioning? How has the family been affected?

- Has the problem affected the client's relationship with her spouse or partner? How has this relationship been affected?

- Does the client feel alienated from friends or other members of her social support network? Does she feel rejected by them? Is this just a perceived consequence, or is the client actually alienated and has she been truly rejected?

- Is the problem interfering with the client's adaptive functioning at home, work, or school? In what ways? For example, does the client have difficulty performing **activities of daily living**? Is there diminished performance at work or school or increased absences? How often do these effects occur?

- Has the client's interest in pleasurable activities changed? Is she more or less active than usual?

- Has the client had any legal difficulties? Legal consequences are particularly likely if the client's symptoms include alcohol or other drug abuse.

5. Client's Beliefs About and Emotional Reaction to Her Problem: A client's beliefs or assumptions about what causes a behavior sometimes serve to maintain it. These beliefs may also pose a barrier to change (e.g., the client may believe that her problem is the result of an innate characteristic or external factor that cannot change). You should also try to find out how significant others in the client's life perceive her behavior since it's possible that they view it in a different way.

Identifying the client's emotional reaction to her problem can be important for a number of different reasons. First, emotions have a potent effect on behavior, and, therefore, a client's emotions may cause her to behave in ways that intensify the problem or create new problems. Second, an intense emotional reaction to an event can become a more significant problem than the event itself – for example, a client may have a debilitating panic reaction in response to receiving a poor evaluation at work. When this is the case, your intervention must address the client's emotional reaction as well as the problematic situation itself.

6. Developmental Considerations: Both normal (expectable) developmental phenomena and transitions from one life stage or role to another can affect a person's social and emotional functioning, and, therefore, you should consider your client's stage of development when attempting to clarify the nature and causes of her problem.

You should explore to what extent a client's problem or symptoms are the result of a normal developmental event or transition versus the result of some other stressful event or an emotional or mental disorder. For example, an "out-of-control" toddler may be exerting her need for increased independence; if the child's behavior is not excessive or dangerous, then you'd want to normalize this developmental event for her parents. In addition, transitions between developmental stages tend to be periods of significant psychological, social, and physical change that, for some people, result in a **maturational crisis**.

7. Family, Work, Educational, and Legal Histories: Information collected for a family, work, educational, and/or legal history may be needed in order to formulate a complete description of the client's problem, including how the problem fits into the wider context of her life, potential sources of her current difficulties, and changes in her level of functioning.

a. Family History: For example, the quality of relationships in the client's family of origin; the quality of her relationship to each significant family member; family composition; birth order; her parents' approach to childrearing and discipline and expectations with regard to education, work, achievement, family interdependence, etc.; whether either parent was ever away from home for an extended period of time (including because of divorce); religious commitments; mental health problems and substance use disorders in immediate family members; the physical environment the client grew up in; and whether there was abuse or neglect in the household.

b. Work History and Educational History: Information about these areas can clarify a client's underlying potential and the effects of her problem or symptoms on her current functioning (e.g., finding out how a client functioned at work before the onset of the problem can reveal whether her functioning has changed). For the work history, other questions you might explore include the following: Has the client changed her career direction many times? Has the client ever been fired? Did the client ever serve in the military? If the client served in the military, what type of discharge did she receive and did she see combat? Has the client pursued any education as an adult? For the educational history, other questions you might explore include the following: What is last grade the client completed? How well did the client do at school? What subjects caused her difficulty? Was she ever diagnosed with a learning disorder? Did she have any conduct problems at school? Was the client ever absent from school for an extended period of time? Did she ever experience school refusal? How old was the client when she progressed from a life of dependency on her parents to one of self-sufficiency?

c. Legal History: Obtaining a legal history is usually important when a client reports intense conflicts with other people, displays signs of aggression or persistent anger, is impulsive, has poor judgment, or abuses alcohol or other drugs. For example, has the client ever been arrested? If so, how old was she and what was the outcome? Has there been a pattern of illegal behavior from adolescence into adulthood?

D. Coping Effort and Coping Skills

Valuable information about a client's difficulties can be learned by exploring how she has tried to cope with her problem. Some examples of functional coping skills and patterns include seeking information, planning, delaying gratification, flexibility, and an ability to consider various solutions to a problem. Because these behaviors represent strengths for the client, they should be pointed out and supported by you. Examples of dysfunctional coping behaviors include denial (which isn't adaptive when it prevents a person from engaging in problem-focused coping), rigidity, impulsiveness, substance use, and a tendency to become angry, overwhelmed, or depressed when facing a life stressor.

Some clients generally lack adaptive coping skills, rely on rigid or dysfunctional coping patterns (e.g., avoidance, alcohol use), or are overly dependent on other people. Others normally have effective coping skills, but are under so much pressure that they are unable to use them to resolve the current problem. If a client who has coped successfully with past problems is unable to cope right now, you should find out what has changed – there may have been an environmental change or the client's level of functioning may have altered in such a way that her ability to cope has been diminished (e.g., perhaps she has become depressed). In addition, the effectiveness of a client's coping skills and patterns may vary in different contexts – perhaps the client copes well in one setting (e.g., home) but not in another (e.g., work).

A coping assessment usually includes consideration of the following factors:

- What are the client's coping skills and coping mechanisms and what resources are available to facilitate coping?

- What coping strategies has the client been using to cope with the current problem? What has worked? What hasn't worked? Is the client relying on ego defense mechanisms?

- How has the client reacted and responded to problems in the past? You should be alert to patterns, both adaptive and maladaptive. For example, is the client able and willing to accept new ideas and weigh all aspects of a situation? This skill, known as cognitive flexibility, has a significant positive impact on coping ability and the capacity to adapt to change.

- How do relevant personal variables affect the client's coping ability (e.g., internal vs. external **locus of control**, sense of **self-efficacy**)? What are the client's beliefs about her own capabilities? How do these beliefs affect her effort, decisions, cognitions, mood, and stress level?

- What skills does the client need to either improve or develop in order to facilitate coping with the current problem and in the future?

E. Other Issues Affecting Functioning

Any number of additional issues, beyond those expressed by the client, may be affecting the presenting problem and/or her capacity to deal with it. Examples include the presence of a health condition, taking prescription medication, using alcohol or other drugs, mental health problems, and exposure to violence. Therefore, you should ask a client about these issues as a routine part of an initial interview. You should ask your questions in a straightforward and nonjudgmental way (e.g., "Are you currently experiencing any health problems?" or "I'd like to know about some of your habits: In an average month, on how many days do you have at least one drink of alcohol?") (Hepworth et al., 2006). The client's answers to these questions will then determine how you follow-up, including which issues you choose to explore in more depth, either yourself or by referring the client for medical or other evaluations. Usually, at a minimum, you will want to follow-up by asking the client how she views the relevant issues in light of her presenting problem (e.g., "How have your daily headaches affected your ability to look for a job?").

F. Biophysical Functioning

Biophysical functioning encompasses physical characteristics, health and genetic factors, and use of alcohol or other drugs. Biophysical factors affecting the client's emotional, cognitive, behavioral, and/or social functioning have practical implications for diagnosis, treatment, and prognosis.

Physical Characteristics and Presentation

Physical characteristics and appearance may be either assets or liabilities for a client and can provide clues about her physical health, mental health, self-esteem, values, and standard of living (Hepworth et al., 2006).

- Take note of distinguishing physical characteristics that may affect the client's social functioning. Examples include her body build, posture, facial features, gait, and any physical abnormalities that may affect her self-image or impose social barriers.

- Take note of how the client presents herself. Clients who move and talk slowly, for example, may be depressed. Minimal changes in facial expressions may also indicate a depressed mood.

- Observe whether the client's dress appropriate for the setting and the weather (e.g., is the client dressed seductively, is she underdressed for cold weather?). Be sure to consider the client's cultural background and values when evaluating her manner of dressing. A disheveled appearance could indicate poverty, a depressed mood, or a more serious mental health problem such as schizophrenia. Or it could merely reflect the way the client likes to dress.

- Take note of facial tics, hand tremors, tense muscles in the face, hands, and arms, and a constantly shifting posture. These may reflect a high level of anxiety or the presence of a physical illness or condition, such as a medication side-effect.

Physical Health

1. Medical History: Basic information about a client's medical history should be sought regardless of the nature of the presenting problem. This information is useful for clarifying the client's problem and current functioning as well as learning how well she complies with the recommendations of health care professionals. It may also reveal the need to refer the client to a medical professional (e.g., physician, psychiatrist, neurologist) for evaluation, treatment, or management. In some cases, the client's reported difficulties will be related to or the direct result of one or more medical problems. You should ask the client about the following issues:

- Begin by asking the client whether she is currently under medical care, and, if not, when she last had a medical examination.

- Ask the client if she is currently taking any prescribed or over-the-counter medications. If so, ask whether the medication is having the desired effect and if she's experiencing any side-effects.

- Ask the client about current and past health problems (e.g., chronic medical conditions, injuries or disorders affecting the central nervous system, malnutrition during childhood). What are/were their effects on her functioning? What medical treatments did the client receive and how did she respond to the treatment? Was she ever hospitalized?

- You may also ask the client about illnesses in her family (perhaps using a genogram to record the information). Explore how the family has been affected by illness, the family's understanding and attitudes toward illness, and how they cope with illness.

- If the client is a member of a group that tends to underutilize health care services (e.g., older adult, homeless, ethnic minority, immigrant or refugee, uninsured, foster child), inquire about her access to health care, including availability, affordability, and acceptability. "Acceptability" refers to whether health services are compatible with her cultural values and traditions.

2. Indicators of Medical Problems: You must be able to recognize when a client may have a medical problem, especially a potentially serious one, that has yet to be diagnosed by a medical professional. The cues listed here should give rise to concern that your client's health could be imminently or gravely threatened; they indicate that an immediate medical referral is probably necessary, especially if the client has not recently been examined by a physician: (a) signs or symptoms of delirium; (b) signs or symptoms of a major neurocognitive disorder (i.e., dementia), especially in an older adult or a person with advanced HIV disease; (c) long-standing depression; (d) abrupt personality change; (e) sudden change in intellectual or behavioral functioning in a child; (f) known or suspected heavy or long-term alcohol or other drug use; (g) known or suspected serious eating disturbance (e.g., emaciated appearance, excessive use of laxatives or diuretics); (h) suspicion of HIV disease; and (i) any other recent alteration or loss of physical functioning (e.g., loss of bladder control) or persistent physical sign or symptom (e.g., dizziness, chest pain, headaches, stomachaches, vomiting).

As a social worker, you are not qualified to provide a client with medical advice even if you are certain that she has a medical condition or other health problem. Instead, your job is to do your best to encourage a client with undiagnosed or untreated physical symptoms to follow your recommendation that she see a medical professional. This may require making a simple referral or you may need to use brokering or case management skills to help the client access the health services she needs. In a medical emergency, of course, you should contact emergency medical services to transport the client to a hospital.

In Appendix I of this chapter, we provide descriptions of medical disorders and diseases that clients may have, including diabetes and HIV/AIDS. Be sure to review this appendix before your exam.

Medication Side-Effects

1. Recognizing Medication Side-Effects: As noted above, you should ask your client whether she is currently taking any prescribed or over-the-counter medication for an emotional, mental, or physical disorder and whether she is experiencing any side-effects. You often need to be explicit when exploring this area because clients may not be aware that certain symptoms they're experiencing could be side-effects of their medication. Therefore, you may need to ask a client directly whether she is experiencing certain symptoms that are often associated with medication side-effects. In particular, symptoms such as tachycardia, tremors, stomach distress, diarrhea or constipation, skin rash, low energy, or sexual problems may be caused by medication prescribed by a physician or psychiatrist, and problems such as anxiety and depression can be exacerbated by certain medications such as pain pills.

If your client is concerned about or distressed by any of these symptoms, you should encourage her to see a medical professional as soon as she can, preferably the one who prescribed the medication. If the client has signs or symptoms of a potentially dangerous medication side-effect (e.g., **tardive dyskinesia**), she should see a medical professional as soon as possible, and, if necessary, you should be active in arranging for her to do so. In addition, a client who is taking too little or too much of her medication, mixing her medication with alcohol or other drugs, or otherwise misusing her medication should be referred for an evaluation by a physician or psychiatrist.

Psychoactive (psychotropic) medications and their side-effects (including tardive dyskinesia, which was mentioned above) are described in Appendix II of this chapter. Be sure to review this appendix before your exam.

2. Medication and Older Adults: An older individual may be taking numerous prescription and/or over-the-counter medications for physiological problems or chronic medical conditions. When assessing an older adult, it is a good idea to consult with her physician (or psychiatrist, for psychotropic drugs) in order to learn about her medication regimen. It's also important to keep in mind the following:

- Because drugs are metabolized differently in older people, side-effects and idiosyncratic reactions are more common, and combinations of several different medications can produce serious side-effects.

- Decreased liver and kidney functioning means that the elimination of medications from the body is less efficient than before, so that older people may have reduced tolerance for the standard dosage of many kinds of medication. This is a particularly serious concern with antianxiety or other sedating medication.

- Older adults may intentionally or unintentionally misuse their medications (e.g., forget dosages, take incorrect dosages, self-medicate, use outdated prescriptions, reduce dosages to save money or because side-effects are intolerable).

3. Abbreviations Used on Prescriptions: Abbreviations used to indicate proper dosages on prescriptions include the following: Q means "every"; QD means "daily" or "every day"; BID means "twice daily"; TID means "three times a day"; QID means "four times a day"; HS means "at bedtime"; PRN means "as needed"; AC means "before meals"; and PC means "after meals."

Use of Alcohol or Other Drugs

The problematic use of alcohol or other drugs may play a role in causing and maintaining a variety of problems reported by clients, including physical health, mental health, and social-role functioning problems. Moreover, substance use disorders are, in and of themselves, problems that usually require intervention by mental health and/or medical professionals.

The presence of one or more of the following indicators should lead you to consider the possibility that a client may have a substance use disorder: (a) alcohol use greater than one or two drinks a day and/or known use of other drugs; (b) certain health problems, such as blackouts, cirrhosis, frequent vomiting, or abdominal pain; (c) memory impairment; (d) certain kinds of social or interpersonal problems, such as withdrawal from family and friends, the loss of friends, and getting into physical fights; (e) a change in work or school performance (e.g., job loss, demotion, tardiness, truancy, a drop in grades); (f) other decreases in normal capabilities (e.g., in habits or efficiency); (g) certain kinds of financial problems (e.g., the client spends money needed for other items on alcohol or other drugs); (h) poor physical appearance, neglect of dress, poor personal hygiene; and/or (i) arrests or other legal problems.

In addition, during an interview you may observe indicators of recent substance use, such as intoxicated behavior (slurred speech, rambling or incoherent speech, unsteady walk, extreme relaxation, reduced inhibitions, impaired coordination, slowed reflexes, etc.); the smell of alcohol; signs of a hangover; and/or glazed eyes or dilated or constricted pupils (or the client is wearing sunglasses to hide her eyes).

For more information on assessing substance use disorders, see Section VIII of this chapter.

Sexual History

Taking a sexual history is indicated when a client's psychosocial problems may be related to sexual behavior. Moreover, sexual health is important to overall health and well-being. Indicators of **sexual health** include the absence of sexually transmitted diseases (STDs) and reproductive disorders, control of fertility, avoidance of unwanted pregnancies, and sexual expression without exploitation, oppression, or abuse. Some clients are not comfortable talking about their sexual history. You should use helping skills to put clients at ease and let them know that taking a sexual history is often a routine part of assessment. Inform them that you explore this area with many of your adult (or, as relevant, adolescent) clients, regardless of their age, gender, marital status, or sexual orientation.

The areas explored in a sexual history may include sexual activity, sexual partners, and sexual practices. For example: Is the client sexually active? Does the client have any difficulties with sexual functioning? Does the client place herself at risk for STDs? Has the client ever experienced any form of sexual abuse or sexual exploitation? The latter topic, in particular, must be explored with due sensitivity to the client's readiness to disclose information and discuss the topic.

G. Emotional Functioning

During an interview, you should attend to how the client describes her mood and emotional functioning and observe the client's verbal and nonverbal behavior and appearance. You should also explore the client's level of subjective distress both during the interview and typically. Even when emotional signs and symptoms are not associated with an underlying mental disorder, they can turn out to be an important focus of attention during treatment.

When assessing emotional functioning, remember to consider the client's cultural background because cultures differ in their approved patterns of emotional expressiveness. On the other hand, a mark of emotional health in any culture is having control over emotions to the extent that one does not become overwhelmed by them.

1. Emotional Control: Difficulties with emotional control (or regulation) involve a tendency to express "too much" emotion (e.g., volatility, excessive irritability). Usually, the key to identifying if an emotional response is excessive is determining whether it is appropriate and proportionate to the triggering stimulus.

- A client may have a persistent or longstanding problem in this area or her difficulties may be the result of tensions associated with a recent or ongoing stressor. Difficulties with emotional control may also be a sign of a mental disorder (e.g., irritability is common in people with a depressive or bipolar disorder).

- Problems with emotional control, whether chronic or acute, will tend to impact a client's relationships with others and overall social-role functioning.

- A client may have legal problems due to a lack of emotional control (e.g., she may engage assaultive behavior).

2. Emotional Range: With an appropriate emotional range, a person can both feel and express many different emotions. The term **anhedonia** is used to describe an inability to feel joy or express many pleasurable emotions.

- A client with a chronically limited emotional range may have interpersonal difficulties (e.g., she may have a pattern of remaining detached, both emotionally and physically, from other people).

- A client with a longstanding inability to experience or express certain emotions may develop acute or chronic psychological problems as a result (e.g., people who chronically blame themselves, placate others, and/or "stuff" their anger may develop symptoms of depression or anxiety).

- A client may experience physical symptoms, such as headaches and ulcers, if she is unable to feel or express her emotions in situations that, for most people, engender anger or sadness.

- A client may have developed psychic mechanisms to protect herself from feelings of rejection, loneliness, and hurt; if so, she may behave as though she is "tough" and doesn't need anyone.

- A client's emotional range may be more limited than it usually is as a result of an overwhelming event or as part of a major depressive episode. This change in emotional functioning may be diminishing the client's ability to cope and function in a variety of settings.

3. Appropriateness of Affect: With **appropriate affect** (healthy affect), a person is in touch with her emotions and can express them spontaneously as she feels them in response to specific emotional or situational stimuli (e.g., she cries when discussing sad material). When evaluating a client's affect, remember that the normal range of expressed affect varies between different cultures and even within the same culture.

- Through observation, you can evaluate whether a client's affect (her expressed thoughts and feelings and facial expressions) is appropriate to her current situation and the material being discussed in the interview. With **inappropriate affect**, the client may, for example, smile or laugh when discussing the death of a loved one. The term "gallows laughter" refers to laughter occurring when discussing painful material. Sometimes, a client will smile constantly no matter what is being discussed.

- A high level of apprehension (muscle tension, fidgeting, lip biting, etc.) would suggest that a client may be fearful, suspicious, or very uncomfortable in unfamiliar interpersonal situations. This may be characteristic of the client's manner in other interpersonal contexts as well, not just in the interview with you. At the other extreme, complete relaxation and openness in a situation that would evoke apprehension and anxiety in most people may reflect denial of the problem or lack of motivation to engage in the problem-solving process.

- **Emotional blunting** (also called **flat affect**) is a muted or apathetic response to stimuli that would normally evoke a stronger response (e.g., a client discusses a traumatic life event in a detached, matter-of-fact way). Emotional blunting may be a medication side-effect or a sign of a mental disorder (e.g., schizophrenia, substance/medication-induced psychotic disorder, severe depression). When flat affect occurs with a thought disorder, you should consider the possibility of psychosis and refer the client for a psychiatric evaluation.

- Elation or euphoria inconsistent with the client's life situation, when combined with flight of ideas, irritability, expansive ideas, and excessive motion, suggest the possibility of a manic episode.

- A highly charming demeanor may reflect a client's skill at projecting a favorable image when it is in her interest do so. In some cases, this is a coping style developed to hide self-centeredness and manipulation or exploitation of others.

4. Anger: Indicators of a problem with anger, or anger control, can include a history of explosive outbursts out of proportion to any precipitating event (which may have led to physically aggressive behavior); overreaction, such as hostility, to minor irritants; use of verbally abusive language; use of passive-aggressive patterns, such as withdrawal or failure to comply with directions or rules; pattern of challenging or disrespecting authority figures; making quick and harsh judgments of other people; and body language cues indicating muscle tension (e.g., a clenched fist or jaw, glaring or refusing to make eye contact).

When attempting to understand a client's anger, consider questions such as the following: (a) What is the source of the anger? Can the client identify the source? (b) What is the intensity, direction, and target of the anger? (c) How does the client normally handle her anger (what are her usual coping strategies)? (d) What is her level of impulse control? (e) Is the anger situational or is it a more pervasive aspect of her personality? (f) Does the client experience guilt about her anger? (g) How does the client express her anger? Verbal aggression? Violent or aggressive behavior? Does the client pose a danger to you or others?

5. Guilt and Shame: The primary feelings associated with guilt are a sense of being bad or evil, remorse, and a fear of punishment. Shame, by contrast, is associated with a sense that one is inadequate, worthless, or disgraced and a fear of being abandoned or excluded by others (e.g., of not belonging). Other indicators of either guilt or shame include self-condemnation, fears of annihilation, and a reluctance to disclose one's flaws.

At the other extreme, a client may appear to lack an appropriate sense of guilt or shame for her behavior (e.g., she may come off as unrepentant, conscienceless, cynical, or unscrupulous). A lack of remorse, when it occurs with a pervasive and longstanding pattern of disregard for and violation of the rights of other people, can be associated with antisocial personality disorder in a client over age 18; a younger client may have conduct disorder.

6. Ambivalence: Barker (2003) defines ambivalence as contradictory emotions that occur at the same time within a person. Extreme ambivalence can lead to indecisiveness and rapidly changing emotional attitudes toward another person or an object. Persistent ambivalence is associated with chronic indecisiveness, mixed feelings, and a sense of being conflicted or stuck. When this is a focus of intervention (but not a mental disorder), it can be associated an identity problem, in which the client is uncertain about multiple issues relating to her identity, including career choice, long-term goals, friendship patterns, sexual orientation, and moral values.

H. Cognitive/Perceptual Functioning

Assessing how clients perceive their world is important because people's perceptions of others, themselves, and events are heavily influenced by how they feel and respond to life experiences in general and problematic situations in particular. In turn, thought patterns are influenced by intellectual functioning, judgment, reality testing, coherence, cognitive flexibility, values, beliefs, self-concept, and cultural belief systems, as well as the ongoing interaction of cognitions, emotions, and behaviors that influence social functioning.

1. Intellectual Functioning (Capacity): Having a rough estimate of a client's intellectual capacity allows you to adjust your verbal communication to a level she can readily understand. It also helps you assess her strengths and deficits and develop goals and tasks that are consistent with her capacities. You can estimate intellectual capacity by noting the client's ability to express herself, grasp ideas, and analyze information. Other useful indicators are her level of educational achievement and vocabulary, but these must be evaluated in light of her educational opportunities, primary language, and any learning disorder she may have. If a client's presentation is inconsistent with her known intellectual capacity or achievement, she may have a medical illness or head injury, be experiencing medication side-effects, or have a problem with alcohol or other drug use.

2. Judgment: Judgment refers to the capacity to make sound, reasoned, and responsible decisions and has a significant impact on problem-solving ability. Sound judgment generally requires planning ability, self-awareness, social cognition, and the ability to control impulses. Deficiencies in judgment may become apparent when you explore in depth a client's problems and the behavioral patterns associated with them. For example, you may discover that a client tends to act with little forethought, engage in wishful thinking rather than deliberate problem solving, or repeatedly act in ways that provide immediate gratification but ultimately result in unwanted consequences, such as job losses, overspending and debt, or arrests. Poor judgment may be associated with a manic episode.

3. Reality Testing: Reality testing refers to the relative ability to judge and evaluate objectively the external world and distinguish between the external world and ideas and values that exist in one's own mind (Barker, 2003). When reality testing is intact, a person is properly oriented to time, place, person, and situation; reaches appropriate conclusions about cause-and-effect relationships; perceives external events and interprets the intentions of others with reasonable accuracy; and can distinguish her own thoughts and feelings from those of others. Whatever their source, problems with reality testing, such as those described below, can pose significant obstacles to motivation and progress in the change process.

Disorientation: **Disorientation** is usually easy to recognize, but if you are uncertain, you ask can a client questions about the date, day of the week, current events, or recent events in her life. Clients who are markedly disoriented may be severely mentally ill, under the influence of drugs, or suffering from a pathological brain syndrome (e.g., delirium).

Distortions of external events and other people's intentions: These range from mild to severe and typically lead to difficulties in interpersonal relationships. Mild distortions may be associated with stereotypical perceptions (e.g., "All men are cheaters"). Moderate distortions may involve obvious misinterpretations of other people's motives (e.g., "My fiancé says he accepted a better job at a new company, but I know he did it so he can meet new women"). Extreme distortions can take the form of **delusions**, which are false beliefs that are firmly held despite what other people believe and/or the existence of clear and indisputable evidence to the contrary.

Psychosis: Severely dysfunctional reality testing (i.e., **psychosis**) may include delusions as well as **hallucinations**, which are sensory perceptions occurring without external stimulation of the associated sensory organ.

You should be aware that reality testing is susceptible to mild and temporary distortion or deterioration under stressful conditions. Additionally, even clients without thought disorders and who are not under stress may exhibit poor reality testing (e.g., a client may choose to blame circumstances when things go wrong in her life, rather than take responsibility for her actions). When a client takes responsibility for her actions, by contrast, you should identify this as an area of strength.

4. Coherence: In some settings, social workers encounter clients who have major thought disorders. Such disorders are characterized by rambling and incoherent speech. **Loose associations**, for example, are characterized by abrupt shifts from one fragmented thought to another, with little if any logical connection between the thoughts. Mild forms of loose association can occur with severe anxiety or depression. More severe forms of loose association, however, as well as flight of ideas, may indicate mania, a thought disorder such as schizophrenia, or acute drug intoxication. With **flight of ideas**, a client's responses seem to "take off" based on a particular word or thought, unrelated to any logical progression or the original point of the communication.

5. Cognitive Flexibility: Cognitive flexibility is marked by an openness to new ideas and ability to consider many different aspects of a situation, and, therefore, is important for effective problem solving and general adaptability. Cognitive *inflexibility*, on the other hand, can result in a variety of personal and interpersonal problems and pose a major obstacle to progress in the change process. Examples of patterns of cognitive inflexibility include thinking in absolute terms (good or bad, success or failure) and adhering to stereotypes. The former pattern can result in depression, relationship problems, workplace conflict, parent-child conflicts, and similar difficulties; the latter pattern can interfere with the capacity to form relationships or cooperate with the members of certain groups (authority figures, the opposite sex, ethnic groups, etc.) as individuals (Hepworth et al., 2006).

6. Values: You should attempt to identify your client's values, assess the role they play in her difficulties, and consider how they may be used to create incentives for her to change. One reason why values often play a role in problems is that values influence behavior. For some clients, value conflicts are central to the presenting problem (e.g., a client is struggling to be both independent and loyal to her family). Value conflicts may also underlie difficulties between a client and other people or between members of a family or couple you are treating – e.g., a child and her parents disagree about appropriate behavior, or spouses have differing beliefs about how they should spend the family's income.

Being aware of a client's values can help you create incentives to encourage her to change dysfunctional behavior. For instance, a client may express strong values about an area of her life and yet behave in direct opposition to them. She might experience **cognitive dissonance** if you help her recognize the inconsistencies between her values and behaviors. Exploring these inconsistencies can help the client see the ways in which her behavior is self-defeating.

Knowing about your client's values is also important because, ethically, you must respect a client's right to both maintain her own values and make decisions that are consistent with them. And, finally, because values result from cultural conditioning, it's important for you to understand your client's cultural reference group, especially if it differs from yours.

7. Misconceptions: Because beliefs are important mediators of emotions and actions, **mistaken beliefs** can play a role in a client's problems. You should identify a client's misconceptions and their sources, and, if they are central to her problem, the intervention may include modifying these misconceptions in order to open the way for behavioral change.

8. Self-Concept: A person's beliefs and ideas about herself are critical determinants of her behavior. Strengths a client may have include high self-esteem and a realistic awareness of her own positive attributes, achievements, and potentials, as well as her own limitations and deficiencies. Alternatively, a client may experience feelings of worthlessness, inadequacy, or helplessness; underachieve because of perceived deficiencies; avoid relationships because she fears rejection; allow herself to be exploited by others; use drugs to overcome feelings of inadequacy, etc. A good way of initiating an exploration of your client's self-concept is to ask an open-ended question, such as, "Tell me how you see yourself" (Hepworth et al., 2006).

I. Mental Disorders (Psychiatric Symptoms)

For a review of diagnostic criteria for specific DSM-5 mental disorders, see Section VII in this chapter.

You should ask your client about previous mental health problems and their treatment and review available records. This information is useful for diagnostic purposes, understanding the client's coping behaviors, estimating the client's willingness to engage in treatment, learning the client's expectations for treatment, and clarifying the meaning the client attaches to her problem or symptoms. Examining this data can reveal, in particular, whether the current problem is a single episode, a recurrent episode, or reflects a progression of problems over time, and what intervention approaches have worked and not worked in the past.

If your client presents with signs and symptoms of a mental disorder, you should explore the duration, frequency, and intensity of the symptoms in order to clarify their effects on her functioning and determine the extent to which she is distressed by the symptoms. Most mental disorders in DSM-5 can be diagnosed only when their symptoms are associated with impairment in important areas of functioning or significant personal distress.

When evaluating this area, you should be aware certain physical symptoms, known as **vegetative symptoms**, may be indicators of a mental disorder, in particular, major depression. Vegetative symptoms include sleep disturbances, changes in appetite or weight, loss of energy or frequent fatigue, and changes in sexual function. They are useful for diagnostic screening purposes because they may indicate a serious mental disorder. If your client reports vegetative symptoms, you should find out whether they reflect a change from her previous functioning.

In addition, you should be familiar with two constructs used to explain the development of certain symptoms: **primary gain** and **secondary gain**. When applied to somatic symptoms, the term "primary gain" suggests that the symptom prevents a person from being consciously aware of a psychological conflict or need, while "secondary gain" suggests that the symptom helps a person avoid unpleasant activities or obtain otherwise unavailable attention from others. When applied to other symptoms (or mental disorders), primary (or paranosic) gain refers to the initial gain achieved through the development of the disorder. For example, a symptom may serve to relieve immediate anxiety (e.g., the primary gain in specific phobia is freedom from the anxiety that accompanies the phobic stimulus). Secondary (or epinosic) gain is said to be present when the symptom (disability or disorder) serves as a means of avoiding unpleasant duties (e.g., a person with agoraphobia who can't leave home is not expected to hold down a job). "Advantage [or gain] by illness" is a similar term used to describe the beneficial effects associated with some mental disorders.

Finally, before concluding that a client's psychiatric symptoms meet the criteria for a primary mental disorder, you must rule out the possibility that they are caused by an underlying medical condition and/or the effects of a substance or medication. This often requires making appropriate referrals for medical evaluations. Moreover, you should be aware that alcohol or other drug use can be either a cause or effect of certain mental health symptoms. For instance, a client with intense, chronic anxiety may "self-medicate" by using alcohol or other drugs or misuse prescription medications to keep her symptoms under control.

J. Personality and Ego Functions

"Personality traits" are patterns of behavior, thinking, and perception that persist throughout adult life. A "personality disorder" can be diagnosed only when the relevant traits are severe enough to cause significant personal distress or marked impairment of functioning. The term **ego syntonic** is descriptive of values, feelings, behaviors, ideas, etc., that are consistent with a person's ego or sense of self; they feel real and acceptable to the person's consciousness. By contrast, the term **ego dystonic** (or ego alien) describes impulses, behaviors, wishes, etc., that are unacceptable to the ego, or to the person's ideal conception of self.

1. Personality Assessment: Most interviews provide cues that can help you understand a client's personality. Examples include evidence of long-term behavior patterns, lifelong patterns of maladjustment or interpersonal conflict, and indicators of low or inflated self-esteem. Specific client behaviors or statements can also reflect prominent character traits (e.g., disinterest, hostility, prejudices, boasting, or argumentativeness). Combined with other biographical data, these cues can suggest a certain personality style (e.g., aggressive, addictive, manipulative, Type A, codependent) or even a personality disorder. Signals suggesting adaptive and positive personality traits should be noted, as well, and conveyed to the client. You can also pose questions designed to uncover what the client was like before the onset of her current problem or symptoms (premorbid personality).

Assessment of a client's current and premorbid personality may entail seeking answers to the following questions: (a) What does the client like best and least about herself? (b) What is the client's mood is normally like? (c) What was the client like as an adolescent? Was there childhood delinquency? (d) What does the client have to say about how others (her family, friends, employers, etc.) view her? (e) What types of interpersonal situations are difficult for the client to handle? (f) What are the client's opinions and impressions of significant people in her life?

2. Functional Personality and Ego Functions: In conceptualizing information about a client's personality functioning, it is helpful to think in terms of the **ego functions** (or ego tasks) on the following list. Notice that many ego functions also reflect aspects of cognitive/perceptual functioning, which were reviewed earlier in this section.

Self-regulation and self-control: This includes impulse control, frustration tolerance, self-awareness of drives, impulses, and affects, and ability to modulate feelings without being overwhelmed.

Judgment: This refers to the capacity to act responsibly. For example, the person can identify possible courses of action, anticipate and evaluate likely consequences, and make decisions about what's appropriate in specific circumstances.

Reality testing capacity: This refers to the capacity to distinguish what's occurring in one's own mind from what's occurring in the external world. This is a critical ego function because negotiating in an adaptive way with the external world requires the ability to perceive and understand stimuli accurately.

Thought processes (cognitive functioning): This includes intelligence level; ability to concentrate and focus attention and use selective inattention to filter irrelevant stimuli; and ability to have logical, coherent, and abstract thoughts and balance concrete and abstract thinking in a way that promotes adaptive functioning. Thought processes can become disorganized in stressful situations.

Capacity for interpersonal relationships (object relations): This refers to the ability to have mutually satisfying relationships, including the ability to perceive oneself and others as whole objects with three-dimensional qualities. For example, the person is able to choose when to initiate and end relationships, has the capacity for intimacy and can regulate the degree of intimacy and distance in her relationships, has the capacity for independence and can regulate her level of independence and dependence in relationships, and has the capacity for an appropriate degree of warmth and empathy in relationships and is able to accept others.

Integrative functioning or synthesis: This refers to the ego's capacity to organize and unify other functions within the personality, which enables a person to think, feel, and act in a coherent manner. For example, the person has the capacity to integrate potentially contradictory experiences, ideas, and feelings (e.g., she can love her husband yet also have angry feelings toward him).

Defensive functioning (ego defense mechanisms): In this context, the healthy use of defense mechanisms is reflected by an ability to effectively limit feelings of depression, anxiety, or other uncomfortable affect in a way that results in adaptive functioning and doesn't significantly disrupt one's personal effectiveness or sense of well-being. All people use defense mechanisms to cope with anxiety, stress, and problems of living (examples of defense mechanisms appear below). However, defensiveness can interfere with a person's ability to accurately perceive reality and get along with others. Rigid or excessive use of defenses impedes realistic problem-solving, and high levels of defensiveness and distortions of reality are characteristic of personality disturbances.

When these ego functions are characteristic of a client's long-term and current functioning (i.e., they haven't disappeared in spite of the stress the client is under), they are associated with effective social and occupational functioning and a subjective sense of personal well-being. Generally, you will evaluate a client's ego functioning as it relates to the problem areas you've identified. For example, if a client exhibits poor judgment, you'll want to explore whether her poor judgment is related to only the presenting problem or, instead, is pervasive. When evaluating a client's ego functions, be aware that there are age-related and culture-based differences in ego functions.

3. Immature, Neurotic, and Mature Defenses: Definitions of many of the defenses (defense mechanisms) mentioned below can be found in Section I of Human Development, Diversity, and Behavior.

a. Immature Defenses: Immature defenses are used in childhood and adolescence. By adulthood, many (but not all) people abandon these defenses because they produce socially unacceptable behavior and/or prevent a person from coping effectively with reality. Immature defenses include the following: (a) denial; (b) distortion (a person grossly reshapes external reality to suit her inner needs); (c) projection; (d) acting out (a person persistently gives in to an impulse to avoid the tension that would result from postponing its expression); (e) blocking (a person temporarily inhibits thinking); (f) hypochondriasis; (g) introjection; (h) passive-aggressiveness (a person expresses aggression indirectly through passivity, turning against herself, etc.); (i) regression; (j) schizoid fantasy (a person avoids interpersonal intimacy and uses eccentricity to repel others); and (k) somatization (a person converts psychic conflict into bodily symptoms). Note that the first three defenses on this list – denial, distortion, and projection – are sometimes called **narcissistic defenses**. These three defenses are almost always pathological because they involve rearranging external reality so that one doesn't have to cope with it.

b. Neurotic Defenses: Neurotic defenses are fairly common in adults and may also be used by some adolescents. They help people cope in the short-term; if overused, however, they tend to cause long-term problems in relationships, academic or occupational functioning, and enjoyment of life. Neurotic defenses the following: (a) controlling (a person tries to manage or regulate events or objects); (b) displacement; (c) dissociation (a person temporarily, but radically, modifies her sense of personal identity to avoid emotional distress); (d) externalization (a person perceives in the external world and objects elements of her own personality); (e) inhibition (a person consciously limits or disowns some ego functions); (f) intellectualization (a person excessively uses intellectual processes to avoid affective experience or expression); (g) isolation of affect; (h) rationalization; (i) reaction formation; (j) repression; and (k) sexualization (a person endows an object or function with sexual significance that it didn't have before in order to deflect anxieties associated with prohibited impulses).

c. Mature Defenses: Mature defenses are ones that are commonly used by "healthy" adults; using them provides a person with pleasure and/or a sense of mastery. Mature defenses include the following: (a) altruism; (b) anticipation (a person realistically anticipates or plans for future inner discomfort); (c) asceticism (a person eliminates the pleasurable effects of experiences); (d) humor; (e) sublimation; and (f) suppression (a person consciously or semiconsciously delays attention to a conscious impulse or conflict).

K. Behavioral Functioning

Information on specific behavioral assessment approaches appears in Section III of this chapter. More generally, you can directly observe a client's communication and social patterns, personal habits, and other characteristic behaviors during individual interviews, and, in conjoint sessions, you can observe the effects these behaviors have on others. When assessing behavior, you should keep in mind that one person's behavior doesn't affect another person's in a simple linear way. Instead, a circular process takes place in which the behavior of all the involved parties reciprocally affects and shapes the behavior of the other parties. Additionally, a critical part of behavioral assessment is identifying the antecedents and consequences of a target dysfunctional behavior (i.e., the events that precede and follow it). You should also explore what thoughts the client has before, during, and following the behavior as well as the intensity of her emotions associated with the behavior.

Many clients have behavioral problems that impair their social functioning, and most of these problems consist of either behavioral excesses or behavioral deficiencies (an absence of needed skills). For **behavioral excesses**, interventions aim to reduce or eliminate the behaviors (e.g., temper tantrums, arguing, consumptive excesses involving alcohol, shopping, or sex). For **behavioral deficiencies**, interventions aim to help clients acquire the skills and behaviors needed to function more effectively (e.g., express their feelings more directly, listen better to others, manage their finances better, resolve conflict).

Finally, as a social worker, you should be skilled at detecting functional behavioral patterns so that you are able to reinforce and make use of your clients' behavioral strengths.

L. Social Functioning

Social functioning, when applied to an individual, is defined as her motivation, capacity, and opportunity to (a) meet her basic needs, including performing tasks necessary for daily living such as obtaining food, shelter, and transportation, and (b) perform her major social roles as defined by her community and culture. Assessment of **social functioning**, therefore, requires you to collect information about a client's need-meeting activities and social role performance. You can then use this information to draw conclusions about the client's current level of social functioning, including both strengths and deficits.

1. Dimensions Social Functioning: Key aspects, or dimensions, of social functioning appear on the list below (Sheafor & Horejsi, 2003). Depending on the nature of the client's presenting problem and life circumstances, some of these aspects will be explored in depth while others will be examined less closely or not at all:

Fundamentals of independent living (e.g., ability to perform self-care tasks, adequacy of literacy skills, ability to meet social-role demands, awareness of personal strengths and limitations).

Personal appearance and hygiene (e.g., ability to maintain a level of personal hygiene that prevents illness and infection, ability to acquire and select appropriate clothing).

Housing and housekeeping (e.g., adequacy and safety of housing, ability to keep her home clean and sanitary).

Nutrition and health care (e.g., diet habits and sleep and exercise patterns, use of alcohol or other drugs, access to and capacity to pay for appropriate medical care).

Adjustments to physical disability (e.g., use of rehabilitation programs, medications, and assistive technology; ability to discuss the disability without embarrassment or apology; willingness to let others know what she can and cannot do).

Coping with ordinary problems of living (e.g., ability to fulfill responsibilities despite frustration, recover at a reasonable rate from depression or anxiety caused by a psychosocial stressor, carefully rebuild relationships after a loss, set priorities and reasonable limits on demands by others, and learn from past experiences; level of comfort with personal identity, self-concept, ethnicity, gender, sexual orientation, economic situation, and life circumstances).

Coping with mental health problems or addiction (e.g., willingness to acknowledge the existence of significant problems and recognize their present and future consequences; use of effective therapies, medications, and support groups).

Spirituality and religious activity (e.g., whether the client has values, beliefs, and perspectives that provide meaning, purpose, and direction in life; ability to attend religious services of her choice).

Citizenship and legal concerns (e.g., whether the client understands right and wrong, legal and illegal activity, and her basic rights and responsibilities as a citizen; willingness and ability to follow laws and moral principles that recognize other people's rights and needs and the common good; ability to avoid situations that could lead her to become involved dangerous or illegal conduct).

Family life (e.g., whether the client has a mutually satisfying relationship with a spouse or partner that meets her needs for intimacy and companionship; whether she experiences nonexploitative sexual activity; the extent to which she is accepting, supportive, and encouraging toward her children, has family members who support and encourage each other, and is willing to make sacrifices for her family and put her children first; whether she has an income sufficient to meet her family's needs).

Friendships and social supports (e.g., ability to maintain satisfying and lasting relationships with family, friends, neighbors, and coworkers; ability to access and willingness to use a social support network for encouragement, information, and tangible assistance; whether the client chooses companions who provide acceptance and encouragement and avoids people who are discouraging, manipulative, or exploiting).

Use of community resources (e.g., awareness of and ability to access needed services and resources such as medical care, mental health services, legal counsel, recreation, and employment services, as well as supports or assistance needed in order to use community resources).

Interaction with the community (e.g., safety of the client's community and neighborhood; extent to which she is limited by discrimination or oppression; extent of participation in social, recreational, and other activities in her community; whether she has a sense of belonging to a positive community; whether she takes initiative to help neighbors and is willing to be helped by them).

Education and training (e.g., ability to effectively compensate for sensory problems that limit learning; awareness of and ability to access education and training needed to develop skills required to perform social roles and fulfill responsibilities at work, home, and school).

Employment and job performance (e.g., whether the client knows how to apply for jobs and behave in job interviews, ability to determine if a job matches her skills and financial needs, whether she has a satisfying job that provides an adequate income and is appropriate to her skill and experience, safety of working conditions, ability to access suitable and affordable day care, whether she is a responsible employee).

Money management and consumer awareness (e.g., whether the client uses budgeting to monitor spending, plans for unanticipated emergencies and seasonal expenses, understands the difference between necessities and wants, avoids unwise expenditures and debt, and understands basic eligibility requirements for assistance from unemployment insurance, SSI, etc., reporting rules, and time limitations).

Recreational and leisure activity (e.g., extent of participation in recreation or leisure activities that provide a break from responsibilities, awareness of various forms of recreation and leisure and willingness to explore them, whether the client chooses safe and wholesome activities and avoids social influences that could be harmful).

2. Understanding Social Role Problems: Signs and symptoms of problems with social functioning are frequently associated with one or more social role problems. You can often determine the specific nature of a social role problem by interpreting interactional dynamics reported by the client and collateral sources. You might also observe certain dynamics yourself during interviews with the client or the client and members of her family.

Broadly speaking, a **social role problem** will involve either difficulties in fulfilling social role obligations or conflicts in relationships with family members and/or people at work or school and/or in the community. Some clients have a distorted view of their social role obligations (e.g., a client feels pressure because she misunderstands how others expect her to behave). For additional information on sources of social role problems and types of social role problems, see Section I of Human Development, Diversity, and Behavior.

Finally, when analyzing problems of role performance and deciding what type of intervention is needed, you should explore the following questions: (a) What is the nature and degree of the discrepancy between the client's actual role performance and role expectation? (b) Is the discrepancy caused by a lack of knowledge or skill? (c) If the discrepancy is caused by a lack of knowledge and skill, how best can this be addressed? (d) If the discrepancy is caused by a rejection of, or lack of interest, in the role, how can this be addressed?

M. Environmental Systems

After evaluating the presenting problem and relevant aspects of the client's functioning, you need to directly assess the client in the context of her environment (the social and physical settings in which she lives). This part of assessment takes a holistic (integrated) view of the client's environment and examines the adequacy of relevant aspects of the environment to meet the client's needs.

1. Adopting an Ecological Perspective: When assessing a client in the context of her environment, you should focus on the transactions between person and environment, or the **goodness of fit** between the client and her environment:

- A client's environment may either provide opportunities and resources that meet her needs and stimulate her growth or, alternatively, present obstacles that make it difficult or impossible for her to fulfill her needs or develop in a healthy manner. When social systems or institutions in a client's environment are failing to effectively or efficiently meet her needs, her social functioning is likely to be impaired.

- When examining client-environment transactions and the strengths and barriers in those transactions, consider issues of affordability, availability, accessibility, and acceptability. As noted earlier, "acceptability" refers to whether services are compatible with the client's cultural values and traditions.

2. Basic Environmental Needs That May be Assessed: In assessing environmental needs, you should give highest priority to those aspects of the environment that are most relevant to the client's particular problem or situation and focus on comparing the client's unique needs against the availability of resources and opportunities in her environment. Basic environmental needs that may be assessed in determining the adequacy of a client's environment include the following (Hepworth et al., 2006):

- An adequate and stable physical environment that fosters health and safety (not only housing, but also surroundings that are free of toxins and other health risks).

- Adequate social support systems (family, relatives, friends, neighbors, organized groups). This is discussed in more detail below.

- Affiliation with a meaningful and responsive faith community. This is discussed in more detail below.
- Access to timely, appropriate, and affordable health care (including physicians, dentists, medications, nursing homes, etc.).
- Access to safe, reliable, and affordable child care and elder care services.
- Access to recreational facilities.
- Transportation (including means of transportation to work, socialize, use resources, vote, etc.)
- Adequate housing that provides sufficient space, sanitation, privacy, and safety from hazards and air/noise pollution.
- Adequate police and fire protection and a reasonable degree of security.
- Safe and healthful work conditions.
- Adequate financial resources to purchase essential resources.
- Adequate nutritional intake.
- A predictable living arrangement with caring others (this is particularly important for children).
- Opportunities for education and self-fulfillment.
- Access to legal assistance.
- Employment opportunities.

3. Assessing Social Support Systems: Social support systems (SSSs) play a critical role in determining a person's social functioning. In particular, adequate social support systems tend to reduce the effects of stressful situations and facilitate successful adaptation. Conversely, lacking adequate social support systems is a vulnerability and may represent a source of distress for the client.

The benefits derived from involvement with social support systems include the following: (a) attachment, which is provided by close relationships that give a sense of belonging and security; (b) social integration, which is provided by membership in a network of people who share one's interests and values; (c) the opportunity to nurture others, which provides incentive to keep going when faced with adversity; (d) physical care when one is unable to care for oneself due to illness, incapacity, or severe disability; (e) validation of personal worth, which promotes self-esteem and is provided by family, friends, coworkers, etc.; (f) a sense of reliable alliance, which is provided primarily by kin; and (g) guidance, child care, financial help, and other assistance in coping with difficulties and crises (Hepworth et al., 2006)

Assessing the social support systems (or **social networks**) in your client's life entails (a) examining their reciprocal interactions with the client, (b) learning the client's perceptions of their importance, and (c) exploring what role they play in the client's problem or ability to overcome her problem. Sometimes a negative support system can be counteracted by helping the client develop a positive network. Other times, the system itself needs to be a focus of intervention (e.g., you work with a client's family members to make them aware of their roles in the client's problem).

4. Spiritual Assessment: Spirituality has been defined in many different ways, but, generally, it is connected to the human search for transcendence, meaning, and connectedness to something beyond the self. It includes three components: a cognitive component (the meaning one gives to past and current events and personal experiences); an affective component (a person's inner life and sense of connectedness to a larger reality); and a behavioral component (the way a person affirms her beliefs, such as though individual prayer or group worship). Therefore, spiritual beliefs may affect a client's response to adversity (spirituality may be a source of strength for her during times of adversity), the coping methods she uses, and the sources of support available to her (e.g., her faith community may be a helpful social network).

Because spirituality influences beliefs, spiritual assessment can help you better understand your client's belief system. And, because connection to a faith community can be a source of tangible resources and social support, spiritual assessment can also help you understand your client's resources. To begin eliciting information about this area, you can ask the client a question such as, "What are your sources of strength and hope," "How do you express your spirituality" or "Do you identify with a particular religion or faith?" (Hepworth et al., 2006).

Another benefit of knowing about your client's spirituality is that it may provide a wider range of appropriate interventions for addressing her problem. If your client has experienced a trauma, for example, an exploration of suffering, good and evil, shame or guilt, and forgiveness may be a central part of the change process. And, if a client is facing a personal or spiritual crisis, it may be important to involve a clergyperson or other leader of her faith in working to address the crisis.

Finally, "religion" is a socially sanctioned institution based on spiritual practices and beliefs, and, in some cases, religious issues may be central to a client's presenting problem – e.g., parents disagree about the spiritual upbringing of their children, or families are in conflict over behaviors forbidden by certain religions, such as premarital sex, contraceptive use, divorce, alcohol use, or homosexuality.

N. Motivation, Resistance, and Ambivalence to Change

1. Motivation: The best indicator of initial level of motivation is whether or not the client has come to your office or agency voluntarily: An involuntary client (one who has been forced into treatment by a family member, the court, etc.) will tend to be less motivated than one who came in on her own. Other information that can help you estimate a client's initial level of motivation include her expressed willingness to be actively involved in treatment and level of subjective distress. A client who appears indifferent to or unconcerned about the problem may not be sufficiently motivated to change.

Other typical obstacles to motivation include the following: the client has no experience with professional helping or had a poor experience with it in the past; the client has difficulty opening up to others; the client is feeling inadequate because she needs help; the client is ashamed of her problem or fears your reaction to it; the client is a member of a cultural group that discourages seeking help from individuals outside the family; or the client has a cultural background that differs from yours.

Both the direction and strength of motivation are important:

- *Direction* – what are the client's goals and expectations for treatment and are they realistic? Unrealistic goals and expectations should be confronted (although gently) so that the client can develop more realistic goals.
- *Strength* – will the client take an active role in the intervention, or does she expect the "cure" to come from you?

Finally, during your early interactions, a client's level of motivation can be influenced by, among other things, the quality of the helping relationship that develops and your ability to establish rapport, understand her goals, and generate relevant incentives. (Strategies for enhancing motivation are described in Section II of Interventions with Clients/Client Systems.)

2. Resistance: Resistance to change is typical simply because people tend toward maintaining the status quo, or keeping things as they are. In addition, some clients are resistant because they feel anxious about needing help and/or are distressed about even the prospect of changing. Change is always difficult and tends to produce feelings of fear or frustration, may bring about personal turmoil, and can provoke conflict among people affected by the change, such as members of a client's family. Some clients are worried about the prospect of experiencing these "side-effects" of change.

Other factors that can influence resistance in the early stage of helping are the nature of the problem (e.g., a client fears disapproval or has feelings of shame, guilt, or fear); personality factors (e.g., low self-esteem, punishing superego, high anxiety); and personal variables (e.g., a multi-problem family, lack of education, negative experiences with social agencies).

In the first phase of helping, examples of client behaviors that may indicate resistance include inattention, intellectualizing (rationalizing or trying to explain away behaviors), long silences, changing the subject, and minimizing her problems. The client may also arrive late for appointments or cancel appointments. Skills and techniques for addressing resistance are described in Section VII of Interventions with Clients/Client Systems.

3. Ambivalence to Change: Ambivalence is present when a client both wants and doesn't want a specific change. A client experiencing ambivalence may feel as though she is pulled in opposite directions and become immobilized and unable to make decisions or take action. You should help a client work through ambivalence to change so that she can engage in the change process and begin making decisions and taking action. One way of doing this is to help her sort through her perceptions of the potential risks and rewards associated with the change she wants, or needs, to make. When the rewards far outweigh the risks, a client will usually be willing to attempt the change. When the risks far outweigh the rewards, however, and/or when the rewards are uncertain, a client will usually remain reluctant to change.

Note that while resistance and ambivalence are related, they are not the same thing. Resistance stems from a wish to maintain the status quo and it may be present even when a person has exhibited a strong desire to change.

O. The Need for External Resources

Assessment may reveal that a client needs services or resources that you or your agency cannot or do not provide. These may include specialized assessments, health care, financial assistance, child care, elder care, job training, etc. When this happens, you should make appropriate referrals to meet the client's needs. Another valuable resource may be the client's natural support system (friends, family, neighbors, etc.). (The referral process is reviewed in depth in Section VI of Interventions with Clients/Client Systems.)

P. Culture and Social Class

1. Assessment of Culturally Diverse Clients: While you must be familiar with the cultural variables that influence your clients, you must avoid stereotyping and should distinguish between patterns that are determined by the client's personality and patterns that are determined by her cultural background. The following guidelines are also important in facilitating assessment of culturally diverse clients:

- Determine the extent to which the client (particularly if she is an immigrant or refugee) has been socialized into the mainstream (dominant or majority) culture. Because culturally diverse individuals belong to two cultures, their functioning should be considered in light of both their culture of origin and the majority culture. For example, how many generations have passed since the client (or her family) came to the United States? Also keep in mind that there may be differences in **acculturation** among members of the same family, with younger members adapting much more quickly and rejecting many of their cultural traditions.

- Bear in mind that cultures vary with regard to a variety of normative patterns that influence interactions and behaviors (e.g., care of elderly relatives, child rearing, adolescent roles, gender roles, mate selection, communication between spouses and between parents and children, style of relating to an authority figure). Thus, certain interactional patterns or behaviors that seem maladaptive to you may be considered adaptive in the client's culture (and vice versa). For example, if you are a middle-class white American, you might view a traditional Hispanic or Arab family as "enmeshed."

- Be aware that you and the client may have differing beliefs about the causes underlying life problems and physical and mental symptoms, and that the client's beliefs may influence her expectations regarding diagnosis and treatment and her willingness to accept a medical or clinical diagnosis and comply with the intervention.

- Bear in mind that various cultural, ethnic, and religious groups attach different meanings and have distinct patterns of response to life events, such as death, physical illness, divorce, pregnancy out of wedlock, etc. They also have differing role expectations for males/husbands and females/wives (e.g., job loss may be more traumatic for a male if men in his culture are expected to provide for the family's material needs).

- Keep in mind that certain behavior that seems unusual to you may be considered normal within the client's cultural reference group. To determine whether a client's behavior is abnormal or not, you must know her cultural definition of what is "normal" or "abnormal" under the circumstances. In addition, the DSM-5 states that an expectable or culturally approved response to a stressor or loss is not a mental disorder. For instance, if a newly arrived immigrant reports anxiety and depression, you would need to assess whether these feelings are understandable in light of the changes in her life as well as what reactions to new situations are typically expected or sanctioned in the client's culture.

- Use psychological testing selectively: (a) Consider whether the client's English language skills are sufficient for her to understand a given test or provide meaningful responses. (b) If you use objective tests, interpret the results carefully, particularly when research indicates that norms are not adequate or that results may be misleading for certain groups. (c) If you use projective tests, be aware that a client who values formality and structure in professional relationships may be uncomfortable with the task of responding to ambiguous stimuli. If so, then non-responsiveness to stimuli may not be a clinical sign. Response content also may be affected by a client's background.

- Be aware that experiences with **discrimination** and **oppression** can produce chronic levels of stress that may play a causal role in the onset and course of certain physical, emotional, behavioral, or social-functioning problems and some mental disorders. Living in poverty can have similar effects.

Finally, if you are unable to collect the relevant information from the client, you should (with permission from the client) try to obtain it from family or friends of the client. Alternatively, you may seek consultation from someone of the client's cultural or ethic group.

2. Assessment of Clients Who are Immigrants or Refugees: When assessing clients who are recent immigrants or refugees, it can be useful to apply concepts associated with the **stages of migration** identified by experts such as Drachman and Halberstadt (1993): premigration and departure, transit, and resettlement. Applying this information reminds you to explore the following areas:

- The client's *departure experience* (which could have been traumatic if the client is a refugee) and feelings about separation from home and, as relevant, family.

- The client's *transit experience* – trauma experienced during transit can make adaptation more difficult during the *resettlement stage.*

- What issues have arisen since the client arrived in the U.S.? Consider adaptation to cultural norms, health and mental health problems, education or employment issues, language barriers, changing family dynamics, and experiences with discrimination or xenophobia. (Xenophobia refers to the fear or hatred of foreigners and other strangers.)

The **culturagram** is an assessment tool that may be used with immigrant families to help understand their worldview (e.g., values, traditions), their strengths, and the challenges they are facing.

3. Assessment of Clients Living in Poverty: The primary determinants of socioeconomic status (or social class) are income, education, and occupation, and the differences between social classes are likely to involve value and lifestyle differences that are even more pronounced, and perhaps more uniform, than religious, racial, or gender differences. In fact, Sue and Sue (2003) argue that social class may be a more powerful determinant of values and behavior than are race or ethnicity and they caution that it can be difficult for therapists from middle- to upper-class backgrounds to relate to the circumstances and hardships affecting clients who live in poverty.

The following guidelines are critical when assessing a client who lives in poverty: (a) Adopt a **strengths perspective**. (b) Be aware that feelings of helplessness, dependence, and inferiority are easily fostered under conditions associated with poverty. If the client feels hopeless, she may respond to her circumstances, as well as to you and other service providers, with passivity and emotional dependency. (c) Avoid attributing client attitudes that result from physical and environmental adversity to her individual or cultural traits. Instead, attempt to understand the client's emotional and mental state and be sensitive to the many obstacles and forces that make it especially difficult for a client living in poverty to change her circumstances.

Although the focus on assessment will depend on the nature of the client's presenting problem or need, you will usually want to collect information about the following areas:

- The client's history of poverty (e.g., is being poor an unexpected development in her life?); current financial situation; and methods of securing housing, food, and clothing; and the adequacy of the housing and food she is able to provide for herself (and her family, if relevant).

- The personal, family, and situational factors contributing to the client's poverty. This can identify barriers to economic self-sufficiency for the client.

- The client's feelings related to her situation. When a person is poor, many aspects of her life are uncertain and beyond her control. This stress often leads to anxiety, fear, and frustration.

- The client's social support network. Relatives, friends, or close associates may be an untapped resource for meeting some of the client's needs.

Finally, a client living in poverty may not have sufficient resources to meet her basic needs or other important requirements, including adequate shelter, food, or medical care for herself and/or her family. You should provide the client with the information she needs in order to apply for services. Because welfare policies, program rules, eligibility criteria, etc., can pose barriers to poor clients in need of assistance, however, you should be prepared to serve as the client's advocate to make sure she obtains all of the services she needs and is entitled to.

III. Assessment Methods and Techniques

A. Client Interviews

Client interviews are often your primary source of data during assessment. With most clients, the first interview begins with your introducing yourself and offering a brief explanation of the purpose of the interview. After this, you start exploring the client's concerns, typically by asking her why she came in. This approach gives the client an opportunity to express her concerns as she sees them and helps you determine what kinds of follow-up questions to ask. (For more information on the first interview, see Section II of Interventions with Clients/Client Systems.)

1. The Client's Verbal Report: Client interviews allow you to hear the client's verbal report. A typical verbal report consists of the presenting problem and information about the client's current and past functioning and life circumstances, including facts, experiences, opinions, and feelings that she discloses spontaneously; information you elicit by questioning her; and impressions you derive about specific functions, such as orientation, concentration, and memory, by observing and interpreting her verbal and nonverbal behavior.

Obtaining a verbal report is relatively easy when a client discloses her concerns, thoughts, and feelings spontaneously or with minimal prompting from you. When a client is hesitant or overwrought with emotion, however, you need to use specific interview skills (open-ended questions, paraphrases, empathic responding, furthering responses, clarification, etc.) to elicit the data you need. Using these skills is effective for increasing the quantity, specificity, and accuracy of the material you elicit. Even if you doubt something the client says, however, you should not challenge her about the content of her verbal report because doing so would be countertherapeutic. Rather, you should assume that a client's report is accurate unless you collect information that contradicts it.

Finally, you usually need to verify and supplement a client's verbal report by speaking to people who know the client well and are familiar with the problem and by reviewing relevant records and reports concerning the client.

2. The Client's Nonverbal Behavior: Observation of a client's nonverbal behavior (e.g., body posture, body language, gestures, eye contact, voice tone, attire) during interviews can provide useful information about her emotions, attitudes, behaviors, and mental status. Behavioral cues can express feelings that a client may be unwilling or unable to put into words, and, in some cases, may contradict or deny a client's verbal messages. In fact, your observations of a client are often more accurate than the client's verbal report because many nonverbal behaviors are performed unconsciously and you have an opportunity to observe them directly. When developing hypotheses based on a client's nonverbal behavior, you must take into consideration her cultural background (e.g., in some cultures, averting one's eyes is a sign of respect).

B. Obtaining Information From Collateral Sources

To verify or supplement a client's verbal report, you will often interview or contact other interested and knowledgeable parties and examine relevant records and reports. Verbal information from collateral contacts is subject to error or bias, but, compared to the client, a collateral source can often provide more objective information (unless the source is directly involved in the problem). A competent assessment may also require you to refer the client to other professionals for specialized evaluations.

Although soliciting collateral information can be useful no matter who the client is, contact with relevant others is particularly important when the client has a serious mental disorder, cognitive limitations, or a substance-related disorder that may prevent her from providing reliable information or when she is heavily invested in the outcome of the assessment.

Before contacting any collateral source, you should have a signed **release of confidential information** from the client or from a minor client's parent or legal guardian, unless a legal exception applies (see Section I of Professional Relationships, Values, and Ethics). In addition, it's worthwhile to explain to the client the purpose and benefits of contacting the source.

1. Family, Teachers, Employers, Etc.: Valuable sources of collateral information include informants who have regular contact with the client and are able to provide meaningful information about relevant aspects of her life (e.g., her previous life history, current characteristics, and behavioral tendencies). Examples include relatives, caregivers, friends, coworkers, employers, teachers, probation or parole officers, and clergy. These individuals (especially family members) may volunteer information, but, more often, you have to actively solicit their input. Your purposes for interviewing these people can be to verify certain facts the client has shared and/or solicit new or more elaborate information, including insight into how they view the client, her situation, and the problem.

2. Life Records and Other Documents: A number of relevant records, files, and reports on the client can provide valuable information about her functioning and key events and experiences in her life. Examples of documents that may exist for a client include physicians' reports, social assessment reports, and medical, mental health, agency, school, employment, arrest, and probation records. Examining relevant documents can alert you to new areas of inquiry and provide a reference against which you can evaluate the client's verbal report. For instance, information documented in a record may inform you that a client's response to a question was incomplete or dishonest.

3. Professionals From Other Disciplines: As a social worker, you may consult with colleagues or professionals from other disciplines or refer a client to one for a number of different reasons. In particular, input from other professionals can sometimes help you clarify the nature and extent of the problem, as well as shed light on other indicators of a client's functioning. This is important when other methods of assessment available to you don't provide a complete picture of the client's functioning.

a. Medical Doctors: You should contact a **medical doctor** whenever a client's physical health is in question or she has psychological symptoms that could be due to the physiological effects of a substance, medication, or underlying medical condition. This can entail obtaining current medical information through referral for relevant evaluations and tests (e.g., a general physical examination, neuroimaging procedures), reviewing a client's existing medical records and speaking directly with her physician, or both.

You may want to recommend a physical exam for any client presenting with psychological symptoms who has not had one in the past year. This is important because a number of medical conditions present as psychological problems (e.g., a depressed client may have an underactive thyroid gland) (see Appendix I in this chapter). Consultation and direct client contact with a physician is critical when you suspect that a client may have a serious, but undiagnosed, health problem or be a heavy user of alcohol or other drugs. In addition, drugs prescribed to alleviate troubling mental or physical symptoms can cause problematic physical side-effects which should be evaluated by an appropriate medical professional.

A **neurologist** is a medical doctor who is trained in the diagnosis and treatment of nervous system disorders, including diseases of the brain, spinal cord, nerves, and muscles. Neurologists perform neurological examinations of the nerves of the head and neck, muscle strength and movement, balance, ambulation (walking and moving about), reflexes, sensation, and memory, speech, language, and other cognitive abilities. They also perform diagnostic tests, such as CAT scans, MRIs/MRAs, and EEGs. Among the signs and symptoms that indicate a client may need to see a neurologist, if she hasn't done so recently, include a change in mental status, forgetfulness, a change in bowel or bladder function, difficulty swallowing, dizziness, double vision, fainting, headaches, numbness, pain in the neck or back, seizures, slurred speech, tingling, and weakness. In addition, the results of neurological testing can facilitate accurate diagnosis of certain mental disorders, including learning disorders, autism spectrum disorders, attention-deficit/hyperactivity disorder (ADHD), Tourette's disorder, other tic disorders, and neurocognitive disorders.

b. Psychiatrist: Consultation with a **psychiatrist** should occur when a client needs, or may need, psychotropic medication to manage the intense, disabling symptoms of an emotional condition, such as grief, or the chronic symptoms of a mental disorder. A medication evaluation is generally indicated when a client who is not currently taking psychotropic medication turns out to have ADHD, a tic disorder, a major neurocognitive disorder (i.e., dementia), schizophrenia or another psychotic disorder, major depressive disorder, a bipolar disorder, and/or obsessive-compulsive disorder. A client with panic disorder, a phobic disorder, or generalized anxiety disorder may also be referred for a medication evaluation.

Referral to a psychiatrist may also be indicated when a client who is taking psychotropic medication reports that the drug is not having the desired effect (e.g., the client continues to feel depressed while taking an antidepressant) or complains of side-effects caused by the medication. And, where relevant, you should consult with any psychiatrist who has treated the client, including any psychiatrist currently prescribing medication for the client. (As noted earlier, information on psychotropic medications and their uses and side-effects appears in Appendix II of this chapter.)

c. Psychologist: You may refer a client to a **psychologist** for psychological testing or consult with a psychologist who has evaluated or treated the client in the past. Psychological testing can be an effective means of uncovering characteristics and personality traits that influence a client's functioning – they can provide information on the client's intellectual capacity, patterns of motivation and coping behavior, self-concept, level of anxiety or depression, and general personality integration – and for detecting learning disorders. Testing by a neuropsychologist can be used to uncover brain damage and its location. You can find a review of major psychological tests later in this section.

Finally, it's also a good idea to contact any social agency, other social worker, family therapist, or other therapist who has assessed, treated, or otherwise assisted the client in the past. You may both consult with these individuals and review their records concerning the client.

C. Observation of Interactions

You can learn more about a client's functioning and circumstances by observing her interactions with family members (e.g., spouse, children, parents) or other significant members of her social support system. Using a technique known as **enactment** allows you to create a situation in which you can observe these interactions directly. Enactment generally entails asking family members or couples to recreate a past conflict in your presence, but can also involve having clients enact a contrived situation to find out how they interact when engaged in common activities such as planning, parenting, and decision-making.

The impressions you derive from observing interactions tend to be more accurate than those gleaned from a verbal report because you're gathering information by direct observation. These observations may be particularly significant when you discover that what you observe is very different from what a client reported about her relationships. When you detect such differences, however, you need to remember that people may behave differently in your presence than they do in "real life" simply because the office/agency setting is artificial or because they want to control the impression they make on you. For this reason, you should ask clients to what extent their enacted behavior corresponds with their behavior in "real-life" situations. You may also visit the clients at their home, since interactions there are more likely to be authentic.

D. Home Visits

Home visits (in-home interviews) with a client (or family) should be scheduled at a mutually convenient time and used in a purposeful manner. They are not simply social visits. When you request an in-home interview, you should provide the client with a clear explanation of how and why it will enhance the effectiveness of the services she receives.

1. Purposes of Home Visits: Home visits can be used to engage clients since many people feel more at ease and accepted at home than they do in an office setting. Home visits are also useful for facilitating a more accurate assessment because they allow you to observe a client in her natural environment. In other cases, home visits are used to deliver services when a client either can't or won't meet you in an office setting.

Although you should generally avoid unannounced visits to a client's home, you might need to make one if you need to speak to a client who doesn't have a phone, can't read a letter or e-mail, or has failed to respond to your efforts to contact her. If you make an unannounced visit, you should explain right away your efforts to contact the client and then attempt to schedule a visit. If the client invites you in, however, it's appropriate to have the in-home interview that day.

2. Benefits of Home Visits: Visiting a client's home is effective for the following purposes: (a) assessing environmental factors affecting the client; (b) gaining a greater understanding of the client by seeing her home environment and observing how she behaves there; (c) seeing how the client interacts with significant others; and (d) gaining first-hand information about home cleanliness, possible drug use, type of neighborhood, financial circumstances, etc. Additionally, arranged home visits can be effective for reducing a client's or family's defensiveness and promoting involvement of the entire family.

3. How to Behave in the Client's Home: It's important to be courteous when visiting a client's home; for example, you should ask the client where she would like you to sit, accept an appropriate offer of food or drink, and show genuine interest in family pictures and other household items that express the client's interests or culture. And, no matter what you find inside the client's home – clutter, odors, extreme cleanliness, or signs of violence, drug use, or impulsivity – you must never show signs of disapproval or shock.

Although the distractions that are commonly present during an in-home interview (e.g., other people coming and going, a loud television, numerous phone calls) may feel disruptive to you, they can provide an accurate picture of the client's (or family's) functioning and environment. When distractions are significant, however, it is appropriate to directly explain to the client the need for privacy during the interview and remind her of the interview's purpose.

If other people are at the client's home during your visit, you should ask the client if it is acceptable to talk about private matters in their presence. If the client wants family or other informal helpers to sit in on the interview, you should respect her preference and allow these people to attend the interview.

E. Clinical Tools for Understanding the Client and Her Situation

1. Life History Grid: The life history grid allows you to organize and graphically depict data related to various periods in a client's life and is useful for identifying major events and the development of significant problems over time. It is especially useful in work with children and adolescents because understanding their experiences during a particular developmental stage is often very useful for clarifying their current functioning. Data from a variety of sources (e.g., interview, agency records, hospital records) are used to develop a life history grid.

2. Life Cycle Matrix: A life cycle matrix is used to graphically depict the developmental stages of all individuals in a household. Because members of a family are usually at different developmental stages and facing different developmental tasks, this tool is particularly useful in work with families. Using this matrix helps you organize your impressions about family members and their physical, psychological, social, and spiritual needs at different stages of development.

3. Tools for Social Assessment:

a. Genogram: A **genogram** is used to obtain and record information about a client's family patterns and history. This tool provides a schematic diagram of the family system describing at least three generations of family relationships, geographical locations, and significant life events. Information included on a typical genogram includes demographics (date of birth, marriages, divorces, deaths); past and current health and psychological status; critical events (moves, illnesses, financial changes); functioning levels; recurrent patterns of behavior (including alcohol or drug use); ethnicity; religion; education; occupations; legal difficulties; and triangulations and other elements of the family's structure. Clarifying these historical patterns can help prepare the client to develop strategies for behavioral change.

b. Ecomap: An **ecomap** is used to help a client acquire a better understanding of her social context so that she can learn effective strategies for changing it. Circles are used to represent the client and the different systems with which she currently interacts (e.g., parents, spouse, children, extended family, friends, school, workplace, church, community organizations, social service agencies, health care agencies). Once these systems are on the map, you ask the client to describe the nature and direction of the energy flow between herself and each system and then record this information on the ecomap using lines that connect the client to each system. For example, a solid line signifies a positive relationship, a broken line signifies a tenuous relationship, a jagged line signifies a stressful relationship, an arrow pointing to the client means that the system primarily influences the client, and an arrow pointing to the system means that the client primarily influences the system.

c. Dual Perspective Worksheet: Norton's dual perspective (1978) can be used to develop a worksheet that depicts the location of both supports and barriers affecting a client's interactions with her social environment. This information allows you and the client to identify areas of strength that might be resources for change and areas that need to be changed. It also helps you determine whether your intervention should target elements of the client's nurturing environment, sustaining environment, or both. (For more information on Norton's dual perspective, see Section VI of Human Development, Diversity, and Behavior.)

d. Social Network Map and Social Network Grid: The Social Network Map or Social Network Grid can be used to assess a client's social support systems. They help identify the client's potential social supports with an emphasis on her perceptions and beliefs about them, and the results can be used to help the client use her social supports more effectively. Using the **Social Network Grid** involves collecting information about key people in the client's social networks, areas of life in which the support occurs, types of support provided by each person, the degree to which support people are important to the client, whether support is reciprocal or not, how close the client is to her support people, the frequency of her contact with her support people, and the length of her relationship with each of them. Because a client may forget to include some of the people in her life or overstate or underestimate their importance, after a grid (or map) is competed, you should discuss with the client how she might reach out to and use the social supports in her life. Finally, because creating grids and maps involves using sort cards, it engages the client in a visual and tactile (kinesthetic) activity, which can be useful for clients who prefer these modalities.

e. Sociogram: A **sociogram** can be used to identify and illustrate a client's friends, associates, and enemies by diagramming the type, frequency, and quality of her contacts with these individuals. To construct a sociogram, you ask the client questions such as, "Who do you talk to the most in your family?" "Who do you talk to the most at work (or school)?" "Who do you spend time with the most?"

Other instruments available to assess a client's social support systems include the Schedule for Social Interaction, the Social Support Network Inventory, the Perceived Social Support Network Inventory, and the Questionnaire on Resources and Stress.

F. Behavioral Assessments

Behavioral assessments attempt to understand behavior by identifying the context in which it occurs. They assume that a behavior can be most effectively understood by focusing on the environmental variables (antecedents and consequences) that control it. Assessment of these variables is known as **functional analysis**. Behavioral assessments are distinguished from other forms of assessment by their emphasis on directly observable behaviors and their view of behavior as both situationally specific and multidimensional (i.e., composed of motor, verbal, and/or physiological responses).

Approaches to behavioral assessment include the following: (a) Behaviorally oriented interviews are used to gain an impression of the presenting problem and the variables maintaining it, as well as collect relevant historical data and identify a client's strengths and past efforts to cope with the problem. (b) Cognitive-behavioral assessments are used to explore a client's cognitions and cognitive strategies and identify which ones contribute to the problem. (c) Behavioral observation (which we discuss in more detail below) is used to observe directly the concerns that are the focus of assessment. **Reactivity** – in which people behave differently because they know they are being observed – can compromise the validity of any observational procedure.

Behavioral observation may be a necessary supplement to an interview or more appropriate than an interview when clients are not old enough to report their problems or are not able to provide a report because of cognitive deficits or the nature of their disorder.

Formal methods of behavioral observation follow an objective and standardized format and require identifying specific behaviors that are observable and measurable. Once a target behavior is defined precisely, an observer writes down each time it occurs and what happened immediately before (antecedent) and after (consequence) the behavior. This information is used to discern patterns of behavior and plan treatment based on those patterns.

Less formal observational procedures, such as observing parent-child interactions in your office or at a client's home, rely more on your recollection and interpretation of what you see. After observing the interactions of a client and her family members or other significant people, you may use a **behavior matrix** to record your observations. What you record will help you determine what positive behaviors should be reinforced, what negative behaviors should be extinguished, and what new behaviors need to be learned by the client.

Specific methods of behavioral observation include naturalistic observation, controlled observation, and self-monitoring:

Naturalistic observation: The client is observed in the environment in which the problem occurs (e.g., her classroom).

Controlled observation: You force the target behavior to take place in a simulated manner (such as via enactment or a role-play) and then observe it firsthand. This may take place in a clinical setting or in a client's natural environment (e.g., her home).

Self-monitoring: With **self-monitoring**, you ask a client to record information about the frequency and conditions surrounding the target behavior. She may also be instructed to maintain a journal or record of other important information, such as her feelings and thoughts before, during, and after each occurrence of the behavior. The results provide detailed information about the nature and magnitude of the behavior and the variables that elicit or reinforce it so that an appropriate intervention strategy can be developed and the effects of intervention can be evaluated.

G. Mental Status Exam

A **mental status exam** (MSE) is used to evaluate a client's current mental functioning. As a social worker, you may see clients who have an undiagnosed mental illness, neurological condition, or neurocognitive disorder (e.g., dementia). Understanding how to use a mental status exam enables you to recognize key symptoms and refer clients for needed psychiatric evaluations and evaluations of medical problems that affect psychological functioning (especially neurological evaluations). In conjunction with other data, information collected from an MSE may also be used to formulate an appropriate clinical diagnosis.

To conduct an MSE, you observe a client's behavior in an informal, systematic way, noting the presence of cognitive, emotional, and behavioral problems. For example, you note the presence of unusual behavior or answers that suggest a mental disorder. You then use your observations to make preliminary decisions about which areas of the client's functioning should be assessed in more detail and, sometimes, more formally. A common practice is to make mental status observations during the course of the interview and then change to direct questioning near the end of the interview to elicit additional information needed for the MSE.

Most MSEs include an evaluation of both behavioral aspects and cognitive aspects. These aspects are described below.

1. Behavioral Aspects: Behavioral functions are evaluated through direct observation of the client's speech and nonverbal behavior during an interview (i.e., you observe certain cues and interpret them as expressions of the client's present functioning).

a. General Appearance and Behavior: The client's appearance and behavior should be evaluated in light of what is generally expected for a person of the client's age, race, sex, socioeconomic status, cultural background, etc.

Physical characteristics: For example, ethnicity, apparent age, posture, disability or disfigurement, and emaciation or obesity. Physical appearance can influence life experiences in significant ways. It may affect self-esteem, how others tend to respond to the client, etc.

Communication barriers: For example, a visual or hearing impairment, impaired speech, and low fluency with the English language.

Alertness/level of consciousness: This can range from alert, to lethargic, to apathetic, to comatose.

Dress and hygiene: For example, quality and appropriateness of clothing and signs of neglect (including self-neglect).

Movement and activity: For example, rate and extent of movement; tense vs. relaxed; excessive motion; tics and other involuntary movements; stereotypies; mannerisms; symptomatic movements (tardive dyskinesia, tremor, autonomic hyperactivity); and mobility, gait, posture, and balance. For instance, fidgeting may indicate anxiety or agitation, and slouching may be a sign of boredom or resentment about coming to see you.

Facial expression: For example, animated vs. fixed facial expression, the client claims to be happy but looks as though she's about to cry, and degree of eye contact (which must always be evaluated within an appropriate cultural context). For instance, a lack of eye contact may signal anxiety or depression, and a client with psychosis may stare at you or repeatedly glance around the room as though she's responding to auditory or visual stimuli that don't actually exist.

Speech behavior: For example, articulation (stuttering, mumbling, clipped speech, immature speech, etc.); voice quality (loud, harsh, barely audible, affected, etc.); phraseology (use of "catch phrases" or baby talk, poor or underdeveloped vocabulary, pseudointellectual, frequent cursing, etc.); productivity (hesitant, rapid, hyperverbal, etc.); and manner (mechanical, responsive, candid, insightful, etc.)

Attitude toward the clinician: This refers to the client's prominent manner of relating to you (e.g., cooperative vs. resistant, friendly vs. hostile, open vs. secretive, involved vs. apathetic). A client's interactional style in an interview may resemble the way she relates to people in other interpersonal settings.

b. Mood and Affect: "**Mood**" refers to a relatively sustained and pervasive emotional state (e.g., anxious, depressed). "**Affect**" is more variable and reactive than mood. It consists of the expression of emotion or feelings displayed to others through facial expressions, hand gestures, voice tone, and other emotional signs such as laughter or tears. Individual affect normally fluctuates according to emotional state, and what is considered a normal range of affect ("broad affect") varies from culture to culture and also within cultures. On an MSE, mood and affect are generally evaluated along several dimensions, including the following:

Type or quality of mood: Usually one mood type will predominate in an interview (e.g., anger, fear, irritation, sadness, happiness).

Lability or reactivity: (a) A client may exhibit a mild restriction in the range or intensity of display of her feelings. This is referred to as **restricted** or **constricted affect**. (b) A client may have **labile affect** (i.e., her affect may be unstable and constantly changing). (c) Conversely, a client may display a significantly reduced variation of mood or affect. As noted earlier in this chapter, the term **affective flattening** (or **blunting**) is used to describe an extremely limited affective range or lack of response to environmental stimuli. Flat affect is associated with schizophrenia and is also found in severe depression and certain neurological conditions. (d) **Bland affect**, in which nothing seems to affect the client, is associated with a major neurocognitive disorder (i.e., dementia).

Appropriateness: Do the client's mood and affect match the current situation and the content of her thought? When a person's mood or affect is significantly inappropriate, this can be a sign of schizophrenia.

c. Flow of Thought: Flow of thought is reflected in a client's flow of speech (i.e., the client's speech is presumed to reflect her thought).

Association: (a) Is the client's speech spontaneous or does it occur only in response to questions? (b) Is there **flight of ideas**? Clients with mania often display flight of ideas, along with pressured speech. (c) Is there tangential speech (answers that seem unrelated to questions)? Are there **loose associations**? Both tangentiality and loose associations are associated with psychosis (often schizophrenia) but may also be found in mania. (d)

Incoherent and rambling speech is often associated with a thought disorder, but may also be a sign of alcohol or other drug intoxication. A client who displays these symptoms must be screened for alcohol and other drug use. (Flight of ideas and loose associations were defined in Section II of this chapter.)

Rate and rhythm of speech: (a) Is there **pressured speech**? This includes rapid speech that is difficult to interrupt and instances in which a client responds extremely quickly to questions (sometimes even before a question is fully asked). Pressured speech is associated with mania; some individuals with mania report that their words can't keep up with their thoughts. (b) Alternatively, a client may take far longer than normal to respond to questions, have long pauses between sentences, speak extremely slowly, and/or provide very brief answers. This is part of **psychomotor retardation** and is associated with severe depression. (c) Other speech cues that may be present include **circumstantial speech** (speech that contains excessive extraneous material in addition to the principal message) and stuttering.

2. Cognitive Aspects: Whereas observation alone can be used to obtain information about behavioral variables, to collect data about cognitive functioning you must also actively question the client to elicit the material you need.

a. Thought Content: Similar to flow of thought, thought content is reflected in the content of a client's speech. Examples of abnormal thought content include **delusions** and morbid preoccupations. Depending on the nature of the abnormal thought content, diagnostic possibilities include a primary psychosis, depressive or bipolar disorder, mental disorder due to another medical condition, or substance/medication-induced mental disorder. Mood-congruent delusions, for example, are associated with a mood disorder, while mood-incongruent delusions are more typical of schizophrenia.

b. Perception: Perception refers to the accuracy of a client's five senses (sight, hearing, touch, smell, and taste) or her ability to correctly perceive external stimuli and her own internal processes. Examples of abnormal perceptions include **illusions** (misperceptions of actual stimuli) and **hallucinations** (perceptions in the absence of actual stimuli). Hallucinations can involve any of the five senses and may be associated with a primary psychosis, mental disorder due to another medical condition, or substance/medication-induced mental disorder. Auditory hallucinations are the most common type among people with schizophrenia, while visual hallucinations are commonly reported by people withdrawing from alcohol who are experiencing delirium tremens. A depressive or bipolar I disorder can also include hallucinations in some cases.

This MSE category also includes anxiety symptoms (e.g., excessive, uncontrollable worry neither directed at nor caused by anything specific the client can identify), phobias, obsessions and compulsions, and thoughts of violence (including suicidal ideation).

c. Consciousness and Cognition: Consciousness and cognition consist of the ability to absorb, process, and communicate information.

Attention and concentration: "Attention" refers to the ability to focus on a current task or topic, while "concentration" is the ability to focus over a sustained period of time. Both abilities require a client to filter out irrelevant stimuli. You can get a sense of a client's attention span and ability to concentrate by observing her behavior during the entire interview. To evaluate these abilities in a more formal way, you can assign mental arithmetic problems, assign tasks such as, "Say the alphabet as quickly as you can" or

"Spell the word 'house' ... now spell it backwards," or name three objects and have the client repeat them. When assessing these areas, you should take into account a client's age, education level, culture, and degree of depression and anxiety.

Orientation: Orientation refers to an accurate awareness of the following: (a) person (e.g., you ask the client, "who are you," "what's your name," "are you married?"); (b) place (e.g., "where are you," "where do you live?"); (c) time (e.g., "how old are you," "what day is today?"); (d) situation (e.g., "who am I," "why are you here?"); (e) familiar objects (e.g., you point to common objects and ask the client to identify them); and (f) other people (e.g., "what's your mother's name?"). For more information on **disorientation**, see Section II in this chapter.

Language: This MSE category evaluates comprehension, fluency, naming of items, repetition, reading, and writing. These language aspects can be partially assessed based on how the client responds to conversation in the interview. They can also be evaluated by means of simple screening tests (e.g., you ask the client to repeat a simple phrase, instruct the client to perform a complex behavior involving a sequence of steps, or ask the client to read or write one or two sentences).

Memory: Memory consists of three types: immediate (within 5 or 10 seconds), short-term, and long-term. Immediate and short-term memory can be evaluated by asking the client to repeat a short list of items immediately (immediate memory) and then after five minutes have passed (short-term memory). To test long-term memory, you can evaluate the client's ability to organize information needed to relate her life history. Depending on the nature of a memory deficit, the primary diagnostic possibilities include a neurocognitive disorder (e.g., dementia), mental disorder due to another medical condition, or substance/medication-induced mental disorder.

Cultural information: This area is concerned with the client's remote memory (long-term memory for things that happened years ago) and general intelligence or intellectual functioning. To test these functions, you can ask a series of questions such as, "name the five most recent presidents," "name the vice president," and "name five large cities." Poor intellectual functioning despite a good educational background can sometimes indicate a neurological problem. As with attention and concentration, however, it's important to consider a client's age, education level, culture, and degree of depression and anxiety when assessing performance in this area.

Abstract thinking: Abstract thinking includes the ability to extract a principle from a specific example. Common ways of assessing abstract thinking include asking a client to interpret some familiar proverbs (e.g., "people in glass houses shouldn't throw stones") or explain the similarities and differences between specific objects (e.g., "How are an apple and an orange alike?"). When evaluating this function, it's important to recognize that abstract thinking depends much more on cultural background, intelligence, and education than mental health. Additionally, proverbs and their interpretations vary across cultures, and clients from some cultural backgrounds may be unfamiliar with the proverbs presented to them.

d. *Insight and Judgment:* To evaluate a client's **insight** (i.e., ideas about her problem and life situation), you can ask a series of questions such as, "do you think you are impaired" and "what strengths do you have?" Insight can be either complete, partial, or nonexistent, and tends to diminish during episodes of illness and improve during periods of remission. Poor insight is associated with neurocognitive disorders, severe depression, psychotic disorders, and mania.

As noted earlier, **judgment** (or common sense) refers to the ability to decide on an appropriate course of action to achieve realistic goals and has a significant influence on decision-making and problem-solving ability. To assess judgment directly, you can ask questions such as, "what do you expect from treatment," "what are your plans for the future," or "you find a stamped, addressed envelop on the sidewalk, what would you do?" Frequent poor judgment can be associated with a manic episode.

H. Structured and Semistructured Diagnostic Interviews

Structured diagnostic interviews provide explicit directions and standard questions that have been carefully developed to elicit specific information about a client's functioning in a consistent way and that are asked in a specific order. Clinical judgment (the subjective component of your decision-making) plays little or no role because you are provided with rules that guide your decisions about what areas to explore and how to sequence your questions and are given a system for rating the client's responses. Some structured diagnostic interviews also provide guidelines for rating the severity of a client's problems. Structured diagnostic interviews have been developed to evaluate specific mental disorders, including depressive disorders, bipolar disorders, anxiety disorders, psychotic disorders, dissociative disorders, eating disorders, psychopathy, and substance use disorders.

Structured diagnostic interviews are associated with certain disadvantages, including the following: (a) In contrast to unstructured and semistructured interviews, structured diagnostic interviews don't allow you to tailor an interview to a client's individual needs. (b) Some clients dislike an interview process that seems mechanized. If an interview is too rigid, a client may be inhibited from volunteering information not directly related to the questions you ask. (c) In focusing closely on decision rules and the wording of questions, you may overlook important observations of the client.

Like structured diagnostic interviews, **semistructured diagnostic interviews** provide standard questions that have been carefully developed to elicit specific information in a consistent way. With semistructured interviews, however, you may deviate from the preset questions to follow-up on important issues raised by the client's responses. An example is the Semistructured Clinical Interview for Children and Adolescents (SCICA).

I. Psychological Testing

Overview of Psychological Testing

Depending on its nature, psychological testing can provide useful information about a client's intellectual capacity, level of anxiety or depression, self-concept, coping behavior, pattern of motivation, and/or general personality integration. Psychological testing, however, emphasizes only certain variables and overlooks others, and, therefore, you should not make decisions based solely on the results of psychological testing. Instead, you must integrate test results with data from other sources.

1. Uses of Psychological Tests: Among the specific uses of psychological tests in clinical settings are the following:

- *Clinical tests* – these are used to assess the existence and severity of specific symptoms and problems (an example is the Beck Depression Inventory-II).

- *Personality tests* – these are used when a personality disorder is suspected or to get information about underlying personality structure to determine how it might be affecting a client's functioning or adaptation.

- *Intelligence tests* – these are used when intellectual disability is suspected, there is deterioration in the intellectual performance of an adult, or there is a discrepancy between a child's expected and actual school performance.

- *Neuropsychological tests* – these are used when brain degeneration or damage is suspected and to determine the nature of the impairment produced by brain pathology.

- *Vocational tests (interest inventories)* – these are used when a client is struggling with an identity issue or life transition, is developmentally stuck, or wants to explore academic or career alternatives.

2. When to Use Psychological Testing: Social workers use most forms of psychological testing selectively. Referral for psychological testing (global personality testing, intelligence testing, neuropsychological testing, etc.) is most appropriate when your own assessment fails to reveal a client's level of functioning or you suspect that a client has a personality disorder, specific learning disorder, or brain damage or dysfunction of some kind. Self-report inventories and checklists (e.g., client self-report standardized rating scales) are a useful alternative to longer psychological tests when the presence or severity of one problem, condition, or symptom is of particular concern.

3. Using Standardized Rating Scales: Many social workers use standardized rating scales to facilitate assessment and diagnosis of specific client problems, determine the need for further assessment in specific areas, and facilitate treatment planning, monitoring, and outcome evaluation. Standardized rating scales include sets of questions that measure well-defined constructs (behaviors, attitudes, feelings, etc.) and have undergone extensive testing to demonstrate their reliability when used with different populations.

Most standardized rating scales are brief, consisting of between 15 and 30 one-sentence statements (e.g., "I feel that I need more self-confidence") that a client is asked to rate on a 3-point to 7-point scale. To prevent clients from failing to consider each item carefully, some items are presented as positive statements and others as negative statements.

Standardized rating scales are available for measuring many different dimensions of client functioning (including social functioning), are easy to administer, and allow you to learn the client's own perception of her problem. Another advantage of standardized rating scales is that they are available for immediate use which can be important in cases when you need to quickly assess the severity of a client's situation. In addition, some standardized rating scales allow for the establishment of "cutting scores" which indicate the point on a scale where a client's score reflects a very serious problem or, at the other end of the scale, doesn't represent a problem that requires professional intervention.

On the flip side, these measures yield limited information. Information derived from these instruments must be supplemented with data from other sources. In addition, before using a scale, you must determine whether the scale is appropriate for the particular client – e.g., has the measure been normed with the cultural group of the client, does the client have the required reading ability, is the scale appropriate for a person in the client's age group?

Although clinician-administered standardized rating scales are available, many clinicians, including many social workers, prefer using client self-report scales. Examples of client self-report (self-administered) scales include the Beck Depression Inventory-II (BDI-II), Clinically Useful Depression Outcome Scale (CUDOS), Patient Health Questionnaire (PHQ-9), Quick Inventory of Depressive Symptomatology (QIDS), Zung Self-Rating Depression Scale, Zung Self-Rating Anxiety Scale, and Depression Anxiety and Stress Scale (DASS). Examples of clinician-administered scales include the Hamilton Rating Scale for Depression (HRSD), Hamilton Anxiety Scale (HAS), Clinician-Administered PTSD Scale for DSM-5 (CAPS-5), and ADHD Rating Scale IV (ADHD RS).

4. Clients' Rights: If you use psychological testing, you should be aware that clients have the right to know the purpose of the testing, names of and rationales for the tests being used, and results of the testing (they even have the right to read the resulting psychological report). They also have the right to know who (through their signed release of information) will have access to testing information (raw scores, test reports) in their records.

5. How to Share Test Results With Clients: If you use psychological testing with a client, you should explain the results to her using words that she can understand and that will not unduly upset her. It would be unethical to give the client only raw test data or to use technical jargon because such information would probably mean little to the client and could lead her to misunderstand her test results.

6. Test Reliability and Validity: Any test that is used must be both reliable and valid. When a test is **reliable**, it provides dependable, consistent results. Validity refers to a test's accuracy: When a test is **valid**, it measures what it is intended to measure.

Brief Symptom-Focused Instruments

1. Symptom Checklist-90-R and Brief Symptom Inventory: The Symptom Checklist-90-R (SCL-90-R) and its shortened version, the Brief Symptom Inventory (BSI), are self-report instruments used to rapidly assess a client's type and severity of symptoms (as well as for treatment planning, monitoring, and outcome assessment). The SCL-90-R is appropriate for individuals age 13 through adulthood.

2. Beck Depression Inventory-II: The Beck Depression Inventory-II (BDI-II) measures the depth of a client's depression, or severity of her complaints, symptoms, and concerns related to her current level of depression. It is designed to be used with psychiatrically diagnosed individuals age 13 and older with at least an 8th-grade reading level. The measure is also useful for treatment planning and is often re-administered during treatment to monitor changes and guide treatment decisions.

The BDI-II is scored by totaling the ratings (0, 1, 2, 3) given by a client for each of 21 items. Generally, cut-off scores when testing depressed clients are as follows: 0-13 reflects minimal depression, 14-19 reflects mild depression, 20-28 reflects moderate depression, and 29-63 reflects severe depression. With normal populations, total scores greater than 15 may indicate depression, but this must be confirmed through an interview with the client.

Similar tests available to assess suicide risk include the **Beck Hopelessness Scale** (BHS) and the **Beck Scale for Suicidal Ideation**. Development of the BHS was based on research showing that hopelessness is a better predictor than depression of suicidal ideation and behavior.

3. Youth Assessment Instruments:

a. Child Behavior Checklist: The **Child Behavior Checklist** (**CBCL**) assesses a child's behaviors via parent report and is useful for treatment planning, monitoring, and outcome assessment. Items describe problem behaviors and symptoms experienced by children ages 6 through 18. The test also includes questions about the child's activities, chores, friends, and grades. Separate scores are obtained on externalizing symptoms (delinquent behavior, aggressive behavior) and internalizing symptoms (anxious/depressed, social problems, attention problems), and scores are compared with national norms. Related instruments include a teacher's version, a self-report form for children ages 11 through 18, preschool and adult versions, a semistructured interview (Semistructured Clinical Interview for Children and Adolescents), and a direct observation form. These instruments are all part of the Achenbach System of Empirically Based Assessment (ASEBA).

b. Conners' Rating Scales-Revised and Connors 3: The **Connors' Rating Scales-Revised** may be used to evaluate problem behavior in youth ages 3 through 17. They include the Conners' Parent Rating Scale-Revised, the Conners' Teacher Rating Scale-Revised, and the Conners-Wells' Adolescent Self-Report Scale, which may be completed by clients ages 12 through 17.

A revised version of these scales, the **Connors 3**, may be used to evaluate behaviors and other concerns in youth ages 8 to 18. In contrast to its predecessor, it offers a more thorough assessment of attention-deficit/hyperactivity disorder (ADHD) and addresses comorbid disorders, such as oppositional defiant disorder and conduct disorder. The Conners 3 includes parent rating scales (Conners 3-P), teacher rating scales (Conners 3-T), and self-report rating scales (Conners 3-SR). The Conners 3 also includes two auxiliary scales: the Conners 3 ADHD Index and the Conners 3 Global Index. The Conners 3 forms are available in paper-and-pencil or computerized format.

c. Other Youth Assessment Instruments: (a) The Behavior Assessment System for Children-2 (**BASC-2**) assesses the emotions and behaviors of youth ages 2 years through 21 years, 11 months. (b) The Child and Adolescent Functional Assessment Scale (CAFAS) is a clinician-rated measure that assesses degree of impairment in youth ages 5 to 19. (c) The Behavioral and Emotional Rating Scale, Second Edition (BERS-2) is used with youth ages 5 to 18 who have behavioral or emotional disorders. It measures functioning across five areas, is based on a strengths perspective, and may be completed as a self-report, or by parents, teachers, or other professionals. (d) The Adolescent Drug Abuse Diagnosis (ADAD) is a semistructured interview instrument that addresses nine areas of functioning (medical, school, social relations, family relations, psychological, alcohol use, and drug use, etc.) and identifies need for treatment in each area.

4. Screening Instruments for Substance Use Disorders: A variety of screening instruments are available to help you determine whether a client may have a substance use disorder.

Examples include the Alcohol Use Disorders Identification Test, or AUDIT, which is a 10-item questionnaire that screens for hazardous or harmful alcohol consumption; AUDIT-C, which is a three-question screen for hazardous or harmful drinking that can be used alone or be incorporated into general health history questionnaires; and the Drug Abuse Screen Test (DAST). The DAST-10 is a 10-item, yes/no self-report instrument condensed from the 28-item DAST. Other available screens include the Simple Screening Instrument for Substance Abuse (SSI-SA), Michigan Alcohol Screening Test (MAST), TCU Drug Screen II (TCUDS II), and CAGE-AID.

Personality Tests

The use of projective personality tests (such as the Rorschach) is based on the assumption that ambiguous and unstructured stimuli can elicit meaningful information about an examinee's personality and underlying conflicts. This assumption is referred to as the **projective hypothesis**. Projective tests are generally less susceptible than objective or structured tests (e.g., MMPI-2, MCMI-III) to "faking" and response sets, and, while structured tests typically identify specific "surface" aspects of the personality, projective tests tend to reveal more unconscious, global aspects.

1. Minnesota Multiphasic Personality Inventory-2: The Minnesota Multiphasic Personality Inventory-2 (**MMPI-2**) is an objective personality test appropriate for individuals age 18 and over with at least an 8th-grade reading comprehension level. For adolescents (ages 14 to 18), the **MMPI-A** is available.

The MMPI-2 has 10 clinical scales and seven validity scales. **Validity scales** provide information about test-taking attitudes and extratest behaviors.

The MMPI-2 is most commonly used to assess personality and behavior (e.g., psychological adjustment, characteristic traits and behavior) through profile analysis.

2. Millon Clinical Multiaxial Inventory: The Millon Clinical Multiaxial Inventory (**MCMI-III**) is an objective personality inventory used to assess lasting personality traits and acute clinical states. It is appropriate for individuals age 18 and over with at least an 8th-grade reading comprehension level. For adolescents (ages 13 to 19) whose reading ability is at or above the 6th-grade level, the **MACI** is available.

The MCMI-III is useful for confirming or ruling out specific disorders (differential diagnosis), but should not be the only source of information used for this purpose. Information about coping behavior, interpersonal style, and personality structure can be derived from analyses of all the clinical scales.

3. The Rorschach: The Rorschach is a projective personality test that can be used with individuals age 5 though adulthood. It consists of a standard set of 10 inkblot cards, each containing a bilaterally symmetrical inkblot.

The major use of the Rorschach is to provide descriptive information about the client as she is at the time of testing (i.e., general and specific information about internal organization and processes). Data provided by the test can also be useful in assessing for or ruling out certain disorders. Rorschach data should not be used alone to construct a treatment plan but can be used to identify potential intervention targets and treatment considerations based on the client's personality style. Data provided about overall personality organization may be used to make general predictions about recurring behavioral patterns, but behavioral predictions made from Rorschach data would be highly speculative.

4. Projective Drawing Tests: Projective drawing tests may be used with both children and adults (e.g., House-Tree-Person or H-T-P test, Draw a Person or DAP test, and Kinetic Family Drawings or KFD). They are best used as a tool for developing working hypotheses and a springboard for discussion with the client.

Intelligence Tests

Intelligence tests are administered for a variety of reasons including assessment of scholastic aptitude, educational and occupational counseling, and identification of intellectual disability, learning disorders, and other mental disorders.

1. Wechsler Adult Intelligence Scale, Fourth Edition: The latest version of the Wechsler Adult Intelligence Scale, the **WAIS-IV**, was published in 2008 and is appropriate for individuals ages 16 through 90 years, 11 months. The WAIS may be used as a screening device and to identify clinical hypotheses for further exploration, but should not be used as the sole means of establishing the presence of a neurological or psychiatric disorder.

Downward extensions of the WAIS are available for younger clients. The Wechsler Intelligence Scale for Children-IV (**WISC-IV**) is appropriate for individuals ages 6 years, 0 months through 16 years, 11 months; and the **WPPSI-III**, is appropriate for children ages 2 years, 6 months through 7 years, 3 months.

2. Stanford-Binet Intelligence Scale, Fifth Edition: The Stanford-Binet Intelligence Scale, Fifth Edition (SB5) is appropriate for individuals ages 2 to 85-plus and may be used as a measure of general cognitive ability and to assist in psychoeducational evaluation, the diagnosis of developmental disabilities and exceptionalities, and forensic, career, neuropsychological, and early childhood assessment.

3. Infant and Preschool Tests: Infant and preschool tests are generally considered valid as screening devices for developmental delays and disabilities. When administered to children age 2 or younger, most have low predictive validity. Most infant tests focus on sensorimotor skills. Examples include the Denver Developmental Screening Test II (Denver II), a screening device for developmental delays in children from birth to 6 years of age; and the Bayley Scales of Infant Development, Second Edition (BSID-II) and Bayley Scales of Infant and Toddler Development, Third Edition (Bayley-III), which assess the developmental status of infants and children ages 1 month to 42 months.

4. Assessment of Intellectual Disability: Measures of adaptive (everyday) functioning that may be used when diagnosing intellectual disability include the following: (a) *Vineland Adaptive Behavior Scales, Second Edition (Vineland-II):* The **Vineland II** is appropriate for individuals from birth to age 90 and designed to evaluate personal and social skills of individuals with intellectual disability, autism spectrum disorders, attention-deficit/hyperactivity disorder (ADHD), brain injury, or major neurocognitive disorders and for assisting in the development of educational and treatment plans. (b) *AAMR*

Adaptive Behavior Scales: These scales assess adaptive functioning on five factors (personal self-sufficiency, community self-sufficiency, personal-social responsibility, social adjustment, personal adjustment). The Adaptive Behavior Scale-School, Second Edition is for individuals from 3 to 21 years of age, and the Adaptive Behavior Scale-Residential and Community, Second Edition is for individuals ages 18 through 80 years.

5. Assessment of Learning Disorders: Measures used to assess learning disorders are designed to assist in diagnosis and identify the nature or pattern of impairment to facilitate planning of appropriate interventions. Examples of these measures include the following: (a) *Illinois Test of Psycholinguistic Abilities, Third Edition (ITPA-III):* This is appropriate for individuals ages 5 through 12 years, 11 months and may be used to evaluate strengths and weaknesses in terms of linguistic abilities, to track a child's progress as the result of an intervention, and to assist in the diagnosis of dyslexia and problems related to phonological coding. (b) *Wide-Range Achievement Test, Revision 4 (WRAT4):* This test measures basic academic skills (reading, spelling, math computation) and is appropriate for individuals ages 5 through 94.

6. Measures for People With Physical Disabilities: The Stanford-Binet, Wechsler tests, Vineland, and several other tests are available in versions that can be used with clients who have visual, hearing, or other impairments. In addition, a number of tests have been developed specifically for people with disabilities. The Columbia Mental Maturity Scale (CMMS) is useful for children ages 3 years, 6 months, through 9 years, 11 months, who have cerebral palsy, brain damage, intellectual disability, speech impairments, hearing loss, or limited English proficiency. The Peabody Picture Vocabulary Test, Fourth Edition (PPVT-IV) is designed for people with orthopedic disabilities, ages 2 years, 6 months, to 90 years; it can be administered to any client who is able to hear the stimulus word, see the drawings, and communicate a response. The Haptic Intelligence Scale is for blind and partially sighted individuals age 16 and older, and the Hiskey-Nebraska Test of Learning Aptitude is appropriate for children ages 3 to 17 who have hearing impairments.

7. Culture-Fair Tests: Most culture-fair tests have reduced cultural content and use a nonverbal format to overcome the cultural loading associated with language. Unfortunately, research suggests that culture-fair tests may be as culturally loaded as traditional tests and less valid as predictors of academic achievement and job performance. Some experts believe that intelligence test performance discrepancies between examinees belonging to different groups are due primarily to differences in test-taking motivation and interest, problem-solving approaches, cognitive styles, and attitudes toward standardized tests, and that these differences have not been eliminated in culture-fair tests. Tests considered culture fair or culture reduced include the Leiter International Performance Scale-Third Edition (**Leiter-III**), a measure of cognitive abilities for individuals ages 3 to 75 years that may also be useful for individuals with language problems or hearing impairment; and **Raven's Progressive Matrices**, a nonverbal measure of general intelligence. The most commonly used version of the Ravens tests is the Standard Progressive Matrices, which is appropriate for individuals ages 6 through 80. The Ravens tests can also be used with individuals who are hearing impaired, non-English-speaking individuals, and individuals with aphasias or physical disabilities.

The **System of Multicultural Pluralistic Assessment (SOMPA)** is designed to assess the educational needs of children ages 5 to 11 years in a racially and culturally nondiscriminatory manner. SOMPA includes three components – medical (physical health conditions affecting learning ability), social system (social-adaptive behaviors), and pluralistic (sociocultural background) – and yields an Estimated Learning Potential (ELP) score, which is then used to estimate the extent to which the child might benefit from programs designed for children with similar backgrounds. Some of the instruments used as a part of SOMPA include the WISC, Adaptive Behavior Inventory for Children (ABIC), Bender-Gestalt (see below), and Health History Inventories.

Neuropsychological Tests

Neuropsychological tests are used to screen for and diagnose neurological disorders. Neuropsychological testing can involve either administering a full battery of tests or choosing a few or only one test to administer.

1. Halstead-Reitan Neuropsychological Battery: Versions of the Halstead-Reitan Neuropsychological Battery are available for individuals age 5 and over. The tests selected for use in the Halstead-Reitan were those found to effectively differentiate between brain-damaged and control subjects. Administration usually includes tests designed to measure sensorimotor, perceptual, and language functioning.

2. Luria-Nebraska Neuropsychological Battery: The Luria-Nebraska Neuropsychological Battery is appropriate for individuals age 15 and above. It is useful as a screening device for brain damage, and, in some cases, can help localize damage. The battery includes the major areas of dysfunction likely to be seen in cases of brain damage (e.g., motor, tactile, vision, speech, memory). A children's version can be used with people ages 8 to 12.

3. The Wechsler Memory Scale, Fourth Edition (WMS-IV): The WMS-IV may be used with individuals ages 16 years through 90 years, 11 months. It provides information on various components of memory and is usually a core component of any thorough cognitive assessment. When used in conjunction with the WAIS, it allows for an examination of the relationship between a client's intellectual and memory functioning.

4. Bender Visual-Motor Gestalt Test, Second Edition: The Bender-Gestalt-II is a screening tool for neuropsychological impairment that may used with individuals age 3 and older.

Interest Inventories (Vocational Tests)

While interest inventories are less valid than intelligence tests for predicting academic and occupational success, a fairly strong relationship has been found between interest inventory scores and occupational choice, satisfaction, and persistence.

Examples of commonly used interest inventories include the following: (a) The **Strong Interest Inventories** include the 1994 Strong Interest Inventory and Newly Revised Strong Interest Inventory; the latter is appropriate for high-school students, college students, and adults. (b) The Kuder Tests include the Kuder Preference Record-Vocational (KPR-V); Kuder Occupational Interest Survey (KOIS) (for high-school juniors and seniors, college students, and adults); Career Planning System, which is an online program that consists of three components (Kuder Galaxy for elementary students, Kuder Navigator for secondary students, and Kuder Journey for postsecondary students and adults); and Kuder Career Search with

Person Match, which is intended to help people appreciate their multipotentiality. (c) The **Career Assessment Inventory** (CAI) is useful for people seeking careers that don't require a four-year college degree or other advanced professional training (although the CAI-Enhanced Version includes occupations that do require advanced education or training). (d) The **Self-Directed Search** (SDS) is a self-administered, self-scored, and self-interpreted inventory that yields scores on Holland's six occupational themes – Realistic (R), Investigative (I), Artistic (A), Social (S), Enterprising (E), and Conventional (C).

J. Computer-Assisted Assessment

Computers may be used in every phase of assessment, from data collection (computer-assisted test administration, in which a client takes a test on a computer) through data interpretation (computer-based test interpretation, or CBTI). Additionally, software packages are available to assess a wide range of areas, including personality, intelligence, vocational interests, neuropsychological functioning, and academic achievement.

Computer-assisted test administration can provide adaptive testing or act as an alternative to standard testing. In **computer adaptive testing** (CAT), the computer tailors the test to an individual client by choosing subsequent items based on the client's previous answers. The primary advantages of CAT are its precision and efficiency (Gregory, 1996): CAT ensures that all clients, regardless of their level or status on the characteristic being assessed, are measured with the same degree of reliability and does so in a way that reduces testing time.

Computer-assisted assessment is also associated with certain drawbacks. For example, **computer-based test interpretations** don't describe the client who took the test so much as they describe what research (and sometimes clinical expertise) has found to be true about people in general who produce the test results found in the client's protocol. Therefore, computer-generated interpretive statements may not describe a client accurately. They may contain misleading or incorrect statements as a result of psychological or environmental characteristics that are unique to the client. You must use your clinical judgment and other client data to identify which statements apply to the client and which do not (Weiner, 2003). In addition, some clients are uncomfortable responding to prompts on a computer screen, which can have a negative impact on the validity of the assessment.

K. Client-Focused Measures

Client-focused measures are techniques developed for a specific client that may be used to assess the extent of her problem, follow her progress during treatment, and determine when treatment can be terminated. While these measures sometimes lack sufficient validity and reliability, they are based on the client's presenting problem, and, therefore, can often provide a more accurate description of the client and her problem than a standardized measure would (Pike, 2002).

Two examples of client-focused measures are **individualized rating scales** and **goal attainment scales**. The former is a scale created by you and the client to measure the intensity, frequency, or duration of a symptom or problem (e.g., a client's worrying could be measured on a scale ranging from none/low to extremely high intensity). These scales are discussed in more depth in the Interventions with Clients/Client Systems chapter, in the section on Practice Evaluation.

Another type of client-focused measure is the client log. **Client logs** are useful for identifying the frequency and duration of a client's problems and the circumstances that control them. The client maintains a log between sessions and brings it to her session each week. An exploratory log helps you and a client better understand the nature of the presenting problem; an interaction log identifies patterns of interaction and communication between a client and significant people in her life; a target problem log is used to identify antecedents that cause or worsen a problem; and an evaluation log contains a specific measurement (e.g., behavioral count) to monitor progress.

IV. Assessment of Families and Children

A. Assessment of Risks in a Family

As a social worker, you may be asked to assess risks in a family (e.g., child abuse, spousal abuse, probation). Standardized risk assessment tools are available to help you predict the probability of future behaviors or maltreatment. Most of these tools emphasize enduring risks for which intervention is indicated, rather than transient risks. Even when called on to assess risk, however, you should attempt to conduct a balanced assessment that also looks for strengths in the family, strengths in their environment, and resilience. One way of achieving this balance is to use the Clinical Assessment Package for Assessing Risks and Strengths (CASPARS), which was developed for families receiving mental health and child welfare services. CASPARS measures both risks and protective factors (strengths) related to family relationships, peer relationships, and sexuality. A similar assessment instrument, ROPES, measures family Resources, Options, Possibilities, Exceptions, and Solutions.

For additional information on assessment of child abuse and neglect and assessment of intimate partner violence, see Section IX in this chapter.

B. Family System Assessment

When evaluating the factors described below, you should consider them in light of the family's ability to carry out important social functions performed by a family, including the stabilization and development of each member, physical and emotional nurturing, problem-solving, child care and socialization, income production, and taking care of the home.

1. Family Composition: A "family" is an organized whole comprised of individuals who reciprocally influence one another over time. Who are the members of the family? What are the characteristics of each member? For example, gender, age, ethnicity, occupation, and coping resources.

2. Family Structure: A "family" has an implicit structure that determines how the members relate to one another. Important elements of a family's structure include its subsystems, boundaries, rules, roles, power hierarchy, and chain of command.

a. Subsystems: What are the significant subsystems in the family? How well does each subsystem perform its functions? For example, do the members of the parent subsystem support each other emotionally on an adult level, help each other learn and perform the role of parent, and cooperate in providing for the family?

b. Boundaries: These include boundaries between members, between subsystems, and between the family and the extended family, larger community, and outside world. Specific questions to explore include the following:

- *How functional are the boundaries between subsystems?* Healthy boundaries are relatively permeable – they protect the integrity of a subsystem while also allowing interaction between subsystems and can adapt to the changing needs of the family system. Some unhealthy boundaries are overly diffuse, allowing too much communication with other subsystems (i.e., **enmeshment**). Other unhealthy boundaries are too rigid, not allowing adequate communication between subsystems (i.e., **disengagement**).

- *Are generational boundaries clear?*

- *How differentiated is each family member?* In other words, how reactive is each member and the family as a whole to the emotions and behaviors of individual members? ("Differentiation of self" refers to a person's ability to separate her intellectual and emotional functioning from the functioning of other family members.)

- *How functional is the boundary between the family and the larger community?* Is the family an **open system**? In other words, is there a relatively permeable boundary allowing interaction with the outside community while maintaining the integrity of the family system? This is considered healthy. Or is the family a **closed system**? In a closed system, the boundary between the family and the outside world is relatively rigid and contact with the environment is minimized. This is considered unhealthy.

c. Family Rules: In a family, "**rules**" are the operating principles that enable the family to perform basic tasks of daily living. Some rules are formulated openly whereas others are implicit and never discussed or negotiated in an overt way (i.e., they are "covert"). In a healthy family, rules are consistent, stated clearly, and enforced fairly over time and can change to adapt to the shifting developmental needs of the family and its members.

Specific questions to explore include the following: (a) What are the explicit rules in the family? How were they negotiated? (b) What are the covert rules in the family? You can often infer these by observing family interactions. (c) What rewards are given for behaving according to rules and who gives these rewards? (d) Are there clear consequences for rule violation? Are these enforced consistently and fairly over time? (e) Are rules contradictory? (f) Do rules support growth, maturation, and individuation? (g) Are rules for each member appropriate to his or her age and developmental needs? (h) Do rules change adaptively in response to new situational or developmental demands or new information?

d. Family Roles: In a family, "**roles**" specify the behaviors each member is expected to perform and those he or she is prohibited from performing. Every member plays several roles at once; examples are spouse, parent, child, sibling, caretaker, hero, victim, martyr, or scapegoat. Ideally, roles are negotiated to meet the developmental needs of each member and to prevent dysfunctional roles such as scapegoat or martyr.

In exploring this area, you might ask the following questions: (a) What do family members expect from one another? How clearly do they communicate their expectations? (b) How well do members meet these expectations? (c) What rewards are given for behaving according to expectations? Who administers the rewards? (d) What punishments are given for violating expectations? Who administers these punishments? (e) Are roles in conflict? (f) Are roles for each member appropriate to his or her age and developmental needs? (g) Are family members satisfied with their roles? (h) Do roles change adaptively in response to new situational or developmental demands or new information?

e. Power Hierarchy and Chain of Command: This element of family structure includes **alignments** (the ways in which members join or oppose one another when dealing with problems) and **power hierarchies** (how members combine forces during times of conflict). Specific questions that might be explored include the following: (a) Does the family have a leader? In some families, one person has absolute decision-making power; in other families, no one has sufficient power to facilitate decision-making processes. (b) Are there power struggles? Over what issues? (c) How and by whom are decisions made? Are conflicts clearly communicated? Are there stable rules for conflict resolution? Does the family accept input and solutions from each member? (d) Do decisions change when new information emerges, new situational demands arise, or the developmental needs of family members change?

3. Family Communication: Family members interact according to patterns of communication which are goal-oriented and regulated. A healthy family can communicate clearly and directly about both emotions and practical, day-to-day matters. Specific questions to consider when assessing family communication include the following: (a) Is communication clear, direct, and specific? (b) Is communication congruent (e.g., are verbal and nonverbal messages consistent)? (c) How well do members give and receive messages and feedback. Do members speak for themselves? Do they use "I-statements" (or "I-messages")? (d) Are there dysfunctional communication patterns (e.g., blaming and criticizing, mindreading, overgeneralizing?). (e) Do communication patterns reveal subgroups? (f) Is it acceptable to communicate a range of negative and positive affect in the family?

4. Family Goals: Consider the following questions: (a) Does the family have explicit goals? Are members aware of the family's primary goals? (b) How are the goals negotiated? (c) Does the family agree about its goals or is a lack of goal consensus a source of conflict? (d) What are the family's implicit goals? These can be inferred by finding out what the family tends to put its energy into accomplishing. Dysfunction can result from unspoken goals. (e) Are members active in pursuit of family goals? (f) Do goals meet the developmental needs of individuals and the family as a whole? (g) Do goals change adaptively in response to new situational or developmental demands or new information?

5. Family Development: Family development includes the growth of individual family members, changes in the structure, tasks, and interactional processes of the family over time, and passages through family life-cycle stages. In exploring this area, you might consider the following questions: (a) Is the family currently in **homeostatic balance**? Or is it in transition or crisis due to a change of some kind? (b) Is one family member's problem or symptom being used to maintain homeostasis? In other words, is there an identified patient? The **identified patient** (IP) is the "symptom bearer" of the family; she is the family member who is usually sent first for treatment and whose symptoms help maintain the family's homeostasis. (c) Does the family allow for individuation and age-appropriate autonomy? (d) Which **family life-cycle transitions** have been experienced? Which ones are anticipated in the near future? (e) How have past transitions been managed? How does this influence current patterns? At any family life-cycle stage, family interactions are influenced by interactions at earlier stages.

6. Family's Adaptation to the Environment: Consider the following questions: (a) In what ways is the family in harmony with extended family, the community, and the world at large? How is it in conflict? (b) How well does the family enable its members to perform their community roles (e.g., to meet the demands of school or work, to handle discrimination)? (c) How well does the environment enable family members to perform their family roles (e.g., provider, nurturer, protector)?

7. Family Strengths: Bear in mind as you assess a family system that every family has strengths and resources that can help its members cope and survive. For example, you might notice that a family is willing to talk about its problems, expresses affection, or demonstrates a commitment to making the changes necessary to overcome its problems. Strengths-based measures for families (and children) include the Family Functioning Style Scale (FSSS) and the Family Resources Scale (FRS).

C. Assessment of Children

Comprehensive assessment of a child (or adolescent) client requires you to obtain information directly from the client. When a child is referred to you for an assessment, however, you will usually also interview the parents or other adults about the presenting problem. The assessment may also include observations of the child alone and interacting with others; behavioral checklists completed by parents, teachers, or other adults who know the child well; a review of relevant documents (such as school records); and, sometimes, psychological testing. Interviews with adults who know the child well and direct observations of the child usually provide a more accurate and complete picture of the child's strengths and problems than the child's own description alone (Bierman, 1983).

In addition, many experts believe that, when evaluating non-white-Anglo children, it is best to use an informal assessment system. For instance, to measure the intelligence of culturally diverse children, you should generally use a flexible and ecologically sensitive assessment approach that takes into account differences in the expression of intelligence and supplement any quantitative psychometric intelligence measures with qualitative and nonpsychometric measures (Gopaul-McNicol & Brice-Baker, 1998).

1. Engaging Clients Under Age 12 and Eliciting the Problem: The following guidelines are useful when attempting to engage a client who is under the age of 12 and working to elicit her problem (Sheafor & Horejsi, 2003):

- To properly structure an interview with a child and interpret her responses, you need to understand her level of cognitive development (e.g., verbal skills, memory, conceptual skills, organizational skills). Before the interview, consider how the child's level of development will affect her capacity to use language and understand situations and events.

- Consider using some form of play to put the child at ease and facilitate communication.

- Allow the child to set the pace of the interview and to move around and explore the room.

- Consider placing yourself physically at the same level as a young child (e.g., sit on the floor with her), particularly if she seems unwilling to talk.

- Begin your interaction with friendly conversation (e.g., ask the child about her favorite TV shows).

- If the child refuses to interact with you, engage in a parallel activity with her and then gradually initiate conversation about the activity (e.g., if the child is playing with a doll, pick up a doll yourself and begin to play with it).

- If the child is frightened of you or the interview process, attempt to normalize the situation (e.g., "When I was your age, I was scared to talk to people I didn't know well"). As needed, reassure the child that being interviewed doesn't mean she's in trouble.

- When the child is *younger than age 6*, much of the information you gather will be from your observations of her play and interactions with you and others. To increase the validity of the inferences you draw from your observations, you should observe the child in more than one setting and at different times of the day. Do not base your conclusions on one observation of the child.

- With a child *under age 6*, consider using play items to set up a make-believe situation relevant to the topics you'd like to explore. You may need to initiate the story-telling, but, once the child is paying attention, you can ask her to continue or complete the story herself. Simply allow her to talk. Active listening techniques, such as paraphrasing and summarization, don't work well with children younger than age 6 or 7.

- A young child may be easily distracted. While it is usually not effective to ask a child to stay with an activity, you, yourself, might return to the activity at a later time and the child may follow you. It's appropriate for you to facilitate the child's expression, but you should not be overly directive. When a young child is very fidgety and unable to pay attention, it may be that she is too tired and the interview should end for the day.

- A child who is *about age 6* will generally be able to express her thoughts and feelings in words and is usually able to answer your questions. (See also the guidelines for interviewing children below.)

- Story-telling, drawing, and play materials may still be necessary when interviewing children between the ages of 7 and 9, but most children *age 9 or older* are able to provide thoughtful answers to your questions.

- Although young children are generally responsive to nonverbal communication, you should avoiding hugging or caressing a child who is your client because this makes many children uncomfortable.

2. Guidelines for Interviewing Children: Note that the research shows that it's possible to obtain reliable and valid data from interviewing children who are as young as age 6. Strategies and techniques that are useful for facilitating interviews with children are described below (Bierman, 1983).

a. Modify Your Questions: (a) Because children may lack the cognitive capacity to respond to broad open-ended questions, modify your questions so that they offer the child a concrete set of answers to choose from (e.g., "What do you like best about your family?" rather than "Tell me about your family"). Appropriately structured open-ended questions elicit more information from a child and reduce the likelihood that the child will be influenced by your questions. Not all open-ended questions are useful, however: Questions that begin with "why" should usually be avoided (e.g., you should ask, "What don't you like about coming here?" rather than, "Why didn't you want to come here?"). (b) Avoid leading questions (e.g., "That probably made you angry, didn't it?") and, at least initially, rely on the child's free recall to obtain the most accurate information about a past event. (c) Avoid "if-then" and other two-part questions because they may confuse the child. (d) Provide the child with visual stimuli to respond to (e.g., have the child draw a picture and then have her talk about the drawing).

b. Other Guidelines:

Offer alternatives to verbally answering questions: If the child lacks the vocabulary or cognitive skills to describe her thoughts and feelings, provide her with other means of expressing herself, such as pictures of faces expressing emotions from which the child can select when responding to questions.

Use descriptive comments: These include objective comments about the child's appearance and positive comments about her behavior or demeanor (e.g., "You look happy today"). Descriptions give attention to the child, encourage the child to continue doing what she's doing, and point out to the child what behavior is expected of her.

Use reflection: Reflective statements mirror what the child says and can be literal or interpretive. Reflection helps clarify and organize the child's thoughts and feelings.

Provide labeled praise: This indicates approval and helps guide and encourage the child to behave in a particular way (e.g., "You're doing a good job of telling me what happened").

Avoid critical statements: Criticism elicits negative emotional reactions and defensiveness from a child and disrupts the development of rapport. Better tactics for altering behavior include making rule-based corrections ("One of the rules in this room is ..."), making invitational statements ("Come and sit at the table"), or ignoring the behavior.

3. Parent and Parent-Child Assessments: Assessment of the parents allows you to identify the extent to which they recognize and understand the existence of their child's problem, contribute to the maintenance of the problem, and support healthy aspects of the child's personality, as well as learn about their lifestyle, values, employment, and financial means. You should observe how the child (or adolescent) and her parents communicate and interact with one another and with you and be alert to indicators of depression, anger, anxiety, aloofness, apathy, helplessness, as well as empathy, support, and a willingness to accept help. During assessment (and afterwards), you must avoid overidentifying with either the child or her parents, becoming infected by the parent's anxieties, or feeling pressured to provide premature recommendations or advice.

When working with minority families, you should consider how different **cultural beliefs** may affect the parents' view of their child's problem and its causes and what they expect from treatment, other services, and resources. You should actively seek information about these areas by asking questions such as, "What do you think caused your child's problem?" "How severe is your child's problem?" "What kind of treatment do you think your child should receive?" "What are the most important results you hope your child will receive from treatment?" "What are the main challenges the problem has caused for you and your child?" "What do you fear most about your child's problem?"

Note that, in some cases, assessment of the parents or the parent-child relationship may reveal that the child's problems actually represent an opening for needed work with her parents on parenting, marital, or individual problems.

4. Assessing the Home Environment: For a child client, assessment of the home environment often includes observation of the home and a semistructured interview conducted in the home with a parent or other primary caregiver. A commonly used measurement is the Home Observation for Measurement of the Environment (HOME) Inventory, which measures the quality and quantity of stimulation and support available to a child in her home.

5. Identifying Developmental Delays: When meeting with a family that includes a pre-school-age child, you may have an opportunity to perform a brief assessment of the child's physical and mental development. If you identify possible developmental delays, you can then make referrals for further evaluation and intervention.

Some early signs of developmental delays and sensory problems include the following:

- *Delays in speech development* – can't say the names of a few familiar objects or people by age 2, doesn't speak in sentences by age 4, can't be understood by people outside the family by age 5.

- *Delays in motor development* – can't walk without help by age 2.

- *Delays in social and mental development* – doesn't react to her own name when called by age 1, doesn't play simple games like peek-a-boo by age 1, can't identify facial features by pointing to them by age 2, doesn't understand simple stories by age 3, doesn't play group games with other children by age 4, doesn't share or take turns by age 5.

- *Vision problems* – holds her head in an awkward position when trying to look at a person or object, one or both eyes are crossed.

- *Hearing problems* – frequent earaches or runny ears, talks in a very loud or very soft voice, doesn't respond when called from another room, delays in language development.

In evaluating these indicators, bear in mind that there is significant variation in the development of normal children at a particular age. In addition, children who are chronically ill or malnourished, have been abused or neglected, or have sensory or neurological problems or intellectual disability will generally fall behind developmental norms.

For detailed information on child development, including developmental milestones, see the chapter on Human Development, Diversity, and Behavior.

6. Meeting the Needs of Children With Disabilities:

a. Early Intervention Programs: Children under age 3 years with special needs (physical disability, intellectual disability, or autism spectrum disorder) are eligible for early intervention programs. When a client family has a child under age 3 with special needs, you should explore whether the family has received early intervention services, and, if not, should inform the parents of these services and assist them (including through advocacy, if needed) to obtain the services they and their child are entitled to.

Early intervention services are usually provided in the child's home or another place familiar to the child. The services provided are written into an **Individualized Family Service Plan** (IFSP) that is reviewed every six months and updated at least once a year. The plan describes services that will be provided to the child as well as services for the parents to help them in daily activities with their child and for siblings to help them adjust to having a sibling with a disability.

b. IDEA and School-Aged Children: The Individuals with Disabilities Education Act (IDEA) (formerly called the Education for All Handicapped Children Act) guarantees individuals with disabilities, including physical disabilities, intellectual disability, learning disorders, and autism spectrum disorders, ages 3 through 21, a free, appropriate public education in the least restrictive setting, including an **individualized education program** and prescriptions. (See Section XVII of Interventions with Clients/Client Systems for more information on the IDEA.)

If a client family has a school-age child with a qualifying disability, you should verify that the child is receiving appropriate attention at school. If the child is not yet receiving appropriate attention at school, you should counsel the parents about discussing their concerns with their child's classroom teacher or the school social worker or counselor and, as necessary, help them arrange for screening and evaluation (observation, standardized testing) of their child through the local school system. Also get permission to review the child's school records.

Note that having attention-deficit/hyperactivity disorder (ADHD) does not automatically qualify a child for special services under the IDEA (i.e., ADHD is not listed as a "qualifying" disability; rather, it is listed as a condition under the Other Health Impaired category). Sometimes students with ADHD may fit the criteria for special assistance based on co-existing conditions, such as a specific learning disorder. Their eligibility for that condition may allow teachers and parents to accommodate the needs of not only the other disability, but also the symptoms of ADHD. If the family has a school-aged child with ADHD and you believe that the child needs accommodations in the classroom, you should counsel the parents to speak with their child's teacher or school social worker or counselor and to request that their child be evaluated for services under the IDEA.

V. Social Histories and Social Assessment Reports

Some authors distinguish between "assessment interviews" and "informational interviews." An informational interview is used to obtain data for a **social history** so that you can make an appropriate decision about the kinds of services you or your agency should offer the client. You don't need to gather comprehensive information about the client's life history. Instead, your goal in this situation is to obtain background information related to the problem, including both objective facts and subjective feelings and attitudes. This information may come from not only the client but also her relatives, friends, and employers, and other agencies that have contact with her (social service agencies, schools, probation police departments, etc.).

1. Social Histories: In a social history, the term "social" refers to the client's interactions with other people and significant systems of her social environment (e.g., family, job, a hospital). Although the specific information contained in a social history varies from agency to agency, a typical social history includes fact-sheet information (name, age, occupation, etc.) plus information about the following: the presenting problem, concern, or request; early childhood experiences and development; family background; dating and marital history; school performance; employment history; contact with other agencies; and the social worker's general impressions concerning the client and her situation.

2. Social Assessment Reports: Social assessment reports are professional reports that describe the social aspects of a client's functioning and her situation (i.e., her social history), with a particular focus on the match or lack of match between a client's needs and the resources available to meet her needs. The "client" may be an individual or a family.

a. Uses of Social Assessment Reports: Social assessment reports are used by social workers to communicate to other professionals (e.g., interdisciplinary teams, doctors, psychologists, school personnel, judges) relevant social information about a client and are particularly useful when decisions are being made about the type of service or program that would be most appropriate for a client and/or when attempting to facilitate a client's adjustment to a new environment (e.g., foster home, nursing home).

b. Characteristics of a Competent Report: The information in a social assessment report should lay the foundation for planning interventions that will help a client resolve her problem or improve her situation. The report contains social data (facts and observations), the social worker's interpretation of the data, and implications of the data for those who will ultimately work with the client.

The organization, format, and content of social assessment reports varies based on an agency's mission and program and the audience for which it is being prepared. Characteristics of a good social assessment report include the following (Sheafor & Horejsi, 2003):

Brevity: Include only information needed by those who will use the report.

Clarity: Avoid professional jargon and psychiatric labels. Describe and give concrete examples of the behavior you discuss.

Usefulness: Keep the report's purpose in mind (i.e., who will read the report and what they need to know).

Objectivity: Express observations in an accurate and nonjudgmental way. Label opinions as such (don't present an opinion as though it were a fact) and support conclusions with data.

Relevance: Include only information that has a clear connection to the client's problem and/or the reason why you and your agency are involved with the client.

Emphasis on client strengths: Avoid focusing on deficiencies, pathology, etc. Emphasize whatever strengths exist.

Consideration of confidentiality: Respect the client's privacy. Assume that the client may want to read the report and has a right to do so. When possible, leave out information that you don't want the client, her family, and/or an attorney to read.

Organized presentation: Use headings to divide the report into clearly defined sections. Headings commonly used in social assessment reports include identifying information (name, date of birth, address, etc.); reason for the report; reason for the social worker's or agency's involvement; statement of the client's problem or concern; family background (family of origin); current family composition and/or household membership; relationships to significant others; ethnicity, religion, and spirituality; physical functioning, health concerns, nutrition, home safety, illness, disabilities, and medications; educational background, school performance, and intellectual functioning; psychological and emotional functioning; strengths, ways of coping, and problem-solving capacities; employment, income, work experience, and skills; housing, neighborhood, and transportation; current and recent use of community and professional services; the social worker's impressions and assessment; and the intervention and service plan.

VI. Diagnosis

Diagnosis is useful for facilitating communication among professionals because it applies a standardized terminology to a client's condition or situation. Barker (2003, p. 118) defines **diagnosis** as, "The process of identifying a problem (social and mental, as well as medical) and its underlying causes and formulating a solution." Barker further notes that, "... many social workers prefer to call this process 'assessment' because of the medical connotation that often accompanies the term 'diagnosis'" (p. 118).

Other authors define diagnosis in a more limited way, as the process by which social workers classify a client's problem, condition, or situation and assign it to a category within a particular **diagnostic taxonomy** such as the Person-in-Environment (PIE) system or the Diagnostic and Statistical Manual of Mental Disorders (DSM). PIE is not a substitute for the DSM; rather, it may be used as a complementary system. These taxonomies will be described a bit later in this section.

1. Comparison of Assessment and Diagnosis: Assessment is a highly individualized process in which you recognize the uniqueness of a client and her situation, focus on her strengths, and attempt to define her problem within its unique context so that you can develop a personalized intervention plan for her. In contrast, many forms of diagnosis (particularly clinical diagnosis) place less emphasis on a client's uniqueness and are not as useful for developing individualized treatment plans. For example, two clients with similar symptoms may both have major depressive disorder (the same clinical diagnosis), but be experiencing very different circumstances and environments.

Additionally, while diagnosis tends to highlight what is "wrong" with a client (e.g., her dysfunction, a mental disorder), assessment also focuses on what is "right" with her, including personal strengths, motivations, resources, and other assets that can be harnessed to resolve her difficulties, improve her functioning, and promote her growth.

2. Traditional Categories of Diagnosis in Social Work: For social workers, diagnosis doesn't usually refer to only clinical diagnosis. Rather, social workers have always tried to develop a broader definition of their clients' problems or needs, one that encompasses interpersonal processes and the person-situation interaction.

Florence Hollis (1964) defined three categories of diagnosis to help social workers formulate a more complete definition of their clients' problems. Hollis's first two categories – etiological and dynamic – emphasize an interactional or transactional view of problem causation.

Etiological diagnosis: Problem causation is usually the result of a convergence of many factors in a client's person-situation complex. Thus, this category includes elements of the person-situation configuration that might be antecedents to a client's problem. These elements may include current interactions as well as prior events that still influence the present and are, therefore, among the causes of a client's problem.

Dynamic diagnosis: This category encompasses, among other things, examining how aspects of a client's personality (including strengths and weaknesses) interact to produce her functioning. It also examines the interplay between a client and other people and systems and the interactions between them. Often, the dynamics of family interaction will be particularly important.

Classificatory diagnosis: Social workers also classify aspects of a client's functioning. This frequently involves assigning a clinical diagnosis (mental disorder), but can also include classifying other aspects of a client's functioning, such as those related to her race, ethnicity, religion, or socioeconomic status, cognitive functioning, medical disease or condition, and family functioning (i.e., a family diagnosis).

Additionally, many social workers use the term **psychosocial assessment** (or psychosocial diagnosis) to describe their summary judgment concerning the problem to be solved (Barker, 2003). A psychosocial assessment (or diagnosis) describes the problem configuration, existing assets and resources, the prognosis, and a plan designed to resolve the problem. Where relevant, it also includes results from psychological tests, information concerning a client's legal status, and any diagnostic labels that apply to the client.

3. Telling a Client About Her Clinical Diagnosis: What you choose to tell a client about her clinical diagnosis depends, in part, on her capacity to understand the information. However, there are general guidelines you should follow when communicating a diagnosis to a client, including the following: (a) Provide an honest, clear, and relatively simple explanation (i.e., convey what the client needs to know but avoid becoming absorbed in the details); (b) do not use jargon that could confuse or worry the client; (c) ask the client questions to ensure her understanding and do your best to answer her questions; (d) emphasize the positive, particularly regarding prognosis; and (e) acknowledge the client's feelings about the diagnosis.

As these guidelines suggest, simply showing the client a summary of the disorder from the DSM-5 or telling her its essential features would not be appropriate. Such an approach would not facilitate as much understanding as clarifying for the client, in layperson's terms, how her behaviors fit the criteria for the diagnosed disorder. Explaining a diagnosis in behavioral terms using terminology the client will understand can often be therapeutic.

4. Person-in-Environment (PIE) System: The Person-in-Environment (PIE) System is used to describe, classify, and code problems in adult social functioning. PIE defines problems relevant to both the person and environment, describes problems in terms of their duration, severity, and the client's ability to solve or cope with them, and seeks to balance problems and strengths. PIE groups client problems into four factors, or general types of problem. The first two factors (problems in social role functioning and problems in the environment) encompass the core of social work practice. The other two factors (mental health problems and physical health problems) enable you to provide a more complete description of a client's problem (Karls, 2002).

Using PIE helps you organize and record your assessment findings in a format that facilitates development of a clear and focused treatment plan, including targets for change in the client's external environment (factor II). In particular, PIE answers the following questions: What problems in social functioning does the client present? What problems exist in the local community's social institutions that are affecting the client? What mental health problems are present? What physical health problems are present? What strengths and resources does the client have to deal with these problems?

As you will see below, each **PIE factor** describes a different feature of a client's problem situation.

> *PIE factor I – Problems in social role functioning:* You begin by identifying all the factor I problems presented by the client – i.e., the problems in social role functioning that are relevant to her performance of activities of daily living required by her community or culture for her age and stage of life. A description of the client's problem(s) in factor I has five components: (a) The social interaction areas or social roles in which the problem is occurring. There are four categories of role problems to select from: familial (parent, spouse, child, sibling, significant other); other interpersonal (lover, friend, neighbor, etc.); occupational (worker/paid, worker/home, volunteer, student); and special life situation (consumer, inpatient/client, outpatient/client, probationer/parolee, prisoner, legal immigrant, undocumented immigrant, refugee, other). (b) The types of problem – i.e., power, ambivalence, responsibility, dependence, loss, isolation, and/or victimization. (c) The severity of each problem. This is noted on a scale of 1 (lowest) to 6 (highest). (d) The duration of each problem (how long each problem has been present). This is noted on a scale of 1 (five years or longer) to 6 (two weeks or less). (e) Clinical judgment of the client's physical, mental, and psychological strength to cope with the problem. This is noted on a scale of 1 (outstanding) to 6 (no coping skills).
>
> *PIE factor II – Problems in the environment:* For factor II, you identify problems in the client's physical or social environment that are affecting her social functioning. A description of a client's factor II problems includes three components: (a) The nature of the environmental or social system problem. PIE includes six groupings of environmental/social system problems to choose from: economic/basic need system (food, shelter, employment, economic resources, transportation); educational and training system; judicial and legal system (police, courts); health, welfare, and safety system (hospitals, clinics, public safety services, social services); voluntary association system (religious institutions, community support groups); and affectional support system (the helping network). The PIE Manual (Karls & Wandrei, 1996) further describes and codes from three to eleven subtypes for each of these problems. (b) The severity of each problem, noted on a scale of 1 (lowest) to 6 (highest). (c) The duration of each problem, noted on a scale of 1 (five years or longer) to 6 (two weeks or less).
>
> *PIE factor III – Mental health problems:* Here, you list the client's mental health problems using the DSM and its codes. You record the clinical disorder itself and, if applicable, the source of the diagnosis.
>
> *PIE factor IV – Physical health problems:* Here, you list the client's physical health problems. These problems may be ones diagnosed by a physician and/or reported by the client.

5. Diagnostic and Statistical Manual of Mental Disorders: In the United States, the most widely used diagnostic classification system is presented in the American Psychiatric Association's Diagnostic and Statistical Manual of Mental Disorders (DSM); and the current version, the DSM-5, was published in 2013. As a social worker, you need to be familiar with the DSM-5 in order to communicate with other professionals about a client's mental disorder and understand reports prepared by psychologists and psychiatrists.

Additionally, in the U.S., health insurance typically will not pay for mental health services unless a DSM-5 diagnosis accompanies the insurance claim. Therefore, knowing how to use the DSM-5 is also important if you rely on third-party payments from Medicaid, Medicare, or private insurance or managed care companies for fees for the services you provide.

The DSM-5 contains separate chapters for 19 diagnostic categories: neurodevelopmental disorders; schizophrenia spectrum and other psychotic disorders; bipolar and related disorders; depressive disorders; anxiety disorders; obsessive-compulsive and related disorders; trauma- and stressor-related disorders; dissociative disorders; somatic symptom disorders; feeding and eating disorders; elimination disorders; sleep-wake disorders; sexual dysfunctions; gender dysphoria; disruptive, impulse control, and conduct disorders; substance related and addictive disorders; neurocognitive disorders; personality disorders; and paraphilic disorders. It also includes chapters called Medication-Induced Movement Disorders and Other Adverse Effects of Medication; Other Conditions That May be a Focus of Clinical Attention; and Other Mental Disorders. The latter chapter provides a residual category that applies to presentations in which there are prominent symptoms characteristic of a mental disorder that cause clinically significant distress or impairment in important areas of functioning but the symptoms don't meet the full criteria for any other mental disorder in the DSM-5.

a. DSM-5's Definition of Mental Disorder: The DSM-5 defines a mental disorder as "a syndrome characterized by clinically significant disturbance in ... cognition, emotion regulation, or behavior that reflects a dysfunction in the psychological, biological, or developmental processes underlying mental functioning" (APA, 2013, p. 20). An expectable or culturally approved response to a stressor or loss is not a mental disorder; and socially deviant behavior (e.g., political religious, sexual) and conflicts that are primarily between the individual and society are not mental disorders unless the deviant behavior or conflict results from a dysfunction in the individual. In addition, mental disorders are "usually associated with significant distress or disability in social, occupational, or other important activities" (APA, 2013, p. 20). The diagnostic criteria for most of the mental disorders in the DSM-5 include the criterion, "the disturbance causes clinically significant distress or impairment in social, occupational, or other important areas of functioning" (or a criterion similar to this). This **criterion for clinical significance** helps to identify disorder thresholds and is useful for determining a person's need for treatment.

The DSM-5 utilizes a categorical approach that divides the mental disorders into types that are defined by a set of diagnostic criteria and requires the clinician to determine whether or not a client meets the minimum criteria for a given diagnosis. To allow for individual differences in symptoms, the DSM-5 includes a **polythetic criteria set** for most disorders that requires a client to present with only a subset of characteristics from a larger list. As a result, two clients can have somewhat different symptoms but receive the same diagnosis.

b. Diagnostic Uncertainty: When using the DSM-5, **diagnostic uncertainty** about a client's diagnosis is indicated by coding one of the following: **Other specified disorder** is coded when the clinician wants to indicate the reason why a client's symptoms don't meet the criteria for a specific diagnosis (e.g., "other specified depressive disorder, recurrent brief depression"). **Unspecified disorder** is coded when the clinician doesn't want to indicate the reason why a client's symptoms don't meet the criteria for a specific diagnosis. "Other specified disorder" and "unspecified disorder" replace the DSM-IV-TR NOS (not otherwise specified) designation.

In addition, the specifier **provisional** may be used when the clinician doesn't currently have sufficient information for a firm diagnosis, but believes the full criteria for the diagnosis will eventually be met.

c. Nonaxial Assessment System: In contrast to previous versions of the DSM, the DSM-5 provides a **nonaxial assessment system** in which all mental and medical diagnoses (former Axis I, Axis II, and Axis III) are listed together with the primary diagnosis listed first, and psychosocial and contextual factors (former Axis IV) and level of disability (former Axis V) are then listed separately.

Psychosocial and contextual factors: Instead of providing a classification of psychosocial and environmental problems (former Axis IV), the DSM-5 uses a selected set of ICD-9-CM V codes (as well ICD-10-CM Z codes). V codes (and Z codes) appear in the DSM-5 chapter on Other Conditions That May Be a Focus of Clinical Attention.

Level of disability: A DSM-5 chapter on Assessment Measures provides the WHO Disability Assessment Schedule 2.0 (WHODAS 2.0) which may be used to assess current disability across six dimensions (i.e., understanding and communicating, getting around, self-care, getting along with people, life activities, and participation in society). Disability (former Axis V) may be assessed with the WHODAS and/or another relevant measure.

d. Cultural Formulation: The DSM-5 provides three tools to help clinicians consider and understand the impact of a client's cultural background on diagnosis and treatment:

Outline for Cultural Formulation: The Outline for Cultural Formulation provides guidelines for assessing four factors: the client's cultural identity; the client's cultural conceptualization of distress; the psychosocial stressors and cultural factors that impact the client's vulnerability and resilience; and cultural factors relevant to the relationship between the client and therapist.

Cultural Formulation Interview (CFI): The CFI is a semi-structured interview consisting of 16 questions designed to obtain information on a client's views regarding the social/cultural context of her presenting problems. It focuses on four domains: cultural definition of the problem; cultural perceptions of cause, context, and support; cultural factors affecting self-coping and past help seeking; and cultural factors affecting current help seeking. Two versions of the CFI are included in the text: a version that is used to interview the client and a version that is used to interview an informant who has knowledge about the client's problems and life circumstances.

Cultural concepts of distress: The DSM-5 defines **cultural concepts of distress** as the "ways that cultural groups experience, understand, and communicate suffering, behavioral problems, or troubling thoughts and emotions" (p. 758). It also distinguishes between three types of cultural concepts: (a) **Cultural syndromes** are clusters of symptoms and attributions that co-occur among individuals from a particular culture and are recognized by members of that culture as coherent patterns of experience. (b) **Cultural idioms of distress** are used by members of different cultures to express distress and provide shared ways for talking about personal and social concerns. (c) **Cultural explanations** refer to the explanatory models that members of a culture use to explain the meaning and causes of symptoms, illness, and distress. The CFI is useful for obtaining information on a client's cultural concepts of distress, and the DSM-5 includes a Glossary of Cultural Concepts of Distress that describes several culture-specific syndromes. For example, **ataque de nervios** is a syndrome recognized by members of certain Latino cultures that is characterized by screaming, crying, trembling, aggression, and a sense of being out of control and often occurs in reaction to a stressful event involving the family.

VII. DSM-5 Mental Disorders and Conditions

A. Neurodevelopmental Disorders

The disorders in this category "typically manifest early in development, often before the child enters grade school, and are characterized by developmental deficits that produce impairments of personal, social, academic, or occupational functioning" (APA, 2013, p. 31). Included in this category are intellectual disability, communication disorders, autism spectrum disorder, attention-deficit/hyperactivity disorder, specific learning disorder, and motor disorders (e.g., tic disorders).

Intellectual Disability (Intellectual Developmental Disorder)

1. Diagnostic Criteria: For a diagnosis of intellectual disability, three diagnostic criteria must be met: (a) deficits in intellectual functions (e.g., reasoning, problem solving, abstract thinking) that are confirmed by a clinical assessment and individualized, standardized intelligence testing; (b) deficits in adaptive functioning that result in a failure to meet community standards of personal independence and social responsibility and impair functioning across multiple environments in one or more activities of daily life (e.g., communication, social participation, independent living); and (c) the onset of intellectual and adaptive functioning deficits during the developmental period.

On individually administered intelligence tests, persons with intellectual disability score about two standard deviations or more below the population mean, with a margin for measurement error (usually 5 points). On tests with a standard deviation of 15 and a mean of 100, this reflects a score of 65-75 (70 ± 5) or below.

2. Degrees of Severity: The DSM-5 distinguishes between four degrees of severity (mild, moderate, severe, and profound) based on adaptive functioning in three domains (rather than IQ scores): (a) The *conceptual* domain includes academic skills, memory, problem solving, judgment in unfamiliar situations, etc.; (b) the *social* domain includes empathy, interpersonal communication skills, friendship abilities, social judgment, etc.; and (c) the *practical* domain includes personal care, task organization, job responsibilities, money management, self-management of behavior, recreation, etc. Adaptive functioning determines the level of support the person needs.

3. Etiology: For cases of intellectual disability with a known cause, about 5 percent are due to heredity (Tay-Sachs, fragile X syndrome, phenylketonuria [PKU]); 30 percent to chromosomal changes and exposure to toxins during prenatal development (Down syndrome, fetal alcohol spectrum disorder); 10 percent to pregnancy and perinatal problems (fetal malnutrition, anoxia, trauma); 5 percent to acquired medical conditions during infancy or childhood (lead poisoning, encephalitis, malnutrition); and 15 to 20 percent to environmental factors and predisposing mental disorders (severe deprivation of nurturance or stimulation, autism spectrum disorder) (Toth & King, 2010). The etiology is unknown in about 30 percent of all cases, and research on risk factors for intellectual disability with an unknown cause indicates that low birth weight is the strongest predictor for all degrees of severity (Croen et al., 2001).

Communication Disorders

1. Childhood-Onset Fluency Disorder:

a. Diagnostic Criteria: Childhood-onset fluency disorder (**stuttering**) is characterized by a disturbance in normal fluency and time patterning of speech that is inappropriate for the person's age and involves sound and syllable repetitions, sound prolongations, broken words, word substitutions to avoid troublesome words, and/or monosyllabic whole-word repetitions.

b. Course: This disorder usually begins between the ages of 2 and 7, and symptoms may become worse when there is special pressure to communicate (e.g., when giving an oral report).

c. Differential Diagnosis: Many preschool children (ages 2 to 4) pass through a period of speech dysfluency and the majority outgrow this and develop normal speech without intervention. With a preschool child, it's usually appropriate to normalize the speech dysfluency and educate the parents. Stuttering is considered atypical if it continues past age 5. With a child older than age 5, referral to a speech pathologist should be considered.

2. Social (Pragmatic) Communication Disorder: Social (pragmatic) communication disorder is characterized by persistent difficulties in the social use of verbal and nonverbal communication. The difficulties limit effective communication, social participation, social relationships, academic achievement, or work performance and are demonstrated by *all* of the following: (a) deficits in using communication for social purposes in a manner that is appropriate for the social context, (b) impairment of the ability to adjust communication to match the context or the listener's needs, (c) difficulties following rules for conversation and storytelling, and (d) difficulties in understanding what is not explicitly stated and nonliteral or ambiguous meanings of language.

3. Language Disorder: Language disorder is characterized by difficulties in acquiring and using language due to deficits in the comprehension or production of vocabulary, sentence structure, and discourse. Language abilities are significantly and quantifiably below those expected for age and result in functional limitations in effective communication, social participation, academic achievement, and/or occupational performance. The difficulties are not attributable to sensory impairment, motor dysfunction, or another medical or neurological condition.

4. Speech Sound Disorder: Speech sound disorder is characterized by difficulty with speech sound production that interferes with intelligibility or prevents verbal communication of messages, and interferes with social participation, academic achievement, or occupational performance. The difficulties are not attributable to congenital or acquired conditions (e.g., cerebral palsy, hearing loss) or other medical or neurological conditions.

Autism Spectrum Disorder

In the DSM-5, the single diagnosis autism spectrum disorder (ASD) encompasses autistic disorder (autism) as well as three other DSM-IV-TR diagnoses – Asperger's disorder, childhood disintegrative disorder, and pervasive developmental disorder NOS. The new name "autism spectrum disorder" reflects current thinking that these formerly separate disorders are, in fact, a single condition with different levels of symptom severity in two key domains: (a) deficits in social communication and social interaction and (b) restricted, repetitive behaviors, interests, or activities.

Diagnosing autism spectrum disorder includes using specifiers to note the individual's unique clinical characteristics (e.g., "with or without accompanying intellectual impairment" and "with or without accompanying structural language impairment") and describe the autistic symptoms, including their severity. For example, many people diagnosed with Asperger's disorder using the DSM-IV-TR criteria would now receive a diagnosis of "autism spectrum disorder, without language or intellectual impairment."

1. Diagnostic Criteria: For a diagnosis of autism spectrum disorder, the individual must exhibit:

- *persistent deficits in social communication and interaction* across multiple contexts as manifested by deficits in social-emotional reciprocity, nonverbal communication, and the development, maintenance, and understanding of relationships;

- *restricted, repetitive patterns of behavior, interests, and activities* as manifested by at least two of the following: stereotyped or repetitive motor movements, use of objects, or speech; insistence on sameness, inflexible adherence to routines, or ritualized patterns of behavior; highly restricted, fixated interests that are abnormal in intensity or focus; hyper- or hyporeactivity to sensory input;

- symptoms during the early developmental period; and

- impairments in social, occupational, or other area of functioning as the result of symptoms.

The DSM-5 distinguishes between three levels of severity: Level 1 (requiring support), Level 2 (requiring substantial support), and Level 3 (requiring very substantial support).

2. Associated Features: Many individuals with autism spectrum disorder have intellectual impairments and/or language abnormalities (e.g., echolalia, pronoun reversal) and typically exhibit an "uneven" profile of cognitive abilities. For example, people with this disorder may perform above average on measures of visual-spatial abilities and mechanical skills and occasionally exhibit savant abilities but do poorly on measures of verbal comprehension and abstract reasoning. They may also have motor deficits and engage in self-injurious behaviors. The earliest signs of the disorder are usually abnormalities in social orienting and responsivity that are apparent by about 12 months of age (e.g., decreased social gaze and eye contact and impaired joint attention).

3. Prognosis: The prognosis for autism spectrum disorder is generally poor. Only about one-third of individuals achieve some degree of partial independence as adults, and few are able to live and work independently. The best outcome is associated with an ability to communicate verbally by age 5 or 6, an IQ over 70, and a later onset of symptoms.

4. Differential Diagnosis: (a) When a person has impairment in social communication and social interactions but doesn't show restricted and repetitive interests or behavior, criteria for SOCIAL (PRAGMATIC) COMMUNICATION DISORDER (instead of autism spectrum disorder) may be met. (b) SCHIZOPHRENIA WITH CHILDHOOD ONSET usually develops after a period of normal, or near normal, development. In addition, hallucinations and delusions are not features of autism spectrum disorder.

5. Specific Assessment Considerations: Ongoing evaluation and monitoring of a client with symptoms of autism spectrum disorder requires a multidisciplinary approach (e.g., psychologist, pediatrician, neurologist, speech-language pathologist, audiologist, child psychiatrist, occupational therapist, physical therapist, educators and special educators).

Diagnosis of autism spectrum disorder in very young children (those less than 16 months of age) depends primarily on the presence of characteristic behaviors such as problems with eye contact and verbal and nonverbal language. For a child who is between 16 and 30 months of age, the Modified Checklist for Autism in Toddlers, Revised (M-CHAT) can be used. For a school-aged client, you should consult with her teachers, and, if needed, help her parents arrange for an evaluation her educational needs (psychoeducational profile). Once the diagnosis is made, you should provide the family and other caregivers with current literature and information about parent support groups and other available community services.

Attention-Deficit/Hyperactivity Disorder

1. Diagnostic Criteria: Attention-deficit/hyperactivity disorder (ADHD) is characterized by a pattern of inattention and/or hyperactivity-impulsivity that has persisted for at least six months, had an onset prior to 12 years of age, is present in at least two settings (e.g., home and school), and interferes with social, academic, or occupational functioning. The diagnosis requires at least six characteristic symptoms of inattention and/or six characteristic symptoms of hyperactivity-impulsivity:

- *Inattention* – e.g., fails to give close attention to details; has difficulty sustaining attention to tasks or play activities; doesn't listen when directly spoken to; fails to finish schoolwork or chores; is easily distracted by extraneous stimuli; is often forgetful in daily activities.

- *Hyperactivity-impulsivity* – e.g., frequently fidgets or squirms in seat; often leaves seat at inappropriate times; frequently runs or climbs in inappropriate situations; talks excessively; has difficulty waiting her turn; interrupts or intrudes on others.

2. Subtypes: Three specifiers are provided to indicate subtype: (a) *Predominantly inattentive* presentation applies when the individual has six or more symptoms of inattention and fewer than six symptoms of hyperactivity-impulsivity; (b) *predominantly hyperactive/impulsive* presentation applies when there are six or more symptoms of hyperactivity-impulsivity and fewer than six symptoms of inattention; and (c) *combined* presentation applies when there are six or more symptoms of inattention and six or more symptoms of hyperactivity-impulsivity.

3. Associated Features: Children and adolescents with ADHD typically test lower on IQ tests than other children even though their intelligence is average or above average, and nearly all exhibit some academic difficulties (Barkley, 2002a). Many also have problems related to social adjustment (e.g., they tend to have few friends and may be the victims of peer rejection). Common co-diagnoses include conduct disorder, a specific learning disorder, oppositional defiant disorder, an anxiety disorder, and major depressive disorder.

Adults with ADHD tend to have low self-esteem and problems related to social relationships; and, compared to peers without ADHD, they have poorer health outcomes and lower educational and occupational achievement (e.g., they are more likely to change jobs frequently and to be fired from a job).

4. Gender: Overall, ADHD is more prevalent in males than females. However gender differences depend on subtype, with the combined subtype being more common for males and the inattentive type being more common for females (e.g., Woo & Keatinge, 2008).

5. Course/Prognosis: Studies suggest that 65 to 80 percent of children with ADHD continue to meet the diagnostic criteria for the disorder in adolescence (Hart et al., 1995; Hinshaw et al., 2006). In addition, up to 15 percent continue to meet the full diagnostic criteria for ADHD as young adults, and up to 60 percent meet the criteria for ADHD in partial remission (Faraone, Biederman, & Mick, 2005).

The symptoms of the disorder vary somewhat over the lifespan: (a) The gross motor activity characteristic of children declines over time; and hyperactivity is often manifested in adults as fidgeting, excessive talking, an inner sense of restlessness, and feeling overwhelmed. (b) In adults, impulsivity typically takes the form of impatience and irritability, problems related to the management of time and money, reckless driving, and impulsive sexuality. (c) In adults, inattention predominates the symptom profile, with common signs of inattention including inconsistency in the ability to concentrate, difficulty establishing and maintaining routines, and an inability to prioritize and complete important tasks (Braun et al., 2004; Miller, 2002).

6. Differential Diagnosis: (a) ADHD must be distinguished from age-appropriate activity levels and from inattention that is the result of an understimulating or disorganized, chaotic environment. (b) In OPPOSITIONAL DEFIANT DISORDER, resistance to tasks that require self-application is due to negativity, hostility, and defiance. In ADHD, resistance to tasks requiring prolonged mental effort is due to impulsivity, difficulty in sustaining attention, and forgetting instructions.

7. Specific Assessment Considerations: If the client is a child or adolescent, have the parents and teachers (and an older child or adolescent) complete behavior rating scales such as the Behavioral Assessment for Children, Second Edition (BASC-2) and the Child Behavior Checklist (CBCL) ADHD Rating Scale. Also consult with the client's teachers and find out if she is receiving appropriate attention at school.

Specific Learning Disorder

1. Diagnostic Criteria: A diagnosis of specific learning disorder is made when a person exhibits difficulties related to academic skills as indicated by the presence of at least one characteristic symptom that persists for at least six months despite the provision of interventions targeting those difficulties. Symptoms include inaccurate or slow and effortful word reading; difficulty understanding the meaning of what is read; difficulties with spelling;

difficulties with written expression; difficulties mastering number sense, number facts, or calculation; and difficulties with mathematical reasoning. The diagnosis also requires that the individual's academic skills are substantially below those expected for her age, interfere with academic or occupational performance or activities of daily living, began during the school-age years, and are not better accounted for by another condition or disorder or other factor such as uncorrected visual or auditory impairment or psychosocial adversity.

The DSM-5 distinguishes between three subtypes (with impairment in reading, with impairment in written expression, and with impairment in mathematics) and provides specifiers for level of severity (mild, moderate, and severe).

Learning difficulties that include problems with word recognition, decoding, and spelling abilities are also called **dyslexia**; and learning difficulties characterized by problems processing numerical information, learning arithmetic facts, and performing accurate or fluent calculations are also referred to as **dyscalculia**.

2. Associated Features: Individuals with specific learning disorder typically have an IQ in the average to above-average range but have higher-than-normal rates of other problems and disorders, including delays in language development and/or motor coordination, attention and memory deficits, and low self-esteem. The most frequent comorbid disorder is ADHD.

3. Etiology: Factors that have been linked to the specific learning disorders include cerebellar-vestibular dysfunction (due, for example, to **otitis media**); incomplete dominance and other hemispheric abnormalities; and exposure to toxins (especially lead). One theory describes the core problem of dyslexia as being deficits in phonological processing (Stanovich, 1993). There is also evidence of a genetic component.

Motor Disorders

1. Tic Disorders: The DSM-5 defines a **tic** as a "sudden, rapid, recurrent, nonrhythmic motor movement or vocalization" (APA, 2013, p. 81). Motor tics include eye blinking, facial grimacing and gestures, jumping, smelling objects, and echokinesis (imitating someone else's movements); while vocal tics include grunting, snorting, barking, echolalia, and coprolalia (repeating socially undesirable words). All forms of tics can be exacerbated by stress as well as diminished during an absorbing activity (e.g., while reading a good book). Tics are usually markedly diminished during sleep.

a. Diagnostic Criteria: The DSM-5 distinguishes between three tic disorders:

Tourette's disorder: **Tourette's disorder** is characterized by the presence of at least one vocal tic and multiple motor tics that may appear simultaneously or at different times, that may wax and wane in frequency but have persisted for more than one year, and that began prior to 18 years of age. For many individuals, the frequency, severity, and disruptiveness of symptoms decline in adolescence or adulthood.

Persistent (chronic) motor or vocal tic disorder: This disorder involves one or more motor *or* vocal tics that have persisted for more than one year and began prior to age 18.

Provisional tic disorder: This disorder is characterized by one or more motor and/or vocal tics that have been present for less than one year and began before age 18.

b. Associated Symptoms: The most common associated symptoms of Tourette's disorder are obsessions and compulsions; and the rate of obsessive-compulsive disorder is higher not only for individuals with Tourette's disorder but also for their biological relatives. Hyperactivity, impulsivity, and distractibility are also common and have been identified as a cause of the high rate of school problems exhibited by children with this disorder (Silver & Hagan, 1990).

c. Etiology: Tourette's disorder has been linked to elevated levels of dopamine and supersensitivity of dopamine receptors in the caudate nucleus (e.g., Segawa, 2003; Wolf et al., 1996).

2. Developmental Coordination Disorder: With developmental coordination disorder, the acquisition and execution of coordinated motor skills is substantially below that expected for the person's chronological age and opportunity for learning and using the skills. The motor skills deficit significantly and persistently interferes with activities of daily living appropriate to chronological age (e.g., self-care) and impacts on academic productivity, prevocational and vocational activities, leisure, and play. The deficits are not better explained by intellectual disability or visual impairment and are not attributable to a neurological condition affecting movement.

3. Stereotypic Movement Disorder:

a. Diagnostic Criteria: Stereotypic movement disorder is characterized by repetitive, seemingly driven, and apparently purposeless motor behavior (e.g., hand waving, body rocking, head banging, self-biting) that interferes with social, academic, or other activities and may result in self-injury. The repetitive motor behavior is not attributable to the physiological effects of a substance or neurological condition and is not better explained by another neurodevelopmental or other mental disorder.

b. Differential Diagnosis: Stereotypic movement disorder does not include the deficits of social communication and reciprocity found in AUTISM SPECTRUM DISORDER. An additional diagnosis of stereotypic movement disorder is not made when motor stereotypies are better explained by the presence of autism spectrum disorder, but an additional diagnosis may be made when stereotypies result in self-injury and become a focus of treatment.

B. Schizophrenia Spectrum and Other Psychotic Disorders

Included in this category are delusional disorder, schizophrenia, schizophreniform disorder, brief psychotic disorder, schizoaffective disorder, substance/medication-induced psychotic disorder, and psychotic disorder due to another medical condition.

1. Characteristic Symptoms of Psychotic Disorders: The disorders in this category are characterized by the presence of one or more of the following:

Delusions: **Delusions** are false beliefs that are firmly held despite what almost everyone else believes or the existence of contradictory evidence. In schizophrenia, delusions are often **persecutory** (the person thinks he is being followed, tricked, or spied on), **referential** (the person believes that passages from books and newspapers or other messages are specifically directed at him), or bizarre. Delusions are **bizarre** if they are clearly implausible, not understandable by one's cultural peer group, and not derived from ordinary life experience. An example is the belief that one's thoughts have been "removed" by an outside force (thought withdrawal). In contrast, **nonbizarre** delusions involve situations that could plausibly happen such as believing that one is under surveillance by the FBI despite a lack of convincing evidence.

Hallucinations: **Hallucinations** are "perception-like experiences that occur without an external stimulus" (APA, 2013, p. 87). They may affect any sensory modality, but auditory hallucinations are most frequent and often take the form of pejorative or threatening voices or a running commentary on the person's thoughts or actions.

Disorganized thinking (disorganized speech): Disorganized thinking is usually inferred from the individual's speech. It often involves a **loosening of associations** that is manifested as incoherence, answers or comments that are unresponsive to questions, and "slipping off the track" from one topic to another.

Grossly disorganized or abnormal motor behavior: Grossly disorganized or abnormal motor behavior can take several forms including unpredictable agitation, a markedly disheveled appearance, clearly inappropriate sexual behavior, or **catatonia** (decreased motor activity and reduced reactivity to environmental stimuli).

Negative symptoms: **Negative symptoms** involve a restriction in the range and intensity of emotions and other functions and include blunted emotional expression, anhedonia (decreased ability to experience pleasure), asociality (lack of interest in social interactions), alogia (diminished speech output), and avolition (restricted initiation of goal-directed behavior).

Note that delusions, hallucinations, disorganized thinking (disorganized speech), and grossly disorganized or abnormal motor behavior are known as **positive symptoms**. Positive symptoms involve an excess or distortion of normal functions.

2. Severity Ratings for Psychotic Disorders: Although a psychotic disorder can be diagnosed without using a severity specifier, severity may be rated by a quantitative assessment of the primary symptoms of psychosis (delusions, hallucinations, disorganized speech, abnormal psychomotor behavior, negative symptoms). The DSM-5 provides a measure called the Clinician-Rated Dimensions of Psychosis Symptom Severity that may be used to perform this assessment. The DSM-IV-TR's subtypes of schizophrenia (paranoid, catatonic, disorganized, etc.) have been eliminated in the DSM-5, and, instead of these subtypes, the DSM-5 offers this dimensional approach to rating severity for the core symptoms of schizophrenia.

Delusional Disorder

1. Diagnostic Criteria: The essential feature of delusional disorder is the presence of one or more delusions that last at least one month. Overall psychosocial functioning is not markedly impaired, and any impairment is directly related to the delusions (e.g., the person loses his job because he's afraid to leave the house and repeatedly misses work).

Specifiers are provided to indicate if delusions are bizarre and to describe the disorder's course (first episode, currently in acute episode; first episode, currently in full remission; multiple episodes, currently in acute episode, etc.).

2. Subtypes: The DSM-5 distinguishes between the following subtypes: (a) erotomanic (the person believes that someone is romantically in love with him); (b) grandiose (the person believes that he has great but unrecognized talent or insight or has made an important discovery); (c) jealous (the person believes that his spouse or lover is unfaithful); (d) persecutory (the person believes that he is being conspired against, cheated, spied on, poisoned, etc.); (e) somatic (the person believes that he has an abnormal bodily function or sensation); (f) mixed; and (g) unspecified.

3. Culture: You must take into account an individual's cultural and religious background in evaluating the possible presence of a delusional disorder.

4. Differential Diagnosis: Delusional disorder (which requires *only* the presence of one or more delusions) is distinguished from SCHIZOPHRENIA and SCHIZOPHRENIFORM DISORDER by the absence of other characteristic symptoms of the active phase of schizophrenia.

Schizophrenia

1. Diagnostic Criteria: The diagnosis of schizophrenia requires the presence of at least two active phase symptoms – i.e., delusions, hallucinations, disorganized speech, grossly disorganized behavior, negative symptoms – for at least one month with at least one symptom being delusions, hallucinations, or disorganized speech. In addition, there must be continuous signs of the disorder for at least six months, and symptoms must cause significant impairment in functioning.

The six or more month period of continuous disturbance may include periods of prodromal or residual symptoms. In other words, an active phase of the illness must be present for at least one month, and, in addition to this, some signs of the disturbance must persist for at least six months – these signs may consist of prodromal and/or residual phase symptoms of schizophrenia. The different **phases of schizophrenia** are defined as follows:

Prodromal phase: The prodromal phase comes before the active phase. It includes a deterioration in functioning and may include only negative symptoms or mild (attenuated) forms of active phase symptoms (e.g., magical thinking instead of full-blown delusions, mildly disorganized speech, eccentric behavior).

Active phase: There are prominent symptoms of the **active phase**, as described with the diagnostic criteria.

Residual phase: The residual phase is similar to the prodromal phase, but it comes after the active phase.

The DSM-5 provides specifiers to describe the course of the disorder (i.e., first episode, currently in acute episode; first episode, currently in partial remission; first episode, currently in full remission; multiple episodes, currently in partial remission; multiple episodes, currently in full remission; continuous; and unspecified) and to indicate if symptoms include catatonia.

2. Associated Features: Common associated features of schizophrenia include inappropriate affect (e.g., laughing for no apparent reason), dysphoric mood, disturbed sleep pattern, and lack of interest in eating. Some individuals have poor insight into their illness (anosognosia) which contributes to treatment noncompliance and is a predictor of relapse. A substance use disorder is a common co-diagnosis, with the rate of tobacco use disorder being particularly high. Contrary to what is commonly believed, there is no evidence that the risk for violent behavior is greater for people with schizophrenia than for people in the general population.

3. Culture: The research suggests that the higher reported rate of schizophrenia for African-Americans is the result of misdiagnosis rather than actual differences in the prevalence of the disorder and that misdiagnosis is due to the fact that African-Americans are more likely to experience hallucinations and delusions as symptoms of depression and other disorders.

4. Course/Prognosis: The onset of schizophrenia is usually between the late teens and early 30s, with the peak age of onset being in the early to mid-20s for males and the late 20s for females. The course is ordinarily chronic with complete remission being rare. A *better prognosis* is associated with good premorbid adjustment, an acute and late onset, female gender, the presence of a precipitating event, a brief duration of active-phase symptoms, insight into the illness, a family history of a mood disorder, and no family history of schizophrenia.

5. Etiology: A number of brain abnormalities have been linked to schizophrenia (e.g., enlarged ventricles).

Evidence of a genetic component is provided by twin and adoption studies and studies showing that the risk for schizophrenia is substantially higher among first-degree biological relatives of people with this disorder than for people in the general population. Additional evidence for a genetic component is provided by studies showing that the relatives of individuals with schizophrenia are not only at increased risk for schizophrenia but also for other schizophrenia spectrum disorders, especially schizotypal personality disorder (e.g., Cannon et al., 1994). (Other disorders that belong to the schizophrenia spectrum include the other psychotic disorders as well as schizoid, paranoid, and avoidant personality disorders.)

The **dopamine hypothesis** was the first biochemical explanation for schizophrenia and attributes it to elevated dopamine levels or oversensitive dopamine receptors. The original dopamine hypothesis has been modified by research suggesting that the role of dopamine may differ for the positive and negative symptoms of this disorder and by studies implicating other neurotransmitters in the disorder's etiology including serotonin, glutamate, and GABA (Downar & Kapur, 2008; Gitlin, 1996).

Finally, in the Northern hemisphere, an abnormally large proportion of people with schizophrenia were born in the late winter or early spring. Some investigators suggest that this seasonal effect is due to higher rates of infectious diseases during the winter months, and this hypothesis is consistent with research showing a link between schizophrenia and prenatal exposure to an influenza virus (Cannon, Barr, & Mednick, 1991).

6. Differential Diagnosis: (a) Schizophrenia requires six months of symptoms. In SCHIZOPHRENIFORM DISORDER, the disturbance lasts for at least one month but less than six months; in BRIEF PSYCHOTIC DISORDER, symptoms last for at least one day but less than one month. (b) Because mood disturbances are common in schizophrenia, the differential diagnosis between schizophrenia, schizoaffective disorder, and major depressive or bipolar disorder with psychotic features can be difficult. However, in schizophrenia, mood symptoms are brief relative to the duration of the disorder, do not occur during the active phase, and do not meet the full criteria for a mood episode. In contrast: (i) In SCHIZOAFFECTIVE DISORDER, prominent mood symptoms occur concurrently with psychotic symptoms for most of the duration of the disorder but there is also a period of at least two weeks during which only psychotic symptoms are present. (ii) When psychotic symptoms occur only during episodes of a mood disturbance, the diagnosis is BIPOLAR or MAJOR DEPRESSIVE DISORDER WITH PSYCHOTIC FEATURES. (c) Schizophrenia must be distinguished from the effects of AMPHETAMINES and COCAINE, which can include delusions and hallucinations.

7. Specific Assessment Considerations: It's important during the initial phase of intervention to determine the appropriate treatment setting for the client, in particular whether the client should be referred for inpatient care. Indications for inpatient hospitalization for clients who have schizophrenia include the following: (a) acute states of psychosis; (b) comorbid intoxication or other substance-related disorder; (c) current suicidality and/or aggression (i.e., protection of the client or others); (d) the need for crisis intervention for other reasons such as to provide safety and relief (e.g., the client may need to be removed from environmental stressors which precipitated or are maintaining his illness); (e) the need for symptom stabilization involving changing or re-establishing a medication regimen; and/or (f) the presence of resistance, decompensation, noncompliance, or a lack of progress in outpatient therapy.

Other important activities during assessment include the following: (a) Evaluate environmental support (e.g., ensure adequate family and community supports away from undue criticism or blame); (b) determine the client's capacity to collaborate in treatment; (c) explore the client's cognitive understanding of his illness and ability to recognize and self-manage the symptoms; (d) determine the client's strengths and weaknesses related to social, vocational, and self-care skills; and (e) assess the role of any damage to the client's self-esteem due to the loss of functioning, interpersonal problems, stigma associated with the illness, etc. If you need supplemental information to substantiate the diagnosis or determine the client's present level of functioning, you may refer the client to a psychologist for psychological testing.

Schizophreniform, Brief Psychotic, and Schizoaffective Disorders

1. Schizophreniform Disorder: The diagnostic criteria for schizophreniform disorder are identical to those for schizophrenia except that the disturbance is present for at least one month but less than six months and impaired social or occupational functioning may occur but is not required. About two-thirds of people with this disorder eventually meet the diagnostic criteria for a diagnosis of schizophrenia or schizoaffective disorder.

2. Brief Psychotic Disorder: Brief psychotic disorder is characterized by the presence of one or more of four characteristic symptoms (delusions, hallucinations, disorganized speech, grossly disorganized or catatonic behavior) with at least one symptom being delusions, hallucinations, or disorganized speech. Symptoms are present for at least one day but less than one month with an eventual return to premorbid functioning. The onset of this disorder often follows exposure to an overwhelming stressor.

3. Schizoaffective Disorder:

a. Diagnostic Criteria: Schizoaffective disorder is characterized by an uninterrupted period of illness during which, at some time, there are concurrent symptoms of schizophrenia and symptoms of a major depressive or manic episode with a period of at least two weeks without prominent mood symptoms.

b. Differential Diagnosis: In schizoaffective disorder, there are prominent delusions and/or hallucinations for at least two weeks in the *absence* of a mood episode. With BIPOLAR or DEPRESSIVE DISORDER WITH PSYCHOTIC FEATURES, psychotic features mainly occur *during* mood episode(s). If the relative proportion of mood to psychotic symptoms changes over time, the diagnosis may change from and to schizoaffective disorder.

C. Bipolar and Related Disorders

Included in this category are bipolar I disorder, bipolar II disorder, cyclothymic disorder, substance/medication-induced bipolar and related disorder, and bipolar and related disorder due to another medical condition.

Bipolar I Disorder

1. Diagnostic Criteria: A diagnosis of bipolar I disorder requires at least one **manic episode** which is a "distinct period of abnormally and persistently elevated, expansive, or irritable mood and abnormally and persistently increased goal-directed activity or energy" (APA, 2013, p. 124). The episode must last for at least one week, be present most of the day nearly every day, and include at least three characteristic symptoms that reflect a clear change from the person's usual behavior: (a) inflated self-esteem or grandiosity, (b) less need for sleep, (c) more talkative than usual or pressure to keep talking, (d) flight of ideas or the feeling that one's thoughts are racing, (e) distractibility, (f) increase in goal-directed activity or psychomotor agitation, and/or (g) excessive involvement in activities that have a high potential for painful consequences. The diagnosis also requires that symptoms cause marked impairment in social or occupational functioning, require hospitalization to avoid harm to self or others, or include psychotic features.

Specifiers are provided for severity (mild, moderate, or severe) based on number and severity of symptoms; type of current or most recent episode (manic, hypomanic, depressed, or unspecified); and accompanying symptoms (e.g., with anxious distress, with mixed features, with rapid cycling, with mood-congruent psychotic features, with mood-incongruent psychotic features, with peripartum onset, with seasonal pattern). The specifier **with rapid cycling** is used when there have been at least four mood episodes in the previous 12 months that meet criteria for a manic, hypomanic, or major depressive episode.

Note: At least one lifetime manic episode is *required* for the diagnosis of bipolar I disorder. In addition, this disorder *may* include one or more episodes of hypomania or major depression. In other words, hypomanic and major depressive episodes are common in bipolar I disorder but they are *not* required for the diagnosis to be made.

2. Associated Features: Bipolar disorder is associated with a number of comorbid conditions, the most common of which are anxiety and substance use disorders (McElroy et al., 2001). In addition, the lifetime risk for completed suicide for individuals with bipolar disorder is about 15 times the risk for the general population (Harris & Barraclough, 1997). People experiencing a manic episode often do not recognize that they are ill and consequently, resist treatment.

3. Etiology: Of the psychiatric disorders, genetic factors have been most consistently linked to the bipolar disorders. For example, family studies have found that the first-degree relatives of individuals with bipolar disorder are at elevated risk for both bipolar disorder and depression (Dubovsky, Davies, & Dubovsky, 2003).

4. Differential Diagnosis: (a) A bipolar disorder may include psychotic features *during* a mood episode. In PSYCHOTIC DISORDERS (e.g., delusional disorder, schizophrenia, schizoaffective disorder), periods of psychotic symptoms occur *in the absence* of prominent mood symptoms. (b) With BIPOLAR II DISORDER, the person has had at least one major depressive episode and at least one hypomanic episode but has *never* had a manic episode.

5. Specific Assessment Considerations: Hospitalization may be necessary if the client is in the midst of a manic episode – i.e., due to a loss of judgment concerning her own behavior, the client may need to be placed in a safe and structured setting. If not, then a client may still need to be taken safely to a physician or psychiatrist for a medication evaluation.

Bipolar II Disorder

1. Diagnostic Criteria: A diagnosis of bipolar II disorder requires at least one hypomanic episode and one major depressive episode. In addition, the person has *never* had a manic episode.

A **hypomanic episode** is "a distinct period of abnormally and persistently elevated, expansive, or irritable mood and abnormally and persistently increased activity or energy" (APA, 2013, p. 132) that lasts for at least four consecutive days and is present most of the day nearly every day. The elevated, expansive, or irritable mood must involve at least three characteristic symptoms that are also associated with a manic episode but are not severe enough to cause marked impairment in social or occupational functioning or require hospitalization. A major depressive episode lasts for at least two weeks and involves five or more characteristic symptoms, at least one of which must be a depressed mood or a loss of interest or pleasure in all or almost all activities.

Specifiers are provided to designate severity, the most recent episode (hypomanic or depressed), and accompanying symptoms.

2. Differential Diagnosis: Bipolar II disorder is distinguished from CYCLOTHYMIC DISORDER by the presence, in bipolar II disorder, of one or more major depressive episodes. That is, in cyclothymic disorder there are numerous periods of hypomanic symptoms and numerous periods of depressive symptoms that don't meet full criteria for a major depressive episode (i.e., either fewer symptoms or a shorter duration).

Cyclothymic Disorder

Cyclothymic disorder is characterized by "numerous periods with hypomanic symptoms that do not meet criteria for a hypomanic episode and numerous periods with depressive symptoms that do not meet criteria for a major depressive episode" (APA, 2013, p. 139) and that cause significant distress or impaired functioning. Symptoms last for at least two years in adults or one year in children and adolescents and are present for at least half the time with the individual not being symptom-free for more than two months at a time.

D. Depressive Disorders

Included in this category are disruptive mood dysregulation disorder, major depressive disorder, persistent depressive disorder, premenstrual dysphoric disorder, substance/medication-induced depressive disorder, and depressive disorder due to another medical condition.

Disruptive Mood Dysregulation Disorder

1. Diagnostic Criteria: Disruptive mood dysregulation disorder is diagnosed in the presence of (a) "severe recurrent temper outbursts manifested verbally (e.g., verbal rages) and/or behaviorally (e.g., physical aggression toward people or property) that are grossly out of proportion in intensity or duration to the situation or provocation" (APA, 2013, p. 156) *and* (b) a chronic, persistently irritable or angry mood between temper outbursts on most days. Symptoms have persisted for at least 12 months and are exhibited in at least two of three settings (home, school, with peers), and temper outbursts are inconsistent with the individual's developmental level and occur, on average, at least three times each week. The diagnosis cannot be assigned for the first time before the individual is 6 years of age or after he is 18 years of age, and the age of onset must be before age 10.

Note: Disruptive mood dysregulation disorder *cannot* co-exist with oppositional defiant disorder (ODD), intermittent explosive disorder, or bipolar disorder; it *can* co-exist with major depressive disorder, ADHD, conduct disorder, and substance use disorders. If criteria for both disruptive mood dysregulation disorder and ODD are met, *only* the diagnosis of disruptive mood dysregulation disorder should be given.

2. Differential Diagnosis: (a) BIPOLAR I and BIPOLAR II DISORDER are episodic conditions (they include discrete periods of mood disturbance that can be differentiated from how the child usually is); disruptive mood dysregulation disorder is *not* an episodic condition. If a child or adolescent has ever had a manic or hypomanic episode, the diagnosis of disruptive mood dysregulation disorder should not be given. (b) Children whose irritability is present only during a major depressive episode (MAJOR DEPRESSIVE DISORDER) or in the context of a PERSISTENT DEPRESSIVE DISORDER (DYSTHYMIA) should receive one of those diagnoses rather than disruptive mood dysregulation disorder. (c) In children whose symptoms also meet criteria for OPPOSITIONAL DEFIANT DISORDER, the following features indicate that disruptive mood dysregulation disorder should be diagnosed instead: (i) the presence of severe and frequently recurrent temper outbursts, and (ii) a persistent disruption in mood between outbursts (i.e., the mood symptoms of disruptive mood dysregulation disorder are rare in children with oppositional defiant disorder).

Major Depressive Disorder

1. Diagnostic Criteria: A diagnosis of major depressive disorder requires the presence of at least five symptoms of a **major depressive episode** nearly every day for at least two weeks, with at least one symptom being depressed mood or a loss of interest or pleasure. The symptoms of a major depressive episode are (a) depressed mood (or, in children and adolescents, a depressed or irritable mood); (b) markedly diminished interest or pleasure in most or all activities; (c) significant weight loss when not dieting, weight gain, or a decrease or increase in appetite; (d) insomnia or hypersomnia; (e) psychomotor agitation or retardation; (f) fatigue or loss of energy; (g) feelings of worthlessness or excessive guilt; (h) diminished ability to think or concentrate or indecisiveness; and/or (i) recurrent thoughts of death, recurrent suicidal ideation, or a suicide attempt. Symptoms cause clinically significant distress or impaired functioning.

Specifiers are provided to indicate severity (mild, moderate, severe); course (single episode or recurrent episode and in partial remission or in full remission); and accompanying features (e.g., with anxious distress, with atypical features, with mood-congruent psychotic features, with mood-incongruent psychotic features, with peripartum onset, with seasonal pattern).

The specifier **with peripartum onset** is applied to major depressive disorder, bipolar I disorder, and bipolar II disorder when the onset of symptoms is during pregnancy or within four weeks postpartum. Symptoms often include anxiety and a preoccupation with the infant's well-being or, in extreme cases, delusional thoughts about the infant (e.g., that the infant is possessed or destined for a terrible fate). About 10 to 20 percent of women experience depression either during pregnancy or the first several months after giving birth (e.g., Gavin et al., 2005), while .1 to .2 percent develop postpartum psychosis (Sit, Rothschild, & Wisner, 2006). Postpartum psychosis is a serious condition involving disorientation, hallucinations, delusions, paranoia, and attempts to harm oneself or one's baby. Major depressive disorder with peripartum onset must be distinguished from the "baby blues," which involves mild transitory mood symptoms and affects up to 80 percent of women during the first two weeks following delivery (e.g., Milgrom, Martin, & Negri, 1999).

The specifier with seasonal pattern is applied to major depressive disorder, bipolar I disorder, and bipolar II disorder when there is a temporal relationship between the onset of a mood episode and a particular time of the year. This condition is also known as **seasonal affective disorder** (SAD) and, in the Northern Hemisphere, most commonly occurs during the winter months. People with SAD usually experience hypersomnia, increased appetite and weight gain, and a craving for carbohydrates. SAD has been linked to several factors including the season-related change in the dark-light cycle that increases melatonin levels; a phase-delay in circadian rhythms; and serotonergic dysfunction (Lam & Levitan, 2000). Phototherapy involves exposure to artificial bright light and has been found to be an effective treatment for this disorder (e.g., Golden et al., 2005).

Finally, the term "**masked depression**" is sometimes used in the literature for depressions in which physical symptoms (pain, loss of appetite, etc.) predominate, and the individual often denies experiencing a depressed mood.

2. Course: The peak age of onset of major depressive disorder is the mid-20s, with the course, duration, and number of episodes varying from person to person. Major depressive episodes – especially the initial episodes – may be precipitated by a severe psychosocial stressor such as the death of a family member or divorce. However, as the number of previous episodes increases, the risk for subsequent episodes is related more to the number of prior episodes than to the occurrence of a life stressor (e.g., Kendler, Thornton, & Gardner, 2001).

3. Age: The symptoms of major depressive disorder vary somewhat with age. Somatic complaints, irritability, and social withdrawal are common in children; while aggressiveness and destructiveness sometimes occur in preadolescents (especially boys). In older adults, memory loss, distractibility, disorientation, and other cognitive symptoms may be present, making it difficult to distinguish depression ("**pseudodementia**") from a major and mild neurocognitive disorder. For more information on this, see Neurocognitive Disorders in this section.

4. Culture: In some cultures, depression is manifested as somatic symptoms. For example, among Latinos, complaints of "nerves" and headaches are common, while Asians often experience depression as weakness, tiredness, or an "imbalance."

5. Etiology: There is evidence that depression has a strong genetic component. For example, major depressive disorder is about 1.5 to 3.0 times more common among first-degree biological relatives of individuals with the disorder than among individuals in the general population.

Two early biochemical theories of major depressive disorder attributed it to lower-than-normal levels of certain neurotransmitters: According to the **catecholamine hypothesis**, some forms of depression are due to a deficiency in norepinephrine, while the **indolamine hypothesis** describes depression as the result of low levels of serotonin. More recently, research on the role of neurotransmitters has focused on the number and sensitivity of postsynaptic receptors (especially serotonin receptors) rather than on the absolute levels of neurotransmitters (e.g., Mintun et al., 2004; Neumeister et al., 2004). Depression has also been linked to elevated levels of the "stress hormone" cortisol (e.g., Sheline, Gado, & Kraemer, 2003).

Several behavioral and cognitive-behavioral theories have been offered as alternatives to biological explanations for depression:

- Lewinsohn's (1974) **behavioral theory of depression** is based on the principles of operant conditioning. It attributes the disorder to a low rate of response-contingent reinforcement for social and other behaviors (e.g., as the result of the death of a partner or change in social environment), which results in extinction of those behaviors as well as in pessimism, low self-esteem, social isolation, and other features of depression that tend to reduce the likelihood of positive reinforcement in the future.

- Seligman's (Abramson, Seligman, & Teasdale, 1978) reformulated **learned helplessness model** describes depression as the result of prior exposure to uncontrollable negative events coupled with a tendency to attribute those events to internal, stable, and global factors. A more recent version of this model (Abramson, Metalsky, & Alloy, 1989) de-emphasizes the role of attributions and, instead, describes hopelessness as the proximal and sufficient cause of depression.

- According to Rehm's (Rehm, Kaslow, & Rabin, 1987) **self-control model**, depression is the result of a combination of problems related to self-monitoring, self-evaluation, and self-reinforcement: People who are depressed attend most to negative events and immediate outcomes; fail to make accurate internal attributions and set stringent criteria for self-evaluation; and have low rates of self-reinforcement and high rates of self-punishment.

- Beck's (1976) **cognitive theory** views depression as being related to negative, illogical self-statements about oneself, the world, and the future (the **depressive cognitive triad**). While some studies confirm Beck's hypothesis, others suggest that negative beliefs may actually reflect a more accurate awareness of reality. For example, Lewinsohn, et al. (1980) found that low self-evaluations by depressed individuals about their social skills were more accurate (more consistent with the evaluations of judges) than the self-evaluations of non-depressed individuals who tended to overestimate their abilities.

6. Differential Diagnosis: (a) Major depressive disorder may be difficult to distinguish from SCHIZOPHRENIA or OTHER PSYCHOTIC DISORDERS when the person's symptoms include delusions, hallucinations, and/or catatonic features. However, when psychotic symptoms occur exclusively during a major depressive episode, the most likely diagnosis is major depressive disorder with psychotic features. (b) A major depressive episode in response to a psychosocial stressor is distinguished from ADJUSTMENT DISORDER WITH DEPRESSED MOOD by the fact that full criteria for a major depressive disorder are not met in adjustment disorder. (c) Major depressive disorder must be distinguished from UNCOMPLICATED BEREAVEMENT, which is included with other conditions that may be a focus of clinical attention. As noted in the DSM-5, a person with uncomplicated bereavement typically experiences his mood as normal.

7. Distinguishing Grief from Major Depressive Episodes (MDE): The DSM-5 also provides the following information to facilitate your understanding of the differences between major depression and grief or bereavement: (a) In grief, the prevailing affect is feelings of emptiness and loss; in an MDE, it is a persistent depressed mood and inability to anticipate pleasure or happiness. (b) In grief, the dysphoria usually becomes less intense as time passes (usually days to weeks) and occurs in waves that typically are associated with thoughts of the person who died; in an MDE, the depressed mood is more persistent and not connected to specific thoughts. (c) Grief may include positive emotions and humor; an MDE involves a pervasive unhappiness. (d) In grief, thought content generally focuses on thoughts and memories of the person who died; in an MDE, thoughts tend to be dominated by self-critical or pessimistic ruminations. (e) In grief, self-esteem is generally unaffected; in an MDE, the person often feels worthless and experiences a sense of self-loathing. (f) In grief, thoughts about death and dying, if they occur, are commonly focused on the person who died and, sometimes, on "joining" him or her; in an MDE, such thoughts are focused on ending one's own life because of feeling worthless or unable to cope with the pain of depression.

8. Specific Assessment Considerations: Because of the association between major depression and suicide risk, it is critical to determine whether a depressed client poses a current danger to himself. In addition to this, you may use a short assessment instrument, such as the Beck Depression Inventory-II, to clarify the severity of the client's symptoms; and should assess for co-existing disorders including a substance use disorder; attempt to gather information from collateral sources (especially when the client's symptoms interfere with concentration and memory); refer the client to a physician to rule out the possibility that another medical condition is responsible for his symptoms; and, once the diagnosis is established, refer the client to a psychiatrist for a medication evaluation. To initiate the development of treatment goals, have the client begin self-monitoring his emotions and the thoughts and events associated with them.

Persistent Depressive Disorder (Dysthymia)

1. Diagnostic Criteria: The essential feature of persistent depressive disorder (dysthymia) is a depressed mood (or in children and adolescents, a depressed or irritable mood) on most days for at least two years in adults or at least one year in children and adolescents as indicated by the presence of at least two of the following symptoms: (a) poor appetite or overeating, (b) insomnia or hypersomnia, (c) low energy or fatigue, (d) low self-esteem, (e) poor concentration or difficulty making decisions, and/or (f) feelings of hopelessness. During the two- or one-year period, the individual has not been symptom-free for more than two months, and the symptoms cause clinically significant distress or impaired functioning.

The following specifiers can be used to describe the most recent two years of an individual's persistent depressive disorder:

- *With pure dysthymic syndrome* – full criteria for a major depressive episode (MDE) have not been met in at least the prior two years.

- *With persistent major depressive episode* – full criteria for an MDE have been met throughout the prior two-year period.

- *With intermittent major depressive episodes, with current episode* – full criteria for an MDE are currently met, but there have been periods lasting at least eight weeks in at least the prior two years with symptoms below the threshold for a full MDE.

- *With intermittent major depressive episodes, without current episode* – full criteria for an MDE are not currently met, but there has been one or more MDEs in at least the prior two years.

2. Differential Diagnosis: The two-year duration distinguishes persistent depressive disorder (dysthymia) from episodes of major depression associated with MAJOR DEPRESSIVE DISORDER. If criteria are met for a major depressive episode at any time during this two-year period, the co-diagnosis of major depression should be noted as a specifier, as shown above.

Premenstrual Dysphoric Disorder

1. Diagnostic Criteria: A diagnosis of premenstrual dysphoric disorder requires, for most menstrual cycles, the presence of at least five characteristic symptoms (see below) during the week before the onset of menses with an improvement in symptoms within a few days after the onset of menses and the absence or presence of minimal symptoms during the week postmenses. The presence of these symptoms should be confirmed by daily ratings during at least two symptomatic cycles (although the diagnosis may be made provisionally before this confirmation). Symptoms must cause clinically significant distress or interfere with usual activities or relationships with others and must not be an exacerbation of another disorder.

Specifically, one or more of the following symptoms must be present: marked affective lability; marked irritability or anger or increased interpersonal conflicts; marked depressed mood, feelings of hopelessness, or self-deprecating thoughts; and/or marked anxiety, tension, and/or feelings of being keyed up or on edge. In addition to this, one or more of the following symptoms must also be present: decreased interest in usual activities; difficulty concentrating; lethargy, easy fatigability, or marked lack of energy; marked change in appetite, overeating, or food cravings; hypersomnia or insomnia; a sense of being overwhelmed or out of control; and/or physical symptoms (e.g., breast tenderness, joint pain, sensation of "bloating," weight gain).

2. Differential Diagnosis: (a) Women with BIPOLAR DISORDER, MAJOR DEPRESSIVE DISORDER, or PERSISTENT DEPRESSIVE DISORDER (DYSTHYMIA) may think they have premenstrual dysphoric disorder, but then realize when they record their symptoms that the symptoms don't follow a premenstrual pattern. (b) PREMENSTRUAL SYNDROME does not require a minimum of five symptoms or the presence of affective symptoms. The presence of physical or behavioral symptoms in the premenstruum (the interval immediately preceding a menstrual period), without affective symptoms, may meet criteria for premenstrual syndrome rather than premenstrual dysphoric disorder.

E. Anxiety Disorders

The anxiety disorders "share features of excessive fear and anxiety and related behavioral disturbances" (APA, 2013, p. 189). Included in this category are separation anxiety disorder, selective mutism, specific phobia, social anxiety disorder, panic disorder, agoraphobia, generalized anxiety disorder, substance/medication-induced anxiety disorder, and anxiety disorder due to another medical condition.

Panic attacks can occur in the context of any anxiety disorder, as well in the context of some other mental disorders (e.g., depressive disorders, posttraumatic stress disorder, substance use disorders) and other medical conditions. As defined in the DSM-5, a **panic attack** "is an abrupt surge of intense fear or intense discomfort that reaches a peak within minutes" (APA, 2013, p. 208) and involves a minimum of four characteristic symptoms – e.g., palpitations or accelerated heart rate, sweating, trembling, feelings of choking, chest pain or discomfort, paresthesias (numbness or tingling), derealization or depersonalization, and/or fear of losing control. Culture-specific symptoms (e.g., tinnitus, headache, uncontrollable crying) should not count as one of the four required symptoms for a panic attack.

There are three types of panic attacks:

Unexpected (uncued) panic attacks: These panic attacks are not associated with a situational trigger (either internal or external) and, instead, occur "out of the blue." Panic disorder requires the presence of recurrent (at least two) unexpected panic attacks. A person with panic disorder may also experience other types of panic attacks, however, particularly later in the course of the disorder.

Situationally bound (cued) panic attacks: These panic attacks are most characteristic of specific phobia and social anxiety disorder (social phobia). They occur almost invariably on exposure to or anticipation of a situational cue or trigger (e.g., the person has an immediate panic attack whenever she thinks about giving a speech at work).

Situationally predisposed panic attacks: These panic attacks are more likely to occur on exposure to a situational cue or trigger, but are not invariably associated with the cue and don't necessarily occur immediately after exposure to it (e.g., a person may be predisposed to having a panic attack while driving a car but doesn't have one every time she drives or doesn't have one until after she's been driving for over an hour). These panic attacks are especially common in panic disorder, but can occur in specific phobia and social anxiety disorder (social phobia) as well.

Finally, panic attack is not a mental disorder and cannot be coded. Instead, when panic attacks are present, they are noted as a specifier (e.g., "posttraumatic stress disorder, with panic attacks"). The exception is panic disorder – in the case of panic disorder, the presence of panic attacks is contained within the diagnostic criteria, and panic attack is not used as a specifier.

Separation Anxiety Disorder

1. Diagnostic Criteria: Separation anxiety disorder involves developmentally inappropriate and excessive fear or anxiety related to separation from home or attachment figures as evidenced by at least three characteristic symptoms – e.g., recurrent excessive distress when anticipating or experiencing separation from home or major attachment figures, persistent excessive fear of being alone, repeated complaints of physical symptoms when separation from an attachment figure occurs or is anticipated. The disturbance must last for at least four weeks in children and adolescents or six months in adults and cause clinically significant distress or impaired functioning.

Separation anxiety disorder is often manifested as **school refusal**, which involves intense anxiety about going to school and is usually accompanied by a stomachache, headache, nausea, and other physical symptoms. School refusal typically occurs at three ages: 5 to 7, 10 to 11, and 14 to 16 years. Onset for younger children is associated with beginning school and is usually a manifestation of separation anxiety; onset for middle-school children is often triggered by a change of schools and may be associated with social anxiety disorder (social phobia); and onset during adolescence is often associated with social anxiety disorder (social phobia), depression, or other disorder and has a poorer prognosis (Csoti, 2003; Elliot, 1999; Rosenhan & Seligman, 1984).

2. Etiology: Children with separation anxiety disorder often come from close, warm families, and their symptoms are frequently precipitated by a major life stress such as the death of a relative or pet, parental divorce, or a move to a new neighborhood.

3. Differential Diagnosis: (a) Fear of separation from loved ones is common following traumatic events. In PTSD, the person experiences, or tries to avoid, intrusive memories of the traumatic event itself; in separation anxiety disorder, the person worries about the welfare of attachment figures and separation from them. (b) With BEREAVEMENT, expected responses include deep longing for the person who died, intense emotional pain, and preoccupation with the deceased or the circumstances of the death; in separation anxiety disorder, the core concern is fear of separation from other attachment figures.

Selective Mutism

1. Diagnostic Criteria: Selective mutism is characterized by a consistent failure to speak in specific social situations in which speaking is expected (e.g., at school) despite speaking in other situations. The disturbance lasts for at least one month (and is not limited to the first month of school); interferes with school or work achievement or social communication; and is not attributable to a lack of knowledge of, or comfort with, the language required in the social situation.

Children with selective mutism often refuse to speak at school, resulting in academic or educational impairment. The disturbance is often marked by high social anxiety.

2. Differential Diagnosis: In COMMUNICATION DISORDERS, the speech disturbance is not limited to specific social situations.

Specific Phobia

1. Diagnostic Criteria: Specific phobia is characterized by intense fear of or anxiety about a specific object or situation (e.g., heights, flying, receiving an injection) with the individual either avoiding the object or situation or enduring it with marked distress. The fear or anxiety is not proportional to the actual danger posed by the object or situation, is persistent (typically lasting for at least six months), and causes clinically significant distress or impairment in functioning.

Specifiers are provided for the following subtypes: animal, natural environment, blood-injection-injury, situational, and other.

2. Etiology: Specific phobia and other anxiety disorders have been linked to biological factors (e.g., abnormal levels of serotonin, norepinephrine, and GABA), cognitive factors, and classical conditioning. With regard to the latter, Mowrer's (1947) **two-factor theory** attributes phobias to avoidance conditioning, which involves a combination of classical and operant conditioning: People first learn to fear a neutral (conditioned) stimulus because of its pairing with an intrinsically fear-arousing (unconditioned) stimulus, and their avoidance of the conditioned stimulus is then negatively reinforced because it keeps them from experiencing anxiety. Because people consistently avoid the conditioned stimulus, they never have an opportunity to extinguish the conditioned fear.

3. Differential Diagnosis: Excessive fears are fairly common in young children – if they are transient and only mildly impairing, they are considered developmentally appropriate and a diagnosis of specific phobia is not given.

Social Anxiety Disorder (Social Phobia)

1. Diagnostic Criteria: The essential feature of social anxiety disorder (social phobia) is intense fear of or anxiety about one or more social situations in which the individual may be exposed to scrutiny by others. The individual fears that she will exhibit symptoms in these situations that will be negatively evaluated; she avoids the situations or endures them with intense fear or anxiety; and her fear or anxiety is not proportional to the actual threat posed by the situations. Fear, anxiety, and avoidance are persistent (typically lasting for at least six months) and cause clinically significant distress or impaired functioning. Situations commonly associated with social anxiety disorder include public speaking, attending parties, initiating conversations, and speaking to authority figures.

2. Differential Diagnosis: (a) Shyness is diagnosable as social anxiety disorder only if it is severe enough to adversely affect important areas of functioning. (b) Individuals with

AGORAPHOBIA who fear and avoid social situations do so because escape might be difficult or help might not be available if they become incapacitated or have panic-like symptoms, not because they fear scrutiny by others. (c) AVOIDANT PERSONALITY DISORDER and social anxiety disorder frequently co-occur. However, avoidant personality disorder is associated with a broader avoidance pattern than social anxiety disorder.

Panic Disorder

1. Diagnostic Criteria: Panic disorder is characterized by recurrent unexpected panic attacks with at least one attack being followed by at least one month of persistent concern about having additional attacks or about their consequences and/or a significant maladaptive change in behavior related to the attack.

Before the diagnosis is assigned, hyperthyroidism, hypoglycemia, cardiac arrhythmia, and other medical conditions that include symptoms of panic disorder must be ruled out.

2. Gender/Age: Females are about twice as likely as males to receive this diagnosis. While prepubertal children may experience the physical symptoms of panic (especially hyperventilation), they rarely receive a diagnosis of panic disorder. According to one theory, this is because children have cognitive limitations that do not allow them to make catastrophic interpretations of their bodily symptoms (Nelles & Barlow, 1988).

Agoraphobia

1. Diagnostic Criteria: The diagnosis of agoraphobia requires the presence of marked fear or anxiety about at least two of the following situations: using public transportation, being in open spaces, being in enclosed spaces, standing in line or being part of a crowd, and/or being outside the home alone. The individual fears or avoids these situations due to concern that escape might be difficult or help will be unavailable in case she develops panic-like, incapacitating, or embarrassing symptoms. Agoraphobic situations nearly always provoke fear or anxiety and are actively avoided, require the presence of a companion, or are endured with intense feelings of fear or anxiety. In addition, the fear or anxiety is not proportional to the actual threat posed by the situations, and the fear, anxiety, or avoidance is persistent (typically lasting for at least six months) and causes clinically significant distress or impaired functioning.

2. Differential Diagnosis: Persons with certain MEDICAL CONDITIONS may avoid situations because of realistic concerns about being incapacitated or embarrassed by medical symptoms. Diagnose agoraphobia only when the fear or avoidance is clearly greater than that typically associated with the medical condition.

Generalized Anxiety Disorder

1. Diagnostic Criteria: Generalized anxiety disorder (GAD) involves excessive anxiety and worry about multiple events or activities that are relatively constant for at least six months, the person finds difficult to control, and cause clinically significant distress or impaired functioning. The anxiety and worry must include at least three of the following symptoms (or at least one symptom for children): restlessness or feeling keyed up or on edge, being easily fatigued, difficulty concentrating, irritability, muscle tension, and/or sleep disturbance.

2. Age: The symptoms of GAD are somewhat age-related. Children and adolescents with this disorder most often worry about performance in school and sports activities or about earthquakes, tornados, or other disasters (APA, 2000). In contrast, young adults worry about work, family, finances, and the future (e.g., Dugas et al., 1998), while older adults worry excessively about personal health and minor or routine matters (e.g., Wetherell, Le Roux, & Gatz, 2003).

F. Obsessive-Compulsive and Related Disorders

Included in this category are obsessive-compulsive disorder, body dysmorphic disorder, hoarding disorder, trichotillomania, excoriation disorder, substance/medication-induced obsessive-compulsive and related disorder, and obsessive-compulsive and related disorder due to another medical condition.

Obsessive-Compulsive Disorder

1. Diagnostic Criteria: Obsessive-compulsive disorder (OCD) is characterized by recurrent obsessions and/or compulsions that are time-consuming or cause clinically significant distress or impaired functioning.

Obsessions are persistent thoughts, impulses, or images that the person experiences as intrusive and unwanted and that he attempts to ignore or suppress. For most individuals, obsessions cause marked anxiety or distress. Examples are repeated thoughts about contamination and repeated doubts about one's actions. **Compulsions** are repetitive and deliberate behaviors or mental acts that the person feels driven to perform either in response to an obsession or according to rigid rules. The goal of the behaviors or mental acts is to reduce distress or prevent a dreaded situation from happening, but they are either excessive or not connected in a logical way to this goal. Examples are compulsive hand-washing, praying, and counting.

Specifiers are provided to indicate the individual's level of insight (with good or fair insight, with poor insight, with absent insight/delusional beliefs) and the presence of tics.

2. Differential Diagnosis: OBSESSIVE-COMPULSIVE PERSONALITY DISORDER does *not* include true obsessions or compulsions. If a person has symptoms of both OCD and obsessive-compulsive personality disorder, however, both diagnoses can be given.

Body Dysmorphic Disorder

Body dysmorphic disorder is characterized by a preoccupation with a defect or flaw in appearance (e.g., spots on the skin, excessive facial hair) that appears minor or is unobservable to others. The person has, at some time during the course of the disorder, performed repetitive behaviors or mental acts because of the defect or flaw (e.g., mirror checking, excessive grooming), and his preoccupation causes clinically significant distress or impaired functioning. People with this disorder often seek plastic surgery or other medical treatment to correct the perceived defect or flaw.

Hoarding Disorder

1. Diagnostic Criteria: Hoarding disorder involves "persistent difficulty discarding or parting with possessions, regardless of their actual value" (APA, 2013, p. 247) due to a need to save the items or to distress associated with parting with them. The inability to discard items causes living areas to be cluttered to the extent that the areas are not usable, and symptoms cause clinically significant distress or impaired functioning.

2. Differential Diagnosis: When a person who meets criteria for hoarding disorder has obsessions typical of OCD that lead to compulsive hoarding behaviors, OCD should be diagnosed instead. On the other hand, if severe hoarding occurs along with other typical symptoms of OCD, but appears to be independent from the OCD symptoms, both hoarding disorder and OCD may be diagnosed.

Trichotillomania and Excoriation Disorder

1. Trichotillomania: Trichotillomania (hair-pulling disorder) is characterized by recurrent pulling out of one's hair resulting in hair loss, along with efforts to reduce or stop hair pulling. The hair pulling causes clinically significant distress or impairment in important areas of functioning.

2. Excoriation Disorder: Excoriation (skin-picking) disorder is characterized by recurrent skin picking resulting in skin lesions, along with efforts to reduce or stop skin picking. The skin picking causes clinically significant distress or impairment in important areas of functioning.

Note that you should not diagnose excoriation disorder if skin-picking is induced by a substance (e.g., cocaine). If such skin picking is clinically significant, consider diagnosing a substance/medication-induced obsessive-compulsive and related disorder.

G. Trauma- and Stressor-Related Disorders

Included in this category are reactive attachment disorder, disinhibited social engagement disorder, posttraumatic stress disorder, acute stress disorder, and adjustment disorders.

Reactive Attachment Disorder

1. Diagnostic Criteria: Reactive attachment disorder is characterized by a consistent pattern of inhibited and emotionally withdrawn behavior toward adult caregivers as manifested by a lack of seeking or responding to comfort when distressed and a persistent social and emotional disturbance that includes at least two of the following symptoms: minimal social and emotional responsiveness to other people; limited positive affect; and/or episodes of unexplained irritability, sadness, or fearfulness when interacting with adult caregivers. The diagnosis also requires that the child has experienced *extreme insufficient care* that is believed to be the cause of the disturbed behavior and is evidenced by at least one of the following: basic emotional needs for comfort, stimulation, and affection are not met by adult caregivers; repeated changes in primary caregivers that limit the ability to form a stable attachment; and/or rearing in an unusual environment that limits opportunities to form selective attachments. Symptoms must be evident before the child is 5 years of age, and the child must have a developmental age of at least 9 months.

2. Differential Diagnosis: Reactive attachment disorder and AUTISM SPECTRUM DISORDER (ASD) can be distinguished based on the following: Children with ASD only rarely have a history of social neglect; children with ASD exhibit restricted interests and repetitive behaviors (which, apart from the possible presence of stereotypic behaviors such as rocking, are not features of reactive attachment disorder); children with ASD show attachment behavior typical for their developmental level (children with reactive attachment disorder do so inconsistently, rarely, or not at all); and children with ASD have selective impairments in social communicative behaviors (children with reactive attachment disorder exhibit social communicative functioning consistent with their level of intellectual functioning).

Disinhibited Social Engagement Disorder

1. Diagnostic Criteria: Disinhibited social engagement disorder is characterized by a pattern of behavior that involves inappropriate interactions with unfamiliar adults as evidenced by at least two of the following: reduced or absence of reticence in approaching or interacting with unfamiliar adults; overly familiar behavior with unfamiliar adults; diminished or absence of checking with an adult caregiver after venturing away from him or her; and/or willingness to accompany an unfamiliar adult with little or no hesitation. For the diagnosis, the child must have a developmental age of at least 9 months and have experienced *extreme insufficient care* that is believed to be the cause of the disturbed behavior and is evidenced by at least one of the following: basic emotional needs for comfort, stimulation, and affection are not met by adult caregivers; repeated changes in primary caregivers that limit the ability to form a stable attachment; and/or rearing in an unusual environment that limits opportunities to form selective attachments.

2. Differential Diagnosis: In contrast to children with ADHD, children with disinhibited social engagement disorder do not have difficulties with attention or hyperactivity.

Posttraumatic Stress Disorder

1. Diagnostic Criteria: The diagnostic criteria for posttraumatic stress disorder (PTSD) vary somewhat, depending on the individual's age.

For *adults, adolescents, and children older than 6 years of age*, the diagnosis of PTSD requires the following:

- *exposure to actual or threatened death, serious injury, or sexual violence in at least one of the following ways:* direct experience of the event; witnessing the event in person as it happened to others; learning that the event occurred to a close family member or friend; repeated or extreme exposure to aversive details of the event (except when exposure is through the media unless such exposure is work-related)

- presence of at least one of the following *intrusion symptoms:* recurrent, involuntary distressing memories of the event (or, in children, repetitive play related to the event); recurrent distressing dreams related to the event (or, in children, distressing dreams without recognizable content); dissociative reactions in which the person feels or acts as if the event is recurring (or, in children, trauma-related reenactment during play);

intense or prolonged psychological distress when exposed to reminders of the event; marked physiological reactions to reminders of the event

- *persistent avoidance of stimuli associated with the event* as evidenced by one or both of the following: avoidance of distressing memories, thoughts, or feelings related to the event; avoidance of external reminders that elicit distressing memories, thoughts, or feelings related to the event

- *negative changes in cognition or mood* associated with the event as evidenced by at least two of the following: inability to remember an important aspect of the event; persistent and exaggerated negative beliefs about oneself, others, or the world; persistent distorted cognitions related to the event's cause or consequences; markedly diminished interest in significant activities; feelings of detachment from others; persistent inability to experience positive emotions

- *marked change in arousal and reactivity associated with the event* as evidenced by at least two of the following: irritable behavior and angry outbursts; reckless or destructive behavior; hypervigilance; exaggerated startle response; impaired concentration; sleep disturbance

For *children 6 years old or younger*, the diagnosis requires the following:

- *exposure to actual or threatened death, serious injury, or sexual violence in at least one of the following ways:* direct experience of the event; witnessing the event in person as it happened to others (especially a primary caregiver); learning that the event occurred to a caregiver

- presence of at least one of the following *intrusion symptoms:* recurrent, involuntary distressing memories of the event that may be expressed during play reenactment; recurrent distressing dreams in which content and/or affect are related to the event; dissociative reactions in which the child feels or acts as if the event is recurring and that may occur during play reenactment; intense or prolonged psychological distress when exposed to internal or external reminders of the event; marked physiological reactions to reminders of the event

- at least one symptom that represents either *persistent avoidance of stimuli related to the event* or *negative changes in cognitions and mood related to the event.*

- *alterations in arousal and reactivity associated with the event* as evidenced by at least two of the following: irritable behavior and angry outbursts; hypervigilance; exaggerated startle response; impaired concentration; sleep disturbance.

For *individuals of all ages*, symptoms must have a duration of more than one month and must cause clinically significant distress or impaired functioning.

Specifiers are provided for dissociative symptoms (depersonalization and derealization); and for delayed expression when the full diagnostic criteria are not met until at least six months after the event.

2. Differential Diagnosis: (a) In ACUTE STRESS DISORDER, the symptom pattern is limited to a duration of three days to one month after exposure to the traumatic event; in PTSD, the duration of the disturbance is more than one month. (b) In ADJUSTMENT DISORDERS, the stressor can be of any type and severity (see also differential diagnosis for adjustment disorders for more information).

Acute Stress Disorder

A diagnosis of acute stress disorder requires exposure to actual or threatened death, severe injury, or sexual violation in at least one of four ways: direct experience of the event, witnessing the event in person as it happened to others, learning that the event occurred to a close family member or friend, and/or repeated or extreme exposure to aversive details of the event. At least nine symptoms from any one of five categories must be present (i.e., intrusion, negative mood, dissociative symptoms, avoidance symptoms, arousal symptoms), and symptoms must have a duration of three days to one month and cause clinically significant distress or impaired functioning.

Adjustment Disorders

1. Diagnostic Criteria: The adjustment disorders involve the development of emotional or behavioral symptoms in response to one or more identifiable psychosocial stressors within three months of the onset of the stressor(s). The symptoms must be clinically significant as evidenced by the presence of marked distress that is not proportional to the severity of the stressor and/or significant impairment in functioning; and symptoms must remit within six months after termination of the stressor or its consequences. This disorder is not diagnosed when symptoms represent normal bereavement.

The following specifiers are provided to describe the predominant symptoms: with depressed mood, with anxiety, with mixed anxiety and depressed mood, with disturbance of conduct, with mixed disturbance of emotions and conduct, unspecified.

2. Differential Diagnosis: (a) Adjustment disorder should only be diagnosed when the level of distress in response to a stressor is greater than what would be expected (taking into account the cultural setting) or when the stressor triggers functional impairment. (b) Do not diagnose adjustment disorder if a person has symptoms that meet criteria for MAJOR DEPRESSIVE DISORDER in response to a stressor. (c) In contrast to PTSD and ACUTE STRESS DISORDER, in adjustment disorders the stressor can be of any severity and type. The required symptom profile for PTSD and acute stress disorder also differentiates them from adjustment disorders. In addition, while adjustment disorders can be diagnosed right after exposure to a traumatic event, PTSD can't be diagnosed until at least one month has passed since such exposure (i.e., for a diagnosis of PTSD, the symptoms must have been present for at least one month); and while adjustment disorders may last for up to six months after exposure to a traumatic event, acute stress disorder lasts for only three days to one month. Finally, diagnosing an adjustment disorder is appropriate when a person has not been exposed to a traumatic event but otherwise exhibits the complete symptom profile of either PTSD or acute stress disorder.

H. Dissociative Disorders

The dissociative disorders include dissociative identity disorder, dissociative amnesia, and depersonalization/derealization disorder. These disorders are "characterized by a disruption of and/or discontinuity in the normal integration of consciousness, memory, identity, emotion, perception, body representation, motor control, and behavior" (APA, 2013, p. 291), and are frequently found in the aftermath of trauma.

1. Dissociative Identity Disorder: Dissociative identity disorder is characterized by the existence in one individual of two or more distinct personality states or the experience of possession, with recurrent gaps in the recall of ordinary events, personal information, or traumatic events that is not consistent with ordinary forgetfulness. Symptoms cause clinically significant distress or impaired functioning.

When considering a diagnosis of a dissociative identity disorder or other dissociative disorder for a client, it's important to take into account potential cultural influences on his symptoms. In some cultures, dissociative states are an acceptable expression of religious or cultural beliefs and do not necessarily constitute a mental disorder.

2. Dissociative Amnesia: A diagnosis of dissociative amnesia requires an inability to recall important personal information that cannot be attributed to ordinary forgetfulness and that causes clinically significant distress or impaired functioning. The DSM-5 provides specifiers to indicate if the disorder is or is not accompanied by dissociative fugue (apparently purposeful travel with an inability to recall some or all of one's past). Dissociative amnesia is often related to exposure to one or more traumatic events.

3. Depersonalization/Derealization Disorder: Depersonalization/derealization disorder is characterized by persistent or recurrent episodes of **depersonalization** (a sense of unreality, detachment, or being an outside observer of one's thoughts, feelings, etc.) or **derealization** (a sense of unreality or detachment involving one's surroundings) that causes clinically significant distress or impaired functioning. Reality testing remains intact during periods of depersonalization or derealization.

I. Somatic Symptom and Related Disorders

The disorders in this category are characterized by physical symptoms that cause distress and impaired functioning and include somatic symptom disorder, illness anxiety disorder, conversion disorder, psychological factors affecting other medical conditions, and factitious disorder.

Somatic Symptom Disorder

1. Diagnostic Criteria: The essential feature of somatic symptom disorder is the presence of one or more somatic symptoms that cause distress or a significant disruption in daily life accompanied by excessive thoughts, feelings, or behaviors related to the symptoms as manifested by at least one of the following: persistent and disproportionate thoughts about the seriousness of the symptoms, persistently high level of anxiety about one's health or symptoms, and/or excessive time and energy devoted to health concerns or symptoms. The disorder is persistent (usually more than six months in duration), although any one symptom may not be continuously present.

The "with predominant pain" specifier is applied when pain is the primary symptom. (This was pain disorder in DSM-IV-TR.)

2. Differential Diagnosis: (a) In DELUSIONAL DISORDER, SOMATIC TYPE, beliefs are held with delusional intensity; in somatic symptom disorder, beliefs may be firmly held but are not of delusional intensity. (b) Persons with BODY DYSMORPHIC DISORDER are preoccupied by perceived defects in their physical appearance, rather than by a fear that somatic symptoms reflect an underlying illness. (c) If a person has extensive concerns about health but no or minimal somatic symptoms, consider ILLNESS ANXIETY DISORDER. (d) CONVERSION DISORDER includes a loss of function; in somatic symptom disorder, the focus is on the distress caused by somatic symptoms.

Illness Anxiety Disorder

1. Diagnostic Criteria: Illness anxiety disorder is characterized by a preoccupation with having a serious illness, an absence of somatic symptoms or the presence of mild somatic symptoms, a high level of anxiety about one's health, and performance of excessive health-related behaviors or maladaptive avoidance of doctors, hospitals, etc. The preoccupation has been present for at least six months, although the specific illness that is of concern may change over time.

2. Differential Diagnosis: (a) In contrast to persons with PSYCHOTIC DISORDERS who experience somatic delusions, persons with illness anxiety disorder are not delusional (they can admit the possibility that the feared disease is not present). (b) In BODY DYSMORPHIC DISORDER, the person's concerns are limited to perceived defects in physical appearance.

Conversion Disorder (Functional Neurological Symptom Disorder)

1. Diagnostic Criteria: A diagnosis of conversion disorder requires the presence of symptoms that involve disturbances in voluntary motor or sensory functioning and suggest a serious neurological or other medical condition (e.g., paralysis, seizures, blindness, loss of pain sensation) with evidence of an incompatibility between the symptom and recognized neurological or medical conditions. Symptoms cause clinically significant distress or impaired functioning.

Specifiers are provided for symptom type (e.g., with weakness or paralysis, with abnormal movement, with anesthesia or sensory loss), course (acute or persistent), and presence or absence of a psychological stressor.

2. Associated Features: Some people with this disorder exhibit la belle indifference (a lack of concern about their symptoms); others respond to their symptoms in an overly dramatic or histrionic manner. Symptoms are often alleviated under hypnosis or during an amytal interview. Some research suggests that suggestion (suggesting to the patient that her symptoms will gradually remit) is the key factor in successful treatment.

Two mechanisms have traditionally been used to explain the etiology of conversion disorder: **Primary gain** occurs when the symptom keeps an internal conflict or need out of conscious awareness, while **secondary gain** occurs when the symptom helps the individual avoid an unpleasant activity or obtain support from the environment.

3. Differential Diagnosis: The diagnosis of conversion disorder does *not* require the judgment that the symptoms are not intentionally produced, since this is difficult to determine reliably. When there *is* clear evidence of feigning, this would suggest a diagnosis of FACTITIOUS DISORDER if the person's aim is to assume the sick role, or MALINGERING if the goal is to obtain an external incentive such as money. In other words, the concept of secondary gain (i.e., deriving external benefits from a symptom) is not specific to conversion disorder, and when there is clear evidence of feigning, the diagnoses that should be considered are factitious disorder and malingering.

Psychological Factors Affecting Other Medical Conditions

1. Diagnostic Criteria: Psychological factors affecting other medical conditions is diagnosed when a person has a medical symptom or condition (other than a mental disorder) and psychological or behavioral factors are adversely affecting the medical condition in one of the following ways: They are (a) affecting the course of the medical condition as shown by a close temporal relationship between the psychological factors and the development or worsening of, or delayed recovery from, the medical condition; (b) interfering with treatment of the medical condition (e.g., poor adherence); (c) creating additional health risks for the person; or (d) affecting the underlying pathophysiology, triggering or worsening symptoms, or necessitating medical attention. The psychological or behavioral factors are not better explained by another mental disorder (e.g., major depressive disorder, panic disorder, PTSD).

It's important to differentiate this disorder from culturally specific behaviors (e.g., using faith healers) that are acceptable within a culture and reflect an attempt to help the medical condition rather than interfere with it. If the behaviors do not unfavorably affect outcomes, they should not be pathologized.

When a person has a co-existing major mental disorder that adversely affects or causes another medical condition, it is usually sufficient to diagnose the mental disorder and the medical condition. Psychological factors affecting other medical conditions is diagnosed when the psychological traits or behaviors do not meet criteria for another mental disorder.

2. Differential Diagnosis: (a) In a MENTAL DISORDER DUE TO ANOTHER MEDICAL CONDITION, the medical condition is deemed to be *causing* the mental disorder through a direct physiological mechanism. In psychological factors affecting other medical conditions, psychological or behavioral factors are judged to *affect the course* of the medical condition. (b) Maladaptive psychological or behavioral symptoms that emerge in response to a medical condition are more appropriately diagnosed as ADJUSTMENT DISORDERS. For instance, a person diagnosed with angina who has developed anxiety as a result of the stress of coping with this illness would be diagnosed with an adjustment disorder, with anxiety; in contrast, a person with angina that is triggered whenever she gets anxious would be diagnosed with psychological factors affecting other medical conditions.

Factitious Disorder

1. Diagnostic Criteria: The DSM-5 distinguishes between two types of factitious disorder – factitious disorder imposed on self and factitious disorder imposed on another. Individuals with **factitious disorder imposed on self** falsify physical or psychological symptoms that are associated with their deception (e.g., they falsify symptoms of depression following the death of a spouse even though the death did not occur); they present themselves to others as being ill or impaired; and they engage in the deceptive behavior even in the absence of an obvious external reward for doing so. Individuals with **factitious disorder imposed on another** (previously called factitious disorder by proxy) falsify physical or psychological symptoms in another person, present that person to others as being ill or impaired, and engage in the deceptive behavior even in the absence of an external reward. For both types, falsification of symptoms can involve feigning, exaggeration, simulation, or induction (e.g., by ingestion of a substance or self-injury).

Note that the *perpetrator* of factitious disorder imposed on another, not the victim, receives the diagnosis. The victim, however, may be given an abuse-related diagnosis (see Other Conditions That May Be a Focus of Clinical Attention later in this section).

2. Differential Diagnosis: Factitious disorder must be distinguished from MALINGERING, which is included with other conditions that may be a focus of clinical attention and is characterized by the intentional production of physical or psychological symptoms for the purpose of obtaining an external reward such as avoiding work, receiving financial compensation, or obtaining drugs.

J. Feeding and Eating Disorders

The disorders in this category are characterized by "a persistent disturbance of eating or eating-related behavior that results in the altered consumption or absorption of food and that significantly impairs physical health or psychosocial functioning" (APA, 2013, p. 329). Included in this category are pica, rumination disorder, avoidant/restrictive food intake disorder, anorexia nervosa, bulimia nervosa, and binge-eating disorder.

Avoidant/Restrictive Food Intake Disorder

1. Diagnostic Criteria: Avoidant/restrictive food intake disorder is characterized by a persistent failure to meet appropriate nutritional and/or energy needs associated with one or more of the following: significant weight loss (or, in children, failure to achieve expected weight gain or slowed growth); significant nutritional deficiency; dependence on oral nutritional supplements or enteral feeding (delivery of nutrients directly to the stomach, such as through a tube); and/or marked interference with psychosocial functioning. The disturbance is not better explained by a lack of available food and is not attributable to a co-existing medical condition or better explained by another mental disorder. If the disturbance occurs in the context of another condition or disorder, its severity exceeds that usually associated with the condition or disorder and needs additional clinical attention.

This disorder replaces the DSM-IV-TR diagnosis of feeding disorder of infancy or early childhood. Examples of the eating or feeding disturbance associated with this disorder include an apparent lack of interest in eating, avoidance of food based on its sensory characteristics, or concern about aversive consequences of eating.

Avoidant/restrictive food intake disorder should not be diagnosed when avoidance of food intake is solely related to specific religious or cultural practices.

2. Differential Diagnosis: Persons with ANOREXIA NERVOSA exhibit a number of additional features that are not present in avoidant/restrictive food intake disorder, including a fear of gaining weight or becoming fat, persistent behavior that interferes with weight gain, and disturbances in the way they experience their body weight and shape. The two disorders should not be diagnosed concurrently.

Anorexia Nervosa

1. Diagnostic Criteria: The essential features of anorexia nervosa are (a) a restriction of energy intake that leads to a significantly low body weight for the person's age, gender, developmental trajectory, and physical health; (b) an intense fear of gaining weight or becoming fat or behavior that interferes with weight gain; and (c) a disturbance in the way the person experiences his body weight or shape or a persistent lack of recognition of the seriousness of his low body weight.

Specifiers are provided for type (**restricting type** or **binge-eating/purging type**); course (in partial remission or full remission); and severity (mild, moderate, severe, or extreme) based on current body mass index.

2. Associated Features: Individuals with anorexia nervosa may engage in excessive exercise, self-induced vomiting, and/or use of laxatives and diuretics, and many are preoccupied with thoughts of food and collect recipes, prepare elaborate meals for others, or hoard food. The studies suggest that over half of individuals with anorexia meet the diagnostic criteria for an anxiety disorder at some time during their life, with the onset of the anxiety disorder (especially social anxiety disorder or OCD) usually preceding the onset of anorexia (Bulik, 2002; Kaye et al., 2004). Depression is also common but may begin either before or after the onset of anorexia (Bulik, 2002). Anorexia is associated with a number of physical symptoms that are caused by starvation including constipation, cold intolerance, abdominal pain, lethargy, bradycardia, and, in females, amenorrhea. When the disorder includes purging, the resulting physical problems may include anemia, impaired renal functioning, cardiac abnormalities, dental problems, and osteoporosis.

3. Age/Gender: The onset of anorexia is most commonly occurs in adolescence or young adulthood and is often associated with a stressful life event. Over 90 percent of individuals with this disorder are female.

4. Differential Diagnosis: (a) Persons with MAJOR DEPRESSIVE DISORDER may lose a lot of weight, but most people with major depression don't have an intense fear of gaining weight or a desire for excessive weight loss. (b) In contrast to persons with anorexia nervosa, individuals with BULIMIA NERVOSA maintain a body weight at or above a minimally normal level.

5. Specific Assessment Considerations: Indicators suggesting that a client with anorexia nervosa should be referred for inpatient care include (a) weight that is 20 percent or more below normal, (b) failure by the client to recognize that there is a problem, (c) belief by the client that he will not improve in outpatient therapy, and/or (d) significant family dysfunction or failure to support the goals of treatment. If the client can be treated on an outpatient basis, refer him to a physician for medical evaluation.

Bulimia Nervosa

1. Diagnostic Criteria: Bulimia nervosa is characterized by (a) recurrent episodes of binge eating that are accompanied by a sense of a lack of control; (b) inappropriate compensatory behavior to prevent weight gain, such as self-induced vomiting, misuse of laxatives or diuretics, fasting, or excessive exercise; and (c) self-evaluation that is unduly influenced by body shape and weight. For the diagnosis, binge eating and compensatory behaviors must occur, on average, at least once a week for three months.

Specifiers are provided for course (in partial remission or full remission) and severity (mild, moderate, severe, or extreme) based on average number of episodes of inappropriate compensatory behavior per week.

Binges are typically triggered by interpersonal stress or a dysphoric mood and continue until the person is uncomfortably full; and, although the type of food consumed varies, it is usually high in calories.

2. Associated Features: Like anorexia, bulimia is associated with anxiety and depression. An anxiety disorder often precedes the eating disturbance, leading some investigators to propose that an early-onset anxiety disorder may play an etiological role in bulimia. Symptoms of depression may occur before or after the onset of the symptoms of bulimia; and depression has been identified as the most common comorbid condition among women with this disorder (Bulik, 2002). Medical complications include fluid and electrolyte disturbances, metabolic alkalosis (from vomiting), metabolic acidosis (from laxative use), dental problems, and menstrual abnormalities. In some cases, electrolyte imbalances are sufficiently severe to cause cardiac arrhythmia and arrest.

3. Age/Gender: Bulimia nervosa usually begins in adolescence or early adulthood, and the onset is often during or after a period of dieting (Hsu, 1993). Over 90 percent of individuals with bulimia are female.

4. Differential Diagnosis: If binge-eating behavior occurs only during episodes of anorexia nervosa, the appropriate diagnosis is ANOREXIA NERVOSA, BINGE-EATING/PURGING TYPE and an additional diagnosis of bulimia nervosa is not given. If a person diagnosed with anorexia nervosa binges and purges but no longer meets the full criteria for anorexia nervosa, binge-eating/purging type (e.g., his weight is normal), bulimia nervosa may be diagnosed only when all criteria for bulimia nervosa have been met for at least three months.

5. Specific Assessment Considerations: Indicators suggesting that a client with bulimia nervosa should be referred for inpatient care include severe medical complications caused by frequent purging, severe accompanying depression, and/or a history of failure in outpatient treatment. If the client can be treated on an outpatient basis, refer him to a physician for medical evaluation.

Binge-Eating Disorder

1. Diagnostic Criteria: A diagnosis of binge-eating disorder requires recurrent episodes of binge eating that involve a sense of lack of control over eating, the presence of at least three characteristic symptoms (e.g., eating more rapidly than usual, eating until feeling uncomfortably full, eating alone due to feeling embarrassed about the amount of food consumed), and the presence of marked distress about binge eating. Binges must occur, on average, at least once a week for three months.

2. Differential Diagnosis: Binge-eating disorder does not include the recurrent inappropriate compensatory behavior (e.g., purging, excessive exercise) seen in BULIMIA NERVOSA. In addition, unlike people with bulimia nervosa, persons with binge-eating disorder usually do not exhibit significant or persistent dietary restriction intended to affect body weight and shape between binge-eating episodes (although they may report frequent attempts at dieting).

Pica and Rumination Disorder

1. Pica: Pica involves persistent eating of non-nutritive, non-food substances (e.g., paint, plaster, insects, clay) for at least one month. For the diagnosis, the behavior must be inappropriate for the individual's developmental level and not part of a culturally sanctioned practice. If the behavior occurs in the context of another mental disorder or medical condition, it must be sufficiently severe to warrant additional clinical attention. Pica can occur at any age, but is most common during childhood.

2. Rumination Disorder: Rumination disorder is characterized by the repeated regurgitation of food over a period of at least one month that is not attributable to an associated gastrointestinal or other medical condition. Regurgitated food may be re-chewed, re-swallowed, or spit out. The disturbance does not occur solely during the course of avoidant/restrictive food intake disorder, anorexia nervosa, bulimia nervosa, or binge-eating disorder, and if the symptoms occur in the context of another mental disorder (e.g., intellectual disability or another neurodevelopmental disorder), they are severe enough to need additional clinical attention.

K. Elimination Disorders

The disorders in this category "involve the inappropriate elimination of urine or feces and are usually first diagnosed in childhood or adolescence" (APA, 2013, p. 355).

1. Enuresis: The essential feature of enuresis is repeated voiding of urine into the bed or clothes at least twice a week for three or more consecutive months. Urination is usually involuntary but can be intentional, and it is not due to use of a substance or a medical condition. This disorder is diagnosed only when the individual is at least 5 years old or the equivalent developmental level.

Specifiers are provided for three subtypes: nocturnal only, diurnal only, nocturnal and diurnal.

2. Encopresis: Encopresis is characterized by repeated involuntary or intentional passage of feces into places not appropriate for that purpose (e.g., the bed, clothing, the floor). Symptoms must occur at least once a month for at least three months, and the child must be at least 4 years old or the equivalent developmental level. The behavior is not due exclusively to use of a substance or a medical condition except one that involves constipation.

Specifiers for two subtypes are provided: with constipation and overflow incontinence and without constipation and overflow incontinence.

3. Specific Assessment Considerations for Elimination Disorders: Referral to (or consultation with) a medical doctor is important to make sure that the symptom is not due to a medical condition or the effects of a substance (e.g., laxative, diuretic). During interviews, clarify precipitating and complicating factors (e.g., emotional stress), explore whether the child has experienced adverse consequences (e.g., teasing, ostracizing), and explore how the parents have attempted to manage the problem and their attitudes toward it.

L. Sleep-Wake Disorders

The disorders in this category are characterized by problems related to the quality, timing, and amount of sleep with resulting daytime distress and impairment. The disorders, or disorder groups, in this category include insomnia disorder, hypersomnolence disorder, narcolepsy, breathing-related sleep disorders (e.g., obstructive sleep apnea hypopnea), circadian rhythm sleep-wake disorders, parasomnias (non-rapid eye movement sleep arousal disorders, nightmare disorder, rapid eye movement sleep behavior disorder, restless legs syndrome), and substance/medication-induced sleep disorder.

Appropriate differential diagnosis of sleep-wake complaints requires consideration of possible co-existing medical or neurological conditions (which are common), as well as possible substance/medication use or withdrawal. If the person is using a substance or taking a medication, the sleep disturbance may improve after he discontinues the substance or medication. Additionally, sleep disorders are often accompanied by depression, anxiety, and cognitive changes that should be addressed in treatment.

1. Insomnia Disorder: A diagnosis of insomnia disorder requires dissatisfaction with sleep quality or quantity that is associated with at least one of the following symptoms: difficulty initiating sleep, difficulty maintaining sleep, and/or early-morning awakening with an inability to return to sleep. The sleep disturbance occurs at least three nights each week, has been present for at least three months, occurs despite sufficient opportunities for sleep, and causes significant distress or impaired functioning.

2. Narcolepsy: Narcolepsy is characterized by attacks of an irrepressible need to sleep with lapses into sleep or daytime naps that occur at least three times per week and have been present for at least three months. The diagnosis requires episodes of cataplexy (loss of muscle tone), a hypocretin deficiency, or a rapid eye movement latency less than or equal to 15 minutes as measured by nocturnal sleep polysomnography (sleep studies). (Hypocretin is a neurotransmitter that regulates arousal, wakefulness, and appetite.)

Many individuals with this disorder experience hypnogogic or hypnopompic hallucinations which are, respectively, vivid hallucinations before or upon falling asleep or just after awakening. Because cataplexy is often triggered by anger, surprise, or other strong emotion, people with this disorder may try to prevent sleep attacks by controlling their emotions.

3. Non-Rapid Eye Movement (NREM) Sleep Arousal Disorders: The essential feature of the non-rapid eye movement sleep arousal disorders is recurrent episodes of incomplete awakening that usually occur during the first third of the major sleep episode (most often during Stage 3 or 4 sleep) and are accompanied by **sleepwalking** (getting out of bed during sleep and walking around) and/or **sleep terror** (an abrupt arousal from sleep that often begins with a panicky scream and is accompanied by intense fear and signs of autonomic arousal). The individual has limited or no recall of an episode upon awakening, and the disturbance causes significant distress or impaired functioning.

Specifiers are provided for two subtypes: sleepwalking type and sleep terror type.

This disorder occurs most often in children, diminishes in frequency with increasing age, and often remits spontaneously during adolescence.

4. Nightmare Disorder: Nightmare disorder is characterized by "repeated occurrences of extended, extremely dysphoric, and well-remembered dreams that usually involve efforts to avoid threats to survival, security, or physical integrity" (APA, 2013, p. 404). Nightmares ordinarily occur during rapid eye movement (REM) sleep in the second half of the major sleep period; and, on awakening from a nightmare, the individual is typically fully alert but may have a lingering sense of anxiety or fear. The sleep disturbance causes significant distress or impaired functioning.

M. Sexual Dysfunctions

The disorders in this category involve "a clinically significant disturbance in a person's ability to respond sexually or to experience sexual pleasure" (APA, 2013, p. 423). The sexual dysfunctions described in the DSM-5 include delayed ejaculation, erectile disorder, female orgasmic disorder, female sexual interest/arousal disorder, genito-pelvic pain/penetration disorder, male hypoactive sexual desire disorder, premature (early) ejaculation, and substance/medication-induced sexual dysfunction. As explained below, the diagnosis of a sexual dysfunction is assigned only when the symptoms are not better explained by a nonsexual mental disorder, relationship distress or other stressor, or the effects of a substance, medication, or medical condition.

1. Subtypes and Specifiers: In describing a sexual dysfunction, subtypes are used to designate the onset of the problem: **Lifelong** describes a sexual problem that has been present from first sexual experiences; and **acquired** describes a sexual problem that emerges after a period of relatively normal sexual function.

Additionally, the specifier **generalized** describes a sexual problem that is not limited to certain types of stimulation, situations, or partners; and the specifier **situational** describes a sexual problem that only occurs with certain types of stimulation, situations, or partners.

2. General Assessment and Diagnostic Considerations for Sexual Dysfunction: The following factors should be considered during assessment of sexual dysfunction because they may be relevant to etiology, treatment, or both: (a) psychiatric comorbidity (e.g., depression, anxiety); (b) medical factors relevant to course, treatment, or prognosis; (c) current stressors (e.g., bereavement, job loss); (d) personal vulnerability factors (e.g., poor body image, history of sexual abuse); (e) partner factors (e.g., partner's sexual problems or health status); (f) relationship factors (e.g., discrepancies in sexual desire, poor communication); and (g) cultural or religious factors (e.g., inhibitions stemming from prohibitions against sexual activity or pleasure). In addition, aging may be associated with a normative decrease in sexual response.

Diagnosis of a sexual dysfunction requires ruling out sexual difficulties that are better explained by a nonsexual mental disorder, by the effects of a drug of abuse or medication, by a medical condition, or by severe relationship distress, partner violence, or other stressors:

- If the sexual dysfunction is mostly explainable by another, nonsexual mental disorder, then only the other mental disorder should be diagnosed.

- If the sexual dysfunction is better explained by the use/misuse or discontinuation of a substance or medication, it should be diagnosed as a substance/medication-induced sexual dysfunction.

- If the sexual dysfunction is attributable to another medical condition, then a sexual dysfunction diagnosis is not made.

- If the sexual difficulties are better explained by severe relationship distress, partner violence, or significant stressors, then a sexual dysfunction diagnosis is not made, but a code for the relationship problem or stressor may be used (see Other Conditions That May Be a Focus of Clinical Attention later in this section).

- If sexual difficulties are the result of inadequate sexual stimulation, then a diagnosis of a sexual dysfunction is not made.

When a client presents with symptoms of a sexual dysfunction, you should refer her to a physician to either rule out or establish a physiological basis (e.g., medical condition, medication) for the symptoms. You should also assess for co-existing mental disorders that may be contributing to or exacerbating the symptoms, especially depressive and substance-related disorders, and get a thorough history regarding the onset and history of the disorder, nature, frequency, and severity of the symptoms, and antecedents and consequences of the symptoms. With a couple, get a history of the relationship, including a sexual history.

N. Gender Dysphoria

Gender dysphoria involves distress or marked impairment related to "incongruence between one's experienced/expressed gender and assigned gender" (APA, 2013, p. 452).

1. Diagnostic Criteria: The DSM-5 provides separate diagnostic criteria for gender dysphoria for children and for adolescents and adults.

For *gender dysphoria in children*, the criteria are a marked incongruence between one's assigned gender at birth and one's experienced or expressed gender as evidenced by a strong desire to be the opposite gender and at least five of the following symptoms: a strong preference for wearing clothes of the other gender; a strong preference for cross-gender roles during play; a strong preference for toys and activities typically used or engaged in by the other gender; a strong preference for playmates of the opposite gender; a strong rejection of toys and activities used or engaged in by the other gender; a strong dislike of one's sexual anatomy; and/or a strong desire for primary and/or secondary sex characteristics of one's experienced gender. Symptoms have a duration of at least six months and cause clinically significant distress or impaired functioning. A specifier for children who have a congenital adrenogenital disorder or other disorder of sex development is provided.

For *gender dysphoria in adolescents and adults*, the marked incongruence between one's assigned gender and experienced or expressed gender must be manifested by at least two characteristic symptoms: a marked incongruence between one's primary and/or secondary sex characteristics and one's experienced or expressed gender; a strong desire to be rid of one's primary and/or secondary sex characteristics; a strong desire for the primary and/or secondary sex characteristics of the opposite gender; a strong desire to be of the opposite gender; a strong desire to be treated as the opposite gender; and/or a strong conviction that one has the feelings and reactions that are characteristic of the opposite gender. Symptoms have a duration of at least six months and cause clinically significant distress or impaired functioning.

Specifiers are provided for individuals who have a disorder of sex development and those who are in posttransition. Individuals who are "posttransition" have transitioned to full-time living as the desired gender and have undergone or are preparing to undergo at least one cross-sex medical procedure or treatment regimen (i.e., gender reassignment surgery or cross-sex hormone treatment).

2. Course/Prognosis: Among clinic-referred children, the onset of gender dysphoria is usually between the ages of 2 to 4 years. Rates of persistence of the disorder from childhood to adulthood vary depending on several factors including natal gender (assigned gender at birth): According to the DSM-5, rates of persistence for natal males range from 2.2 to 30 percent, while rates for natal females range from 12 to 50 percent. For those exhibiting persistence of the disorder, most are sexually attracted to individuals of their natal gender.

3. Differential Diagnosis: (a) Gender dysphoria must be distinguished from simple nonconformity to stereotypical gender-role behaviors (e.g., "tomboyish" or "sissyish" behavior). (b) A person with BODY DYSMORPHIC DISORDER wants to change or remove a body part because he perceives it as abnormally formed, not because he wants to be of the other gender. If criteria are met for both gender dysphoria and body dysmorphic disorder, however, both diagnoses can be given. (c) In TRANSVESTIC DISORDER, a heterosexual or bisexual adolescent or adult male derives sexual excitement from cross-dressing behavior; this behavior causes distress and/or impairment, but the person does not repudiate his assigned gender. A person with transvestic disorder who also has clinically significant gender dysphoria, however, can be given both diagnoses.

O. Disruptive, Impulse-Control, and Conduct Disorders

The disruptive, impulse-control, and conduct disorders include "conditions involving problems in the self-control of emotions and behaviors ... that violate the rights of others (e.g., aggression, destruction of property) and/or that bring the individual into significant conflict with societal norms or authority figures" (APA, 2013, p. 461). The disorders in this category include oppositional defiant disorder, intermittent explosive disorder, conduct disorder, pyromania, and kleptomania.

Oppositional Defiant Disorder

1. Diagnostic Criteria: The essential feature of oppositional defiant disorder is a recurrent pattern of angry/irritable mood, argumentative/defiant behavior, or vindictiveness that is demonstrated by four or more symptoms (see below), and is exhibited with at least one person who is not a sibling:

Angry/irritable mood: Often loses temper, is often touchy or easily annoyed, and/or is often angry and resentful.

Argumentative/defiant behavior: Often argues with authority figures (or, for children and adolescents, with adults); often actively defies or refuses to obey rules or comply with requests from authority figures; often intentionally annoys others; and/or often blames others for her mistakes or misbehavior.

Vindictiveness: Has been spiteful or vindictive two more times in the past six months.

Symptoms have persisted for at least six months and have caused distress for the individual or others in her immediate social environment (e.g., family, peers, work colleagues) or have had a negative impact on important areas of functioning.

For children *younger than age 5 years*, the symptomatic behavior should occur on most days for at least 6 months, unless otherwise noted. For persons age *5 years or older*, the symptomatic behavior should occur at least once per week for at least 6 months, unless otherwise noted.

2. Differential Diagnosis: (a) The temper outbursts associated with DISRUPTIVE MOOD DYSREGULATION DISORDER are more severe, more frequent, and more persistent. Do not diagnose oppositional defiant disorder (even if all criteria are met) if the person's mood disturbance is severe enough to meet criteria for disruptive mood dysregulation disorder. (b) The behaviors of CONDUCT DISORDER are more severe and, unlike oppositional defiant disorder, include physical aggression toward people or animals, destruction of property, and a pattern of theft or deceit. The aggression associated with oppositional defiant disorder usually includes temper tantrums and *verbal* arguments with authority figures. Additionally, persons with oppositional defiant disorder have problems with emotional dysregulation (i.e., angry and irritable mood); such problems are not characteristic of conduct disorder. When criteria are met for both disorders, both diagnoses can be made.

Intermittent Explosive Disorder

1. Diagnostic Criteria: Intermittent explosive disorder is characterized by recurrent behavioral outbursts that are related to an inability to control aggressive impulses as manifested by (a) verbal or physical aggression that occurs, on average, twice a week and has persisted for at least three months *or* (b) three behavioral outbursts that caused damage or destruction of property and/or physical assault that injured people or animals during a 12 month period. The severity of the aggressiveness is not proportional to the provocation or precipitating social stressor. The outbursts are not premeditated or committed to achieve a tangible outcome and they cause significant distress, impaired functioning, or financial or legal consequences. The diagnosis can be assigned only to individuals who are at least 6 years of age or equivalent developmental level.

This diagnosis can be made along with a diagnosis of autism spectrum disorder, ADHD, oppositional defiant disorder, or conduct disorder only when repeated impulsive aggressive outbursts are in excess of those usually seen in these disorders and require independent clinical attention.

2. Differential Diagnosis: Persons with CONDUCT DISORDER sometimes display impulsive aggressive outbursts but the type of aggression specified by the diagnostic criteria for conduct disorder is proactive and predatory. With intermittent explosive disorder, the aggression is impulsive, unpremeditated, and not committed to achieve a tangible goal.

Conduct Disorder

1. Diagnostic Criteria: The diagnosis of conduct disorder requires a persistent pattern of behavior that violates the basic rights of others and/or age-appropriate social norms or rules as evidenced by the presence of at least three characteristic symptoms (see below) during the past 12 months and at least one symptom in the past six months. The characteristic symptoms are divided into four categories:

Aggression to people and animals: Often bullies, threatens, or intimidates others; often starts physical fights; has used a weapon that can cause serious physical harm to others; has been physically cruel to people; has been physically cruel to animals; has stolen while confronting a victim; and/or has forced someone into sexual activity.

Destruction of property: Has deliberately set fires with the intention of causing serious damage and/or has deliberately destroyed others' property (other than by fire setting).

Deceitfulness or theft: Has broken into a house, building, or car; often lies to get goods or favors or to avoid obligations (i.e., "cons" others); and/or has stolen items of value without confronting a victim.

Serious violations of rules: Often stays out at night despite parental prohibitions, starting before age 13 years; has run away from home overnight at least twice while living with parents or parent surrogates, or once without returning for a long time; and/or is often truant from school, starting before age 13.

Symptoms must cause significant impairment in functioning, and the disorder cannot be assigned to individuals over age 18 who meet diagnostic criteria for antisocial personality disorder.

The DSM-5 provides specifiers for three **subtypes**: *childhood-onset type* for individuals who exhibit at least one symptom prior to age 10; *adolescent-onset type* for individuals who exhibit no symptoms prior to age 10; and *unspecified onset* when the onset of symptoms is unknown. The childhood-onset type is associated with a higher degree of aggressiveness, a greater risk for continued aggressiveness in adulthood, and an eventual diagnosis of antisocial personality disorder and/or a substance use disorder.

The DSM-5 also provides specifiers for individuals with limited prosocial emotions (lack of remorse or guilt, callous/lack of empathy, unconcerned about performance, and shallow or deficient affect); and for severity (mild, moderate, or severe) based on the number of conduct problems.

2. Etiology: Moffitt (1993) distinguishes between two types of conduct disorder that differ in terms of age of onset, symptom severity, and etiology. The **life-course-persistent type** begins early (symptoms are sometimes apparent by age 3) and involves a pattern of increasingly serious transgressions that continues into adulthood. Moffitt attributes this type to a combination of neurological impairments (especially deficits in verbal skills, executive functioning, and memory), a difficult temperament, and adverse environmental circumstances. In contrast, the **adolescence-limited type** is a temporary form of antisocial behavior that reflects a "maturity gap" between the adolescent's biological maturation and lack of opportunities for adult privileges and rewards. For individuals with this type, antisocial acts are usually committed with peers and are inconsistent across situations (e.g., the individual may shoplift with friends but adhere to rules at school).

3. Gender: Conduct disorder is more common in males than in females; and, in females, symptoms may be somewhat different and often include lying, truancy, running away, and substance use. Also, males are likely to exhibit both physical and relational aggression, while females exhibit more relational aggression.

4. Differential Diagnosis: Conduct problems may occur in children and adolescents with MOOD DISORDERS, but persons with conduct disorder exhibit conduct problems during periods when there is no mood disturbance. When criteria for both conduct disorder and a mood disorder (a bipolar disorder, major depressive disorder, or disruptive mood dysregulation disorder) are met, however, both diagnoses can be made.

5. Specific Assessment Considerations: Adolescents with conduct disorders (or delinquency) rarely seek treatment on their own. Typically, the parents, school, or a community agency make the initial contact with you. Moreover, some parents who bring their child or adolescent in do so only because of pressure from the school or juvenile court and, therefore, may be poorly motivated to cooperate with treatment.

During assessment, you should usually do the following: (a) screen for a substance use disorder; (b) assess functioning in multiple domains (e.g., emotional, behavioral, cognitive, interpersonal) and settings (e.g., home, school); (c) explore the client's perceptions of and feelings about her behavior and determine whether she experiences guilt and remorse; (d) have parents and teachers complete rating scales (e.g., the Parent Daily Report checklist) to identify the frequency and duration of problematic behaviors; and (e) perform a family evaluation (family dynamics may be a contributory factor). You should also explore the family's responses to the problematic behavior – the parents may over- or under-react to the behavior or role model violent solutions to problems. If relevant, collect information from court personnel (probation officers, etc.).

It's also important to determine whether treatment can take place on an outpatient basis. Inpatient or residential treatment may be indicated initially if the client poses a danger to others, is incapable of feeling empathy or guilt, and/or cannot form meaningful relationships with others. Residential treatment may also be indicated if the family is unwilling to follow through on treatment and/or incapable of exercising appropriate behavioral control.

Pyromania and Kleptomania

1. Pyromania: Pyromania is characterized by deliberate and purposeful fire setting on two or more occasions and tension or affective arousal before setting fires; pleasure, gratification, or relief when setting fires or witnessing or participating in their aftermath; and fascination with, interest in, curiosity about, or attraction to fire and its situational contexts. The fire setting is not done for monetary gain, as an expression of sociopolitical ideology, to hide criminal activity, to express anger or vengeance, to improve one's circumstances, in response to a delusion or hallucination, or as a result of impaired judgment, and is not better explained by a manic episode, conduct disorder, or antisocial personality disorder.

2. Kleptomania: Kleptomania is characterized by recurrent failure to resist impulses to steal items that are not needed for personal use or their monetary value and a growing sense of tension immediately before committing the theft and pleasure, gratification, or relief at the time of committing the theft. The stealing is not committed to express anger or vengeance and is not in response to a delusion or a hallucination and is not better explained by a manic episode, conduct disorder, or antisocial personality disorder.

P. Substance-Related and Addictive Disorders

Additional information on substance use disorders appears in Section VIII of this chapter.

This category includes substance use and substance-induced disorders for 10 classes of substances and one non-substance-related disorder – gambling – which the DSM-5 identifies as a behavioral addiction. The 10 classes of substances are alcohol; caffeine; cannabis; phencyclidine and other hallucinogens; inhalants; opioids; sedatives, hypnotics, or anxiolytics; stimulants; tobacco; and other/unknown.

Substance Use Disorders

1. Diagnostic Criteria: The substance use disorders are characterized by "a cluster of cognitive, behavioral, and physiological symptoms indicating that the individual continues using the substance despite significant substance-related problems" (APA, 2013, p. 483) as manifested by at least two characteristic symptoms during a 12-month period. The characteristic symptoms can be categorized in terms of four groups:

- *Impaired control* – substance used in larger amounts or for a longer period of time than intended; persistent desire or unsuccessful efforts to cut down or control use; great deal of time spent in activities related to obtaining the substance or recovering from its effects; and/or craving for the substance.

- *Social impairment* – recurrent substance use that results in a failure to fulfill major role obligations at home, school, or work; recurrent substance use despite persistent social problems caused or worsened by substance use; and/or important activities given up or reduced due to substance use.

- *Risky use* – recurrent substance use in situations in which it is physically dangerous to do so; and/or continued substance use despite knowing that doing so creates or worsens a physical or psychological problem.

- *Pharmacological criteria* – **tolerance** (need for increased amounts of the substance to achieve the desired effect or markedly diminished effect with continued use of the same amount of the substance); and/or **withdrawal** (characteristic withdrawal symptoms or continued use of the substance to avoid withdrawal).

A diagnosis of substance use disorder can be applied to all 10 classes of drugs except caffeine. If a person meets criteria for more than one substance use disorder (e.g., alcohol use disorder and cannabis use disorder), each diagnosis should be recorded.

Note that the term "addiction" is not a diagnostic criterion in the DSM-5, but it often appears in the literature and is described as involving a compulsion to use a drug, development of tolerance for the drug, and experience of withdrawal symptoms when the drug is not taken.

2. Severity Ratings and Specifiers:

a. Severity Ratings: A general estimate of severity for a substance use disorder is the following: *Mild* (presence of two to three symptoms), *moderate* (four to five symptoms), and *severe* (six or more symptoms).

b. Course Specifiers: (a) *In early remission:* After full criteria were met before, no criteria have been met for at least three months but less than 12 months ("craving" may be met). (b) *In sustained remission:* After full criteria were met before, no criteria have been met at any time for 12 months or longer ("craving" may be met).

c. Descriptive Features Specifiers: These include "*on maintenance therapy*" and "*in a controlled environment.*" The latter may be used if the person is in remission and in an environment where access to the substance is restricted.

Substance-Induced Disorders

The substance-induced disorders include (a) substance intoxication, (b) substance withdrawal, and (c) substance/medication-induced mental disorders. The latter disorders "are potentially severe, usually temporary, but sometimes persisting central nervous system (CNS) syndromes that develop in the context of the effects of substances of abuse, medications, or toxins" (APA, 2013, p. 487), and they include substance/medication-induced psychotic disorder, substance/medication-induced bipolar and related disorder, substance/medication-induced depressive disorder, substance/medication-induced anxiety disorder, substance/medication-induced obsessive-compulsive and related disorder, substance/medication-induced sleep disorder, substance/medication-induced sexual dysfunction, and substance/medication-induced major or mild neurocognitive disorder.

1. Substance Intoxication: Substance intoxication involves the development of a reversible substance-specific syndrome due to the recent ingestion of a substance. The maladaptive behavioral or psychological changes associated with intoxication are attributable to the physiological effects of the substance on the central nervous system and arise during or shortly after the substance is used. The symptoms are not better explained by another mental disorder and are not due to another medical condition. This diagnosis does not apply to tobacco.

2. Substance Withdrawal: Substance withdrawal involves substance-specific behavioral changes, with cognitive and physiological features, that develop due to termination of, or reduction in, heavy and long-term substance use. Withdrawal is usually, but not always, associated with a substance use disorder and is typically accompanied by an urge to begin using the substance again to reduce the symptoms. The symptoms are not better explained by another mental disorder and are not due to another medical condition and they cause clinically significant distress or impairment in important areas of functioning. When a person has substance intoxication and/or withdrawal involving several substances, each diagnosis should be recorded separately.

3. Substance/Medication-Induced Mental Disorders: Each substance/medication-induced mental disorder has unique diagnostic criteria, but all share the following features: (a) The disorder involves a clinically significant symptomatic presentation of a mental disorder. (b) There is evidence from a history, physical exam, or laboratory results that the disorder developed during or within one month of substance intoxication or withdrawal or of taking a medication and that the substance or medication is capable of producing the mental disorder. (c) The disorder cannot be better explained by another mental disorder or medical condition. (d) The disorder does not occur only during the course of delirium. (e) Symptoms cause clinically significant distress or impaired functioning.

A substance/medication-induced mental disorder should be diagnosed, instead of substance intoxication or substance withdrawal, *only* when the symptoms defined in the diagnostic criteria for the substance/medication-induced mental disorder (e.g., delusions or hallucinations, elevated or depressed mood, anxiety, sleep disturbance, etc.) predominate in the clinical picture and are severe enough to warrant specific clinical attention.

Specific substance-induced mental disorders are described below.

a. Alcohol-Induced Disorders: Alcohol is associated with all of the substance-induced disorders except obsessive-compulsive and related disorders. Characteristics of some of these disorders are summarized below:

Alcohol intoxication: Symptoms of alcohol intoxication include maladaptive behavioral and psychological changes (e.g., inappropriate sexual or aggressive behaviors, impaired judgment, mood lability) with at least one of the following symptoms: slurred speech, incoordination, unsteady gait, nystagmus (involuntary eye movement), impaired attention or memory, and/or stupor or coma.

Alcohol withdrawal: **Alcohol withdrawal** is diagnosed in the presence of at least two of the following symptoms within several hours to a few days following cessation or reduction of alcohol consumption: autonomic hyperactivity (e.g., sweating, tachycardia); hand tremor; insomnia; nausea or vomiting; transient illusions or hallucinations; anxiety; psychomotor agitation; and/or generalized tonic-clonic seizures.

Alcohol withdrawal delirium: Alcohol withdrawal delirium (**delirium tremens** or DTs) involves prominent disturbances in attention, awareness, and cognition following cessation or reduction of alcohol consumption that are sufficiently severe to warrant clinical attention. Common associated features include autonomic hyperactivity, vivid hallucinations, delusions, and agitation.

Alcohol-induced major neurocognitive disorder: This disorder is characterized by evidence of a significant decline in one or more cognitive domains that interferes with independence in everyday activities. The DSM-5 provides two specifiers for this disorder – nonamnestic-confabulatory type and amnestic-confabulatory type. The amnestic-confabulatory type is also known as **Korsakoff syndrome**, and it is characterized by anterograde and retrograde amnesia and confabulation (attempts to compensate for memory loss by fabricating memories) and has been linked to a thiamine deficiency. ("Anterograde amnesia" involves difficulty acquiring new information, and "retrograde amnesia" refers to an inability to recall previously learned material.)

b. Other Substance-Induced Disorders: Features of some of the other substance-induced disorders are summarized below:

Stimulant intoxication: The stimulant drugs include amphetamine-type drugs and cocaine. Stimulant intoxication is characterized by maladaptive behavioral and psychological changes (e.g., euphoria or affective blunting, hypervigilance, anxiety or anger, impaired judgment) and the development of at least two of the following symptoms during or shortly after drug use: tachycardia or bradycardia; pupillary dilation; elevated or lowered blood pressure; perspiration or chills; nausea or vomiting; weight loss; psychomotor agitation or retardation; muscular weakness, respiratory depression, or cardiac arrhythmias; and/or confusion, seizures, or coma.

Stimulant withdrawal: Stimulant withdrawal is diagnosed in the presence of at least two of five physiological changes that occur within a few hours to several days after cessation of or reduction in prolonged stimulant use: fatigue; vivid, unpleasant dreams; insomnia or hypersomnia; increased appetite; and/or psychomotor agitation or retardation. Withdrawal after repetitive high-dose use can cause a "crash" that involves intense lethargy, depression, and increased appetite.

Sedative, hypnotic, or anxiolytic intoxication: This diagnosis requires maladaptive behavioral and psychological changes (e.g., inappropriate aggressive or sexual behaviors, impaired judgment, mood lability) with at least one of the following symptoms as the result of recent drug use: slurred speech; incoordination; unsteady gait; nystagmus (involuntary eye movement); impaired cognition; and/or stupor or coma.

Sedative, hypnotic, or anxiolytic withdrawal: A diagnosis of this disorder requires the development of at least two of the following symptoms within several hours to a few days following cessation or reduction in drug use: autonomic hyperactivity; hand tremor; insomnia; anxiety; nausea or vomiting; transient hallucinations or illusions; psychomotor agitation; anxiety; and/or grand mal seizures.

Opioid intoxication: The opioids include heroin, morphine, codeine, methadone, oxycodone, and fentanyl. Opioid intoxication involves clinically significant problematic behavioral or psychological changes (e.g., initial euphoria followed by apathy or dysphoria, psychomotor agitation or retardation, and impaired judgment), pupillary constriction, and the development of at least one of the following symptoms during or shortly after drug use: drowsiness or coma; slurred speech; and/or impaired attention or memory.

Opioid withdrawal: Opioid withdrawal occurs following cessation or reduction in the use of an opioid following prolonged or heavy use or administration of an opioid antagonist following a period of opioid use. The diagnosis requires the presence of at least three of the following symptoms: dysphoric mood; nausea or vomiting; muscle aches; lacrimation (excessive secretion of tears) or rhinorrhea (excessive mucus secretion from the nose); sweating, pupillary dilation, or piloerection ("goose bumps" or erection of hair on the skin); diarrhea; yawning; fever; and/or insomnia.

Inhalant intoxication: This disorder is characterized by maladaptive behavioral and psychological changes following short-term, high-dose exposure to an inhalant (e.g., toluene or gasoline) with at least two of the following symptoms: dizziness; nystagmus (involuntary eye movement); incoordination; slurred speech; unsteady gait; lethargy; depressed reflexes; psychomotor retardation; tremor; generalized muscle weakness; blurred vision; stupor or coma; and/or euphoria.

Caffeine intoxication: This disorder is characterized by the development of five or more of the following symptoms during, or shortly after, caffeine use: restlessness; nervousness; excitement; insomnia; flushed face; diuresis (increased production of urine); gastrointestinal disturbance; muscle twitching; rambling flow of thought and speech; tachycardia or cardiac arrhythmia; periods of inexhaustibility; and/or psychomotor agitation. A manic episode, panic disorder, and generalized anxiety disorder can cause a clinical presentation that is similar to that of caffeine intoxication.

Tobacco withdrawal: Tobacco withdrawal is characterized by the development of at least four characteristic symptoms within 24 hours of abrupt cessation or reduction in the use of tobacco – i.e., irritability or anger, anxiety, impaired concentration, increased appetite, restlessness, depressed mood, and/or insomnia.

Gambling Disorder

Gambling disorder is characterized by persistent and recurrent gambling behavior leading to clinically significant distress or impairment as shown by four or more of the following in a 12-month period: (a) needs to gamble with increasing amounts of money to achieve the sought-after excitement; (b) is restless or irritable when trying to cut down or stop gambling; (c) has made repeated unsuccessful attempts to control, cut back, or stop gambling; (d) is often preoccupied with gambling; (e) often gambles when feeling distressed; (f) after losing money gambling, often returns another day to get even; (g) lies to hide the extent of involvement with gambling; (h) has jeopardized or lost a significant relationship, job, or educational or career opportunity because of gambling; and/or (i) relies on others for money to relieve financial problems caused by gambling.

Q. Neurocognitive Disorders

The disorders in this category have deficits in cognitive functioning as their core feature and "are syndromes for which the underlying pathology, and frequently the etiology as well, can potentially be determined" (APA, 2013, p. 591). The neurocognitive disorders in the DSM-5 include delirium and the syndromes of major neurocognitive disorder and mild neurocognitive disorder and their etiological subtypes (e.g., neurocognitive disorder due to Alzheimer's disease, vascular neurocognitive disorder, neurocognitive disorder due to HIV infection, substance/medication-induced neurocognitive disorder, etc.).

Except in the case of delirium, the first step in the diagnostic process is to differentiate between normal neurocognitive function, mild neurocognitive disorder, and major neurocognitive disorder. This is achieved through careful history taking and objective assessment. The second step is to assign an etiological category, such as neurocognitive disorder due to Alzheimer's disease.

The diagnostic criteria for neurocognitive disorders are based on six cognitive domains: (a) *Complex attention* – sustained attention, divided attention, selective attention, and processing speed. (b) *Executive function* – planning, decision-making, working memory, responding to feedback/error correction, overriding habits/inhibition, and mental flexibility. (c) *Learning and memory* – immediate memory, recent memory (free recall, cued recall, recognition memory), very-long-term memory (semantic, autobiographical), and implicit learning (unconscious learning of skills). (d) *Language* – expressive language (naming, word finding, fluency, grammar, syntax) and receptive language. (e) *Perceptual-motor* – abilities subsumed under the terms visual perception, visuoconstructional (assembly skills requiring hand-eye coordination), perceptual-motor, praxis (integrity of learned movements), and gnosis (perceptual integrity of awareness and recognition, such as recognition of faces). (f) *Social cognition* – recognition of emotions and theory of mind (the ability to consider someone else's mental state or experience).

Delirium

1. Diagnostic Criteria: A diagnosis of delirium requires (a) a disturbance in attention and awareness that develops over a short period of time (ordinarily hours to a few days), represents a change from baseline functioning, and tends to fluctuate in severity over the course of a day (often worsening in the evening and at night); and (b) at least one additional disturbance in cognition – e.g., impaired memory, disorientation, impaired language, deficits in visuospatial ability, or perceptual distortions. Symptoms must not be due to another neurocognitive disorder and must not occur in the context of a severely reduced level of arousal (e.g., during a coma), and there must be evidence that symptoms are the direct physiological consequence of a medical condition, substance intoxication or withdrawal, and/or exposure to a toxin.

2. Differential Diagnosis: Both delirium and MAJOR or MILD NEUROCOGNITIVE DISORDERS include memory impairment, but major or mild neurocognitive disorders don't include reduced consciousness. Thus, careful assessment of attention and arousal is helpful for differentiating a major or mild neurocognitive disorder from a persistent delirium. In addition, while the symptoms of other neurocognitive disorders are usually fairly stable, delirium symptoms tend to fluctuate.

Major and Mild Neurocognitive Disorders

The DSM-5 distinguishes between major and mild neurocognitive disorders based on the severity of symptoms. **Major neurocognitive disorder** subsumes the DSM-IV-TR diagnosis of dementia and is diagnosed when there is evidence of *significant* decline from a previous level of functioning in one or more cognitive domains that interferes with the individual's independence in everyday activities and does not occur only in the context of delirium. **Mild neurocognitive disorder** subsumes the DSM-IV-TR diagnosis of cognitive disorder NOS and is the appropriate diagnosis when there is evidence of a *modest* decline from a previous level of functioning in one or more cognitive domains that does *not* interfere with the individual's independence in everyday activities (but may require greater effort or compensatory strategies) and does not occur only in the context of delirium.

For both major and mild neurocognitive disorder, the DSM-5 identifies 13 types based on etiology: Alzheimer's disease, frontotemporal lobar degeneration, Lewy body disease, vascular disease, traumatic brain injury, substance/medication use, HIV infection, prion disease, Parkinson's disease, Huntington's disease, another medical condition, multiple etiologies, and unspecified.

1. Neurocognitive Disorder Due to Alzheimer's Disease:

a. Diagnostic Criteria: Neurocognitive disorder due to Alzheimer's disease is diagnosed when the criteria for major or mild neurocognitive disorder are met, there is an insidious onset of symptoms and a gradual progression of impairment in one or more cognitive domains (or at least two domains for *major* neurocognitive disorder), and the criteria for *probable* or *possible* Alzheimer's disease are met:

- For *major neurocognitive disorder, probable* Alzheimer's disease is diagnosed when there is evidence of a causative genetic mutation, clear evidence of a decline in memory and at least one other cognitive domain, a steadily progressive and gradual decline in cognition without extended plateaus, and no evidence of a mixed etiology. Otherwise, *possible* Alzheimer's disease is diagnosed.

- For *mild neurocognitive disorder, probable* Alzheimer's disease is diagnosed when there is evidence of a causative genetic mutation, while *possible* Alzheimer's disease is diagnosed when there is no evidence of a causative genetic mutation, clear evidence of a decline in memory and learning, a steadily progressive and gradual decline in cognition without extended plateaus, and no evidence of a mixed etiology.

It is often difficult to obtain direct evidence of Alzheimer's disease, so it is ordinarily diagnosed only when all other causes of a major or mild neurocognitive disorder have been ruled out. A definitive diagnosis requires an autopsy or brain biopsy that confirms extensive neuron loss and other specific indicators of the disease.

b. Prevalence/Course: Alzheimer's disease is the single-most common cause of dementia and, according to the DSM-5, accounts for 60 to over 90 percent of all cases, with a late onset (in the eighth or ninth decade) being more common than an early onset. It is characterized by a gradual onset of symptoms and a slow, progressive decline in cognitive functioning that can be described in terms of the following stages:

Stage 1 (1 to 3 years): Anterograde amnesia (especially for declarative memories); deficits in visuospatial skills (wandering); indifference, irritability, and sadness; and anomia (difficulty recalling words or names).

Stage 2 (2 to 10 years): Increasing retrograde amnesia; flat or labile mood; restlessness and agitation; delusions; fluent aphasia (aphasia in which speech is well articulated and grammatically correct but lacking in content); acalculia (loss of the ability to engage in arithmetic calculation); and ideomotor apraxia (an inability to translate an idea into movement).

Stage 3 (8 to 12 years): Severely deteriorated intellectual functioning; apathy; limb rigidity; and urinary and fecal incontinence.

2. Vascular Neurocognitive Disorder: Vascular neurocognitive disorder is diagnosed when the criteria for major or mild neurocognitive disorder are met, the clinical features are consistent with a vascular etiology (e.g., stroke), and there is evidence of cerebrovascular disease from the individual's history, a physical examination, and/or neuroimaging that is considered sufficient to account for her symptoms. This disorder often has a stepwise, fluctuating course with a patchy pattern of symptoms that is determined by the location of the brain damage, and the timing and extent of recovery depends on the cause. Risk factors for vascular neurocognitive disorder include hypertension, diabetes, cigarette smoking, obesity, high cholesterol levels, and atrial fibrillation.

3. Neurocognitive Disorder Due to HIV Infection: Individuals with neurocognitive disorder due to HIV infection exhibit symptoms characteristic of neurocognitive disorders that affect subcortical areas of the brain including the following: impaired concentration and memory (especially difficulty learning new information); slowed psychomotor speed; apathy and depression; and/or movement disorders such as tremor, clumsiness, or saccadic (rapid, jerky) eye movements (Watkins et al., 2011). The advanced form of HIV infection is referred to as acquired immune deficiency syndrome (AIDS); and, in the literature, neurocognitive disorder due to HIV disease is also known as **AIDS dementia complex** (ADC).

4. Differential Diagnosis for Major and Mild Major Neurocognitive Disorders: MAJOR DEPRESSIVE DISORDER – especially in older adults – may resemble a major or mild neurocognitive disorder in terms of cognitive symptoms; this form of depression is sometimes referred to as **pseudodementia**. In pseudodementia, the onset of cognitive symptoms is likely to be abrupt and the person is typically concerned (sometimes overly concerned) about her impairments; in a major or mild neurocognitive disorder, cognitive deficits usually have a gradual onset and progressive course and the person denies or is unaware of her impairments.

5. Specific Assessment Considerations: If you suspect that a client may have a major or mild neurocognitive disorder, you should begin by screening for the disorder. This assessment should cover the client's history and current functioning in adaptive, behavioral, cognitive, and emotional domains, including the extent to which she can function independently (perform activities of daily living) and safely. A standardized brief mental status inventory may be used (e.g., Folstein Mini Mental State Exam). Informal tests of memory may also be used (e.g., asking the client to recall a list of words recently studied). If you continue to suspect a major or mild neurocognitive disorder after screening, you should refer the client to a neuropsychologist for further evaluation. Referral for medical evaluations is also indicated (e.g., physical and neurological exams, lab tests), as is exploring the client's current and past substance use and possible toxin exposure.

R. Personality Disorders

Overview of the Personality Disorders

As defined in the DSM-5, a personality disorder "is an enduring pattern of inner experience and behavior that deviates markedly from the expectations of the individual's culture, is pervasive and inflexible, has an onset in adolescence or early adulthood, is stable over time, and leads to distress or impairment" (APA, 2013, p. 645). The DSM-5 groups the personality disorders into three clusters based on descriptive similarities: Cluster A personality disorders (paranoid, schizoid, schizotypal) are marked by odd or eccentric behaviors. Cluster B personality disorders (antisocial, borderline, histrionic, narcissistic) are characterized by dramatic, emotional, or erratic behaviors. Cluster C personality disorders (avoidant, dependent, obsessive-compulsive) include anxiety or fearfulness. If an individual has personality features that meet criteria for more than one personality disorder, each one can be diagnosed. This category also includes the diagnosis personality change due to another medical condition.

The following is a general description of personality disorders that applies to each personality disorder in the DSM-5:

- There is an enduring pattern of inner experience and behavior that deviates markedly from the expectations of the person's culture. This pattern is demonstrated in two or more of the following areas: cognition (i.e., how the person perceives and interprets self, others, and events); affectivity (i.e., the range, intensity, lability, and appropriateness of emotional response); interpersonal functioning; and/or impulse control.

- The pattern is inflexible and pervasive across a wide range of personal and social situations.

- The pattern leads to clinically significant distress or impairment in important areas of functioning.

- The pattern is stable and longstanding and its onset can be traced back at least to adolescence or early adulthood.

- The pattern is not better explained as an expression or consequence of another mental disorder and is not attributable to the physiological effects of a substance or another medical condition.

1. General Assessment Considerations for Personality Disorders: Psychological (e.g., personality) testing often plays a role in the diagnosis of a personality disorder. If you are not qualified to administer or interpret personality tests, you should refer the client to a clinical psychologist. Because the diagnostic criteria require the presence of an enduring, longstanding pattern, it's important to get a thorough history regarding the client's psychosocial, emotional, and behavioral functioning and family of origin. For a personality disorder diagnosis to be made, the enduring pattern cannot be due to the direct physiological effects of another medical condition (e.g., head trauma) or a substance. You should refer the client to a physician for medical evaluations. You must also assess for co-existing mental disorders, especially depressive and substance use disorders.

2. Children/Adolescents and Personality Disorders: Personality disorders are seldom diagnosed in children and adolescents, but in unusual cases in which the maladaptive traits appear to be pervasive and persistent, are unlikely to be limited to a particular developmental stage, and are not the result of another mental disorder, these diagnoses can be made in individuals under age 18 years. The exception to this is antisocial personality disorder, which requires that the person be at least 18 years old. To diagnose someone under age 18 with a personality disorder, the features must be present for at least one year.

3. Culture-Related Diagnostic Issues: It is critical to take into account the client's ethnic, cultural, and social background when evaluating his personality functioning. Problems associated with acculturation after immigration or with the expression of habits, customs, or religious or political values supported by the person's culture of origin are not personality disorders.

4. Gender-Related Diagnostic Issues: Some personality disorders (e.g., antisocial personality disorder) are diagnosed more frequently in males, and others (e.g., borderline, histrionic, and dependent personality disorders) are diagnosed more frequently in females. Be cautious not to overdiagnose or underdiagnose particular personality disorders in males or in females because of social stereotypes about conventional gender roles and behaviors.

5. General Differential Diagnostic Considerations for Personality Disorders: (a) Distinguish personality disorders from personality traits that don't reach the threshold for a personality disorder. Personality traits should be associated with a personality disorder only when they are maladaptive, inflexible, and persistent and cause significant personal distress or impairment of functioning. (b) Many personality disorders have features that are also found in episodes of other mental disorders. A personality disorder should be diagnosed only when the essential features appeared before early adulthood, are typical of the person's long-term functioning, and do not occur solely during an episode of another mental disorder.

(c) Personality disorders that may be associated with PSYCHOTIC DISORDERS (i.e., paranoid, schizoid, schizotypal) have an exclusion criterion stating that the defining behavior has not occurred solely during the course of a psychotic disorder or bipolar or depressive disorder with psychotic features. If a person with a persistent mental disorder (e.g., schizophrenia) has a pre-existing personality disorder, the personality disorder should also be recorded, followed by "premorbid" in parentheses. (d) In persons with SUBSTANCE USE DISORDERS, do not diagnose a personality disorder based only on behaviors that are consequences of substance intoxication or withdrawal or that are engaged in to maintain substance use (e.g., stealing or other antisocial behavior).

Paranoid Personality Disorder

1. Diagnostic Criteria: The essential feature of paranoid personality disorder is a pervasive pattern of distrust and suspiciousness that entails interpreting the motives of others as malevolent. The diagnosis requires that the person have at least four of the following symptoms: (a) suspects, without adequate basis, that others are exploiting, harming, or deceiving him; (b) is preoccupied with unwarranted doubts about the loyalty or trustworthiness of others; (c) is reluctant to confide in others because of an unjustified fear that the information will be used against him; (d) reads hidden demeaning or threatening meanings into harmless remarks or events; (e) persistently bears grudges; (f) perceives attacks on his character or reputation that others don't perceive and is quick to react angrily or counterattack; and/or (g) is persistently suspicious, without good reason, about the fidelity of his spouse or sexual partner.

2. Differential Diagnosis: (a) People with SCHIZOID PERSONALITY DISORDER are often seen as aloof and strange but they don't usually have prominent paranoid ideation. (b) SCHIZOTYPAL PERSONALITY DISORDER has similar traits of suspiciousness, interpersonal detachment, and paranoid ideation, but it also includes magical thinking, odd thinking and speech, and unusual perceptual experiences.

Schizoid Personality Disorder

1. Diagnostic Criteria: A diagnosis of schizoid personality disorder is made when a person displays a pervasive pattern of detachment from interpersonal relationships and a restricted range of emotional expression in social settings. At least four of the following symptoms must be present: (a) doesn't want or enjoy close relationships, including being part of a family; (b) almost always chooses solitary activities; (c) has little interest in sexual experiences with another person; (d) takes pleasure in few activities; (e) lacks close friends or confidants other than first-degree relatives; (f) seems indifferent to praise or criticism; and/or (g) exhibits emotional coldness, detachment, or flattened affectivity.

2. Differential Diagnosis: (a) SCHIZOTYPAL PERSONALITY DISORDER includes cognitive and perceptual distortions that are not found in schizoid personality disorder. (b) Social isolation in AVOIDANT PERSONALITY DISORDER is due to a fear of being embarrassed and concerns about being rejected; schizoid personality disorder is marked by a more pervasive detachment and a limited desire for close relationships.

Schizotypal Personality Disorder

1. Diagnostic Criteria: Schizotypal personality disorder is diagnosed in the presence of pervasive social and interpersonal deficits involving acute discomfort with and reduced capacity for close relationships and eccentricities in cognition, perception, and behavior. The diagnosis requires the presence of at least five characteristic symptoms: (a) ideas of reference (excluding delusions of reference); (b) odd beliefs or magical thinking (inconsistent with subcultural norms) that influences behavior; (c) bodily illusions and other unusual perceptual experiences; (d) odd thinking and speech (e.g., vague, circumstantial, metaphorical, overelaborate, stereotyped); (e) suspiciousness or paranoid ideation; (f) inappropriate or constricted affect; (g) odd, eccentric, or peculiar behavior or appearance; (h) lack of close friends or confidants, other than first-degree relatives; and/or (i) extreme social anxiety that doesn't diminish with familiarity and tends to involve paranoid fears rather than negative judgments about self.

2. Differential Diagnosis: (a) PARANOID and SCHIZOID PERSONALITY DISORDERS don't include cognitive or perceptual distortions or marked eccentricity or oddness, which are essential features of schizotypal personality disorder. (b) Individuals with AVOIDANT PERSONALITY DISORDER want relationships with others but are held back by their fear of rejection; those with schizotypal personality disorder don't appear to want relationships and are persistently detached from others.

Antisocial Personality Disorder

1. Diagnostic Criteria: Antisocial personality disorder (APD) is characterized by a pattern of disregard for and violation of the rights of others that has occurred since age 15 and involves at least three characteristic symptoms: (a) failure to conform to social norms with regard to lawful behaviors (i.e., repeatedly engages in acts that are grounds for arrest); (b) deceitfulness (e.g., repeated lying or conning others for personal profit or pleasure); (c) impulsivity or failure to plan ahead; (d) irritability and aggressiveness (i.e., repeated physical fights or assaults); (e) reckless disregard for the safety of self or others; (f) consistent irresponsibility (i.e., repeated failure to maintain consistent work behavior or honor financial obligations); and/or (g) lack of remorse (i.e., is indifferent to or rationalizes hurting or mistreating others or stealing from them). For the diagnosis, the person must be at least 18 years of age and have a history of conduct disorder before the age of 15.

When considering a diagnosis of antisocial personality disorder, it's important to consider the economic and social context in which the client's "antisocial" behavior is occurring. For example, seemingly antisocial behavior may be part of a "protective survival strategy" for a client from a low socioeconomic level and/or an urban area.

The DSM-5 states that the likelihood of developing antisocial personality disorder in adult life is increased if the individual experienced childhood onset of conduct disorder (before age 10 years) and accompanying ADHD; and that child abuse or neglect, unstable or erratic parenting, or inconsistent parental discipline may increase the chance that conduct disorder will evolve into antisocial personality disorder. Although antisocial personality disorder is chronic, its symptoms (especially involvement in criminal behavior) often become less severe and pervasive by the fourth decade of life.

2. Differential Diagnosis: For persons age 18 years and older, CONDUCT DISORDER can be diagnosed only if criteria for antisocial personality disorder are not met.

Borderline Personality Disorder

1. Diagnostic Criteria: The essential feature of borderline personality disorder (BPD) is a pervasive pattern of instability in interpersonal relationships, self-image, and affect, and marked impulsivity that began during early adulthood and is apparent in multiple contexts. At least five characteristic symptoms must be present for the diagnosis: (a) frantic efforts to avoid abandonment (other than suicidal or self-mutilating behavior, which appears elsewhere in these criteria); (b) a pattern of unstable, intense interpersonal relationships that are marked by fluctuations between idealization and devaluation; (c) persistent instability of self-image or sense of self (i.e., identity disturbance); (d) impulsivity in at least two areas that may be self-damaging such as sex, spending, substance abuse, or binge eating (do not count suicidal or self-mutilating behavior here, as it appears elsewhere in these criteria); (e) recurrent suicidal behavior, gestures, or threats, or self-mutilating behavior; (f) affective instability due to a marked reactivity of mood; (g) chronic feelings of emptiness; (h) inappropriate, intense anger or difficulty controlling anger; and/or (i) transient, stress-related paranoid ideation or severe dissociative symptoms.

Individuals with borderline personality disorder are intensely fearful of real or imagined abandonment, and the perception of impending separation or rejection or loss of external structure can lead to profound changes in self-image, affect, cognition, and behavior. They may experience intense anger and/or engage in impulsive and extreme behaviors (suicide attempts, self-mutilation) when faced with a realistic time-limited separation or when there are unavoidable changes in plans (e.g., when a therapist suddenly announces the end of the hour or when a significant other must cancel an appointment). In relationships, they exhibit a pattern of idealizing potential caregivers (including therapists) or lovers during initial encounters (demanding to spend a lot of time together, sharing intimate details about themselves), but then quickly switching to devaluating the person (e.g., saying that the person doesn't care enough or doesn't give enough). This shift may occur suddenly or dramatically.

2. Etiology: Several psychodynamic theories of borderline personality disorder have been proposed. According to Kernberg (1984), borderline personality disorder can be traced to adverse, unpredictable caregiver-child interactions that alternate between rejection and smothering. These interactions produce an insecure ego that relies on primitive defense mechanisms, especially **splitting**, which involves dichotomizing the self and others into "all good" and "all bad" aspects.

Linehan's (1987) **biosocial model** describes borderline personality disorder as due to an interaction between biological and environmental factors. According to Linehan, **emotion dysregulation** is the core feature of borderline personality disorder and is the result of excessive emotional vulnerability, an inability to modulate strong emotions, and exposure to an invalidating environment (i.e., an environment in which the individual's experiences are consistently labeled by significant others as incorrect or inappropriate).

3. Differential Diagnosis: (a) PARANOID and NARCISSISTIC PERSONALITY DISORDERS may also be marked by angry reactions to minor stimuli, but they do not include the pervasive instability of self-image, self-destructiveness, impulsivity, and abandonment concerns that are found in borderline personality disorder. (b) HISTRIONIC PERSONALITY

DISORDER can also be marked by attention seeking, manipulative behavior, and rapidly shifting emotions, but it does not include the self-destructiveness, angry disruptions in relationships, and chronic feelings of emptiness that are found in borderline personality disorder.

Histrionic Personality Disorder

1. Diagnostic Criteria: Histrionic personality disorder is characterized by a pervasive pattern of emotionality and attention-seeking. For the diagnosis, at least five characteristic symptoms must be present: (a) feels uncomfortable when not the center of attention; (b) is inappropriately sexually seductive or provocative; (c) displays rapidly shifting emotions and shallow expression of emotions; (d) consistently uses physical appearance to attract attention; (e) uses excessively impressionistic speech that is lacking in detail; (f) displays self-dramatization, theatricality, and exaggerated expression of emotion; (g) is suggestible; and/or (h) considers relationships to be more intimate than they are.

2. Differential Diagnosis: (a) Persons with NARCISSISTIC PERSONALITY DISORDER typically want praise for their presumed superiority; those with histrionic personality disorder are willing to appear fragile or dependent if this gets them attention. (b) Persons with DEPENDENT PERSONALITY DISORDER are overly dependent on others for guidance and praise but they lack the exaggerated emotional features of people with histrionic personality disorder.

Narcissistic Personality Disorder

1. Diagnostic Criteria: Narcissistic personality disorder (NPD) involves a pervasive pattern of grandiosity, a need for admiration, and a lack of empathy as indicated by at least five of the following symptoms: (a) has a grandiose sense of self-importance (e.g., expects to be acknowledged as superior without corresponding achievements); (b) is preoccupied with fantasies of unlimited success, power, brilliance, beauty, or ideal love; (c) believes that he is "special" and unique and can only be understood by, or should only associate with, other special or high-status people or institutions (his own self-esteem is likely to be enhanced, or mirrored, by the idealized value he assigns to those with whom he associates); (d) needs excessive admiration; (e) has a sense of entitlement. (i.e., expects favorable treatment or automatic compliance with his wishes); (f) is interpersonally exploitative; (g) lacks empathy for others' feelings or needs; (h) often envies others or believes that others envy him; and/or (i) exhibits arrogant, haughty behaviors or attitudes.

Because their self-esteem is vulnerable, people with narcissistic personality disorder are very sensitive to criticism or defeat; they may be haunted by feelings of humiliation and degradation, even though they don't show these feelings outwardly, and may react with rage or withdrawal in the face of criticism. Sustained feelings of humiliation or shame and the resulting self-criticism may be associated with social withdrawal, depressed mood, and persistent depressive disorder (dysthymia) or major depressive disorder. Sustained periods of grandiosity may be associated with a hypomanic mood.

2. Differential Diagnosis: (a) Grandiosity may occur as part of a MANIC or HYPOMANIC EPISODE. The associated mood change or alterations in functioning differentiates these episodes from narcissistic personality disorder. (b) While persons with BORDERLINE or

HISTRIONIC PERSONALITY DISORDER also may require a lot of attention, only people with narcissistic personality disorder require attention that is admiring.

Avoidant Personality Disorder

1. Diagnostic Criteria: Avoidant personality disorder is characterized by a pervasive pattern of social inhibition, feelings of inadequacy, and hypersensitivity to negative evaluation, as indicated by at least four characteristic symptoms: (a) avoids school or work activities involving interpersonal contact due to a fear of criticism, disapproval, or rejection; (b) is unwilling to get involved with people unless he is certain that he will be liked; (c) shows restraint in intimate relationships due to a fear of being shamed or ridiculed; (d) is preoccupied with being criticized or rejected in social situations; (e) is inhibited in new interpersonal situations because of feelings of inadequacy; (f) views himself as socially inept, unappealing, or inferior; and/or (g) is very reluctant to take personal risks or engage in new activities because they may prove embarrassing.

2. Differential Diagnosis: In DEPENDENT PERSONALITY DISORDER, the person is concerned about being taken care of; in avoidant personality disorder, the person is focused on avoiding humiliation and rejection.

Dependent Personality Disorder

1. Diagnostic Criteria: People with dependent personality disorder display a pervasive and excessive need to be taken care of, which leads to submissive, clinging behavior and a fear of separation. The diagnosis requires the presence of at least five symptoms: (a) has difficulty making decisions without excessive advice and reassurance; (b) needs others to assume responsibility for most major areas of his life; (c) fears disagreeing with others because it might lead to a loss of support or approval; (d) has difficulty initiating or doing things alone due to a lack of self-confidence; (e) goes to great lengths to get nurturance and support from others, even volunteering to do unpleasant things; (f) feels uncomfortable or helpless when he is alone due to exaggerated fears of being unable to care for himself; (g) urgently seeks another relationship as a source of care and support when a close relationship ends; and/or (h) is unrealistically preoccupied with fears of being left to take care of himself.

A childhood history of chronic illness or separation anxiety disorder is common.

Because the extent to which dependent behaviors (e.g., passivity, deferential conduct) are considered appropriate varies across cultures and age groups, sociocultural and age factors must be taken into consideration when evaluating this disorder. To qualify as a symptom, a dependent behavior must be clearly in excess of the client's cultural norm or reflect an unrealistic concern.

2. Differential Diagnosis: Persons with AVOIDANT PERSONALITY DISORDER withdraw from relationships until they're sure they'll be liked; those with dependent personality disorder seek and maintain connections to others.

Obsessive-Compulsive Personality Disorder

1. Diagnostic Criteria: Obsessive-compulsive personality disorder is diagnosed when a person displays a persistent preoccupation with orderliness, perfectionism, and mental and interpersonal control that severely limits his flexibility, openness, and efficiency. At least four characteristic symptoms must be present: (a) is preoccupied with details, rules, lists, order, organization, or schedules to such an extent that the major point of the activity is lost; (b) shows perfectionism that interferes with task completion; (c) is excessively devoted to work and productivity to the exclusion of leisure activities and friendships (not accounted for by economic necessity); (d) is overconscientious, scrupulous, and inflexible about matters of morality, ethics, or values (not accounted for by cultural or religious identification); (e) is unable to discard worn-out or worthless objects even when they have no sentimental value; (f) is reluctant to delegate tasks or to work with others unless they are willing to do things exactly his way; (g) has a miserly spending style toward self and others (money is seen as something to be hoarded for future calamities); and/or (h) shows rigidity and stubbornness.

2. Differential Diagnosis: OBSESSIVE-COMPULSIVE DISORDER includes the presence of true obsessions and compulsions; obsessive-compulsive personality disorder does not. When criteria for both disorders are met, both diagnoses should be made.

S. Paraphilic Disorders

The paraphilic disorders are characterized by an "intense and persistent [at least six months] sexual interest other than sexual interest in genital stimulation or preparatory fondling with phenotypically normal, physically mature, consenting human partners ... [that] is currently causing distress or impairment to the individual or ... has entailed personal harm, or risk of harm, to others" (APA, 2013, pp. 685-686). Included in this category are voyeuristic disorder, exhibitionistic disorder, frotteuristic disorder, sexual masochism disorder, sexual sadism disorder, pedophilic disorder, fetishistic disorder, and transvestic disorder.

Individuals with paraphilias tend to seek treatment only because of conflicts with sexual partners or because they have come to the attention of the legal system. Many claim that their sexual behaviors cause them no distress and that their only problem is the reactions of other people. Others, however, report experiencing extreme shame, guilt, and depression. Symptoms of depression may be accompanied by an increase in the frequency and intensity of the paraphilic behavior.

With the exception of sexual masochism, the paraphilias are almost never diagnosed in females.

1. Pedophilic Disorder: For at least six months, the person has experienced recurrent, intense sexually arousing fantasies, sexual urges, or behaviors involving sexual activity with a prepubescent child or children (generally age 13 years or younger). The person has acted on these urges, or the urges or fantasies cause marked distress or interpersonal difficulty. The person is at least age 16 years and at least five years older than the child(ren). (*Note:* Do not include a person in late adolescence involved in an ongoing sexual relationship with a 12- or 13-year-old.) The existence of multiple victims is sufficient, but not required, for this diagnosis to be made – i.e., a person can meet the diagnostic criteria by simply acknowledging intense or preferential sexual interest in children.

A person with pedophilic disorder may be sexually attracted to males, females, or both, and may be attracted to only children (exclusive type) or to both children and adults (nonexclusive type). The person's characteristic behavior can range from undressing the child and looking at him or her, exposing himself, masturbating in the presence of the child, and touching or fondling the child, to performing oral sex on the child and/or penetrating the child's mouth, anus, or vagina with his fingers, penis, or foreign objects. The person is likely to excuse and rationalize his behavior (he is "teaching the child," the child is "sexually provocative"). He may limit his activities to his own children or other relatives (which is indicated by using the DSM-5 specifier "limited to incest") or may also victimize children outside his family. Some (but not all) individuals with pedophilic disorder threaten the child to prevent disclosure. Except in cases where the individual also has sexual sadism disorder, he is likely to be quite attentive to the child's needs in order to gain his or her affection, interest, and loyalty and to prevent the child from disclosing the sexual activity.

The diagnostic criteria for pedophilic disorder can apply both to persons who disclose this paraphilia and persons who deny sexual attraction to prepubertal children despite significant objective evidence to the contrary.

> *Persons who disclose:* If they also report that their sexual attraction to prepubertal children is causing psychosocial difficulties, they may be diagnosed with pedophilic disorder. However, if they report feeling no guilt, shame, or anxiety about their paraphilic impulses, are not functionally impaired by their impulses, and have *never* acted on their impulses (as indicated by self-report and legally recorded history), then they have a pedophilic sexual orientation but *not* pedophilic disorder.

> *Persons who deny:* Because they deny sexual experiences, impulses, or fantasies involving children, they may also deny feeling distressed. Therefore, as long as there is evidence of recurrent behaviors for six months and evidence that they have acted on their sexual urges or experienced interpersonal difficulties as a result of the disorder, they may be diagnosed with pedophilic disorder even in the absence of self-reported distress.

This application of the diagnostic criteria both to individuals who disclose the paraphilia (i.e., "admitting individuals") and to those who deny it also pertains to the other paraphilic disorders that involve a nonconsenting partner.

2. Other Paraphilic Disorders: The other paraphilic disorders in the DSM-5 are (a) voyeuristic disorder (spying on others who are engaged in private activities); (b) exhibitionistic disorder (exposing the genitals); (c) frotteuristic disorder (touching or rubbing against a nonconsenting person); (d) sexual masochism disorder (undergoing humiliation, bondage, or suffering); (e) sexual sadism disorder (inflicting humiliation, bondage, or suffering); (f) fetishistic disorder (using nonliving objects or having a highly specific focus on nongenital body parts); and (g) transvestic disorder (engaging in sexually arousing cross-dressing). For each of these disorders, the person has either acted on the urges with a nonconsenting person (for paraphilic disorders that involve a nonconsenting partner) or the urges or fantasies cause clinically significant distress or impairment in important areas of functioning.

Finally, the diagnosis of transvestic disorder has been reported almost exclusively in males, and the majority of males identify as heterosexuals "although some individuals have occasional sexual interaction with other males, especially when they are cross-dressed" (APA, 2013, p. 703).

T. Other Conditions That May be a Focus of Clinical Attention

As noted earlier in this section, the DSM-5 no longer provides a classification of psychosocial and environmental problems (former Axis IV). Instead, the DSM-5 uses a selected set of ICD-9-CM "V codes" (as well ICD-10-CM "Z codes"). These V codes (and Z codes) appear in the DSM-5 chapter, Other Conditions That May Be a Focus of Clinical Attention.

These conditions and problems are not mental disorders but may be a focus of clinical attention or may otherwise affect the diagnosis, course, prognosis, or treatment of a client's mental disorder.

Coding one (or more) of these conditions or problems is appropriate if it (a) is a reason for the client's current visit; (b) helps to explain the need for a test, procedure, or treatment; and/or (c) provides useful information on circumstances that may affect the client's care, regardless of its relevance to the current visit.

1. Relational Problems:

a. Problems Related to Family Upbringing:

Parent-child relational problem: For example, inadequate parental supervision; parental overprotection; scapegoating; threats of physical violence; or feelings of sadness, apathy, or anger about the other person in the relationship.

Sibling relational problem: This category can be used for either children or adults.

Upbringing away from parents: This may be applied to children under state custody and placed in foster care or kin care; children living, without a court mandate, in a nonparental relative's home or with friends; and children living in group homes or orphanages. It does not apply to children in boarding schools.

Child affected by parental relationship distress: Negative effects of parental relationship discord (e.g., high levels of conflict, distress) on a child, including effects on the child's mental or other medical disorder.

b. Other Problems Related to Primary Support Group:

Relationship distress with spouse or intimate partner: For example, conflict resolution difficulty, withdrawal, or overinvolvement; chronic negative attributions of the other's intentions or dismissals of the partner's positive behaviors; or chronic sadness, apathy, and/or anger about the other partner. This category excludes spousal or partner abuse problems and sex counseling.

Disruption of family by separation or divorce: Partners in an intimate adult couple are living apart due to relationship problems or are in the process of divorce.

High expressed emotion level within family: Hostility, emotional overinvolvement, and criticism directed toward a family member who is an identified patient.

Uncomplicated bereavement: **Uncomplicated bereavement** is a normal reaction to the death of a loved one. (Be aware, however, that the duration and expression of "normal" bereavement vary considerably among different cultural groups.) Some people who are grieving present with symptoms characteristic of a major depressive episode (e.g., sadness, insomnia, poor appetite, weight loss); while these people typically regard their depressed mood as "normal," they may seek treatment for associated symptoms such as insomnia or poor appetite.

2. Abuse and Neglect: In addition to codes for a confirmed or suspected episode of abuse or neglect, codes are also provided to indicate if the current encounter is to provide mental health services to the victim or the perpetrator. A separate code is also provided for recording a past history of abuse or neglect.

a. Child Maltreatment and Neglect Problems: (a) Child Physical Abuse (physical discipline, such as spanking, is not considered abuse as long as it is reasonable and causes no bodily injury to the child). (b) Child Sexual Abuse. (c) Child Neglect (e.g., abandonment; lack of appropriate supervision; failure to attend to emotional or psychological needs; failure to provide shelter, clothing, nourishment, education, and/or medical care). (d) Child Psychological Abuse.

b. Adult Maltreatment and Neglect Problems: (a) Spouse or Partner Violence, Physical. (b) Spouse or Partner Violence, Sexual. (c) Spouse or Partner Neglect (i.e., an act or omission in the past year by a partner that deprives a dependent partner of basic needs and results, or has a reasonable potential to result, in physical or psychological harm to the dependent partner). (d) Spouse or Partner Abuse, Psychological. (e) Adult Abuse by Nonspouse or Nonpartner (i.e., acts of physical, sexual, or emotional abuse by another adult who is not an intimate partner).

3. Educational and Occupational Problems:

a. Academic or Educational Problem: For example, illiteracy; lack of access to schooling; problems with academic performance or underachievement; or discord with teachers, school staff, or other students.

b. Problem Related to Current Military Deployment Status: Psychological reactions to deployment are not included in this category because such reactions would be better captured as an adjustment disorder or another mental disorder.

c. Other Problem Related to Employment: For example, unemployment; recent job change; threat of job loss; job dissatisfaction; stressful work schedule; uncertainty about career choices; discord in the work environment; or hostile work environment.

4. Housing and Economic Problems:

a. Housing Problems: (a) Homelessness. (b) Inadequate housing (e.g., lack of heat, infestation by rodents, overcrowding). Consider cultural norms before assigning this category. (c) Discord with neighbor, lodger, or landlord. (d) Problem related to living in a residential institution (note that psychological reactions to a change in living situation would be better captured as an adjustment disorder).

b. Economic Problems: (a) Lack of adequate food or safe drinking water. (b) Extreme poverty. (c) Low income. (d) Insufficient social insurance or welfare support (e.g., a person meets eligibility criteria for social or welfare support but is not receiving such support or receives support that is insufficient to meet needs). (e) Unspecified housing or economic problem.

5. Other Problems Related to the Social Environment:

a. Phase of Life Problem: A problem adjusting to a life-cycle transition (e.g., entering or finishing school, leaving parental control, getting married, starting a new career, becoming a parent, adjusting to an "empty nest" after children leave home, retiring).

b. Problem Related to Living Alone: For example, chronic feelings of loneliness, isolation, or lack of structure in carrying out activities of daily living, including irregular meal and sleep schedules or inconsistent performance of home maintenance chores.

c. Acculturation Difficulty: Difficulty in adjusting to a new culture (e.g., following migration).

d. Social Exclusion or Rejection: For example, bullying, teasing, and intimidation by others; being targeted by others for verbal abuse and humiliation; or being purposefully excluded from activities with peers, coworkers, or others in one's social environment.

e. Target of (Perceived) Adverse Discrimination or Persecution: Discrimination against or persecution of a person based on her membership (or perceived membership) in a specific category (e.g., gender or gender identity, race, ethnicity, religion, sexual orientation, country of origin, political beliefs, disability status, caste, social status, weight, physical appearance).

f. Problems Related to Crime or Interaction With the Legal System: (a) Victim of crime. (b) Conviction in civil or criminal proceedings without imprisonment. (c) Imprisonment or other incarceration. (d) Problems related to release from prison. (e) Problems related to other legal circumstances.

g. Other Health Service Encounters for Counseling and Medical Advice: (a) Sex counseling. (b) Other counseling or consultation (i.e., counseling or advice/consultation for a problem not specified elsewhere in this DSM-5 chapter). Examples include spiritual or religious counseling, dietary counseling, or counseling on nicotine use.

h. Problems Related to Other Psychosocial, Personal, and Environmental Circumstances: (a) Religious or spiritual problem (e.g., loss or questioning of faith, problems associated with conversion to a new faith, questioning of spiritual values unrelated to an organized church or religious institution). (b) Problems related to unwanted pregnancy. (c) Problems related to multiparity (multiple birth). (d) Discord with social service provider, including probation officer, case manager, or social services worker. (e) Victim of terrorism or torture. (f) Exposure to disaster, war, or other hostilities. (g) Other problem related to psychosocial circumstances. (h) Unspecified problem related to unspecified psychosocial circumstances.

i. Other Circumstances of Personal History:

Problems related to access to medical and other health care: (a) Unavailability or inaccessibility of health care facilities. (b) Unavailability or inaccessibility of other helping agencies.

Nonadherence to medical treatment: Reasons for nonadherence may include discomfort resulting from treatment (e.g., medication side-effects), expense of treatment, personal values or religious or cultural beliefs about a proposed treatment, age-related incapacity, or the presence of a mental disorder (e.g., schizophrenia, personality disorder). This category should be used only when the problem is severe enough to warrant independent clinical attention and does not meet diagnostic criteria for PSYCHOLOGICAL FACTORS AFFECTING OTHER MEDICAL CONDITIONS.

Malingering: **Malingering** involves the intentional production of false or grossly exaggerated physical or psychological symptoms, motivated by external incentives (e.g., avoiding work or military duty, getting financial compensation, evading criminal prosecution, getting drugs). Malingering should be strongly suspected if any combination of the following is present: (a) medicolegal context (e.g., the person is referred by an attorney or self-refers while a legal case or criminal charges are pending); (b) marked discrepancy between the person's claimed stress or disability and the objective findings and observations; (c) a lack of cooperation during the diagnostic evaluation and in complying with treatment; and/or (d) the presence of antisocial personality disorder. Malingering is differentiated from CONVERSION DISORDER and other somatic symptom and related mental disorders by the intentional production of symptoms and obvious external incentives associated with it. Also, the motivation for symptom production in malingering is an external incentive; in FACTITIOUS DISORDER, external incentives are absent.

Wandering associated with a mental disorder: A person with a mental disorder (such as major neurocognitive disorder or neurodevelopmental disorder) whose desire to walk about leads to substantial clinical management or safety concerns. This category does not include persons whose intent is to escape an unwanted housing situation or who walk or pace as a result of medication-induced akathisia. (A condition known as **sundown syndrome**, or sundowning, involves the occurrence or increase of certain symptomatic behaviors in a circadian rhythm usually during the late afternoon, evening, or night. A person who is sundowning may exhibit mood swings and become more demanding, suspicious, agitated, or disoriented. In persons with Alzheimer's disease or other major neurocognitive disorders, sundowning may co-occur with wandering which can result in an emergency in which the person walks away from her home or other residence during the night – i.e., elopement at night.)

Borderline intellectual functioning: Differentiating borderline intellectual functioning and MILD INTELLECTUAL DISABILITY requires careful assessment of intellectual and adaptive functioning, particularly when the person has a co-occurring mental disorder that may affect compliance with standardized testing procedures (e.g., schizophrenia).

Additional conditions: (a) Overweight or obesity. (b) Other personal history of psychological trauma. (c) Personal history of self-harm. (d) Personal history of military deployment. (e) Other personal risk factors. (f) Problem related to lifestyle (e.g., lack of physical exercise, inappropriate diet, high-risk sexual behavior, poor sleep hygiene). A problem attributable to a symptom of a mental disorder is not coded unless it is a focus of treatment or directly affects the course, prognosis, or treatment of the client, and, in such cases, both the mental disorder and the lifestyle problem should be coded. (g) Adult antisocial behavior (e.g., the behavior of some professional thieves, racketeers, or dealers in illegal substances). (h) Child or adolescent antisocial behavior (e.g., isolated antisocial acts by children or adolescents).

VIII. Understanding and Assessing Addictive Behaviors

In this section, the word "drug" when used by itself refers collectively to alcohol and all other drugs of abuse. For information on the substance-related disorders described in the DSM-5, see Section VII of this chapter.

Chemical dependency experts usually identify drug addiction as a biopsychosocial disease because the development of addiction is thought to be influenced by biophysical, psychological, and social factors, and, over a period of time, addiction is expected to have adverse effects on a person's biophysical, psychological, and social functioning.

A. Dependence, Tolerance, and Withdrawal

Physical (or tissue) dependence refers to the biological adaptation of the body to a drug – after prolonged exposure to a drug, the body adapts to it and may stop producing neurochemicals that are analogous to the drug. The body begins to "expect" the drug to be present and to tolerate its effects. **Tolerance** refers to a condition of diminished responsiveness to a drug as a result of repeated exposure to it: The same amount of the drug begins to have decreasing effects, and, as tolerance progresses, increased amounts of the drug are required to achieve the desired effects.

Once physical dependence and tolerance have developed, **withdrawal** may emerge when the person stops taking the drug suddenly or decreases the amount of the drug that she takes. Thus, while the development of tolerance will tend to increase a person's use of a drug, the wish to avoid withdrawal symptoms will tend to prolong her drug use. During withdrawal, which can include intense physical and emotional symptoms, the body gradually adjusts to the absence of the drug on which it has been physically dependent. Acute withdrawal from a drug can represent a medical emergency requiring urgent medical care (e.g., hospitalization for detoxification).

Different drugs have different potentials for abuse. For example, sedatives, amphetamines, and opiates are considered to have high overall potentials for abuse, while marijuana and hallucinogens are considered to have moderate potentials for abuse. Drugs also differ with regard to their potential for producing psychological and physical dependence. Sedatives are associated with high potentials for both psychological and physical dependence; amphetamines are associated with a high potential for psychological dependence and a low potential for physical dependence; and hallucinogens are associated with a low potential for both psychological and physical dependence.

B. Etiology and Risk Factors for Addiction

1. Etiology of Alcoholism:

a. Genetic Hypothesis: A significant amount of research has found that the rates of alcoholism are higher among biological relatives than in the general population. Adoption studies conducted in Scandinavia in the 1970s, for example, found genetic, but not adoptive, transmission of alcoholism – that is, the biological sons of alcoholics adopted in infancy and studied into adulthood were four times more likely to be alcoholic than were the biological sons of non-alcoholics; no such relationship with alcohol abuse in the adoptive parents was found (Cloninger et al., 1985). Other research has found greater concordance rates in alcoholism for identical versus fraternal twins (Goodwin, 1979). Critics of the genetic hypothesis point out that the high rates of alcoholism found in certain families may be due to social (e.g., modeling) rather than genetic factors. (See also the review of Addiction Risk Factors, below.)

b. Biological Mechanisms: Some researchers have proposed that alcoholism is due to a biological or physical factor that is present in people with alcoholism, but not in non-alcoholics. One theory proposes that drinking alcohol produces a morphine-like chemical in the brains of certain individuals (i.e., those with alcoholism) (Davis & Walsch, 1970). Others relate alcoholism to dysfunction in the endocrine system (e.g., hypoglycemia) or to metabolic processes, such as the accumulation of acetaldehyde (a product of alcohol metabolism) following drinking – in one study, men with familial histories of alcoholism were found to show levels of acetaldehyde after drinking that were double the levels of those without such histories (Schuckit & Rayses, 1979).

In other individuals, metabolic processes may serve to inhibit the development of alcoholism. For instance, Chinese and Japanese individuals experience a more rapid onset of uncomfortable physiological reactions to alcohol, such as facial reddening, accelerated heartbeat, and increased blood pressure, and, relative to other American cultural groups, Asian Americans have low rates of alcoholism. Critics of this hypothesis point out that Eskimo and American Indian individuals tend to exhibit the same uncomfortable physiological reactions to alcohol, and yet have relatively high rates of alcoholism.

c. The Disease Model: The **disease model** has been summarized by Mann (1968), who described alcoholism as a progressive disease that manifests itself chiefly by the "uncontrollable drinking of the victim" and that, if left untreated, grows progressively worse. Many proponents of the disease model rely on concepts developed by **Jellinek** (1960), who proposed that alcoholism is not a single disease but, rather, a disorder involving several types of alcoholism; and that, without intervention, certain of types of alcoholism will progress through a series of declining stages. Jellinek described five distinct types of alcoholism:

- *Alpha alcoholism* is characterized by psychological dependence in which drinking is used increasingly to help the alcoholic cope with problems.

- *Beta alcoholism* includes physical problems (e.g., cirrhosis, stomach problems) resulting from alcohol use, but no signs of physical or psychological dependence.

- *Gamma alcoholism* includes physical addiction (in which withdrawal symptoms occur whenever drinking is stopped), a progression from psychological to physical dependence, and a loss of control over the ability to regulate alcohol intake. Gamma alcoholism is associated with the most severe damage to the alcoholic's physical health, emotional well-being, and social functioning. On the other hand, this form of alcoholism is marked by periods of abstinence. Because Gamma alcoholics often sense their loss of control, they may be highly motivated for treatment.

- *Delta alcoholism* is similar to Gamma alcoholism except that the alcoholic is able to control her consumption of alcohol in certain situations. On the other hand, Delta alcoholism is associated with a high degree of both psychological and physical dependence, making abstinence for even a short period of time impossible

- *Epsilon alcoholism* is characterized by periodic, unpredictable drinking binges.

Jellinek further proposed that individuals with Gamma or Delta alcoholism will pass through the following series of declining stages:

Prealcoholic (warning) phase: The drinker consumes alcohol with increasing frequency to relieve tension or otherwise feel good. As drinking increases during this phase, a tolerance to alcohol is developed.

Prodromal (early alcoholic) phase: The drinker begins to experience blackouts (periods of amnesia while or immediately after drinking), surreptitious drinking, preoccupation with drinking, and feelings of guilt about inappropriate behaviors engaged in while intoxicated. In addition, the person begins to gulp drinks.

Crucial phase: The drinker loses control of her alcohol intake, rationalizes her drinking and assigns blame to others, has frequent blackouts, and begins to experience social, occupational, and other problems. This phase marks the beginning of physical addiction.

Chronic phase: This phase is associated with a total obsession with drinking, a complete loss of control over alcohol intake (e.g., the person may consume any form of alcohol), a loss of tolerance for alcohol, morning drinking, memory loss, moral deterioration, and severe physical symptoms.

The disease model has been accepted by many treatment professionals and individuals with alcoholism, in part because it provides a straightforward goal for treatment (total abstinence from alcohol); its assumptions underlie many treatment programs for alcoholism, including Alcoholics Anonymous. Critics of the disease model point out that it ignores the sociocultural factors that might produce alcoholism and offers people with alcoholism a "sick role" that can interfere with successful treatment.

d. Psychological Theories: Psychological correlates may underlie the development of alcoholism to an extent; however, many experts now believe that characteristic "alcoholic" traits such as depression, anxiety, low self-esteem, and poor frustration tolerance play an even greater role as consequences of persistent and heavy alcohol use.

Personality theory: Personality theory proposes that alcoholism is the result of an "alcoholic personality" characterized by high levels of impulsiveness, aggression, emotionality, agitation, and frustration. The results of research on this hypothesis have been mixed, however, and it remains unclear whether these personality characteristics cause or are caused by excessive drinking.

Psychodynamic theory: Proponents of a psychodynamic theory of alcoholism reject the conceptualization of alcoholism as a disease. Many psychodynamic theories hypothesize that problem drinking is associated with ungratified needs (e.g., a need for power) and with the ways that alcoholics learned to satisfy those needs in childhood. These theories further suggest that individuals with psychological conflicts who develop alcoholism are those with a genetic predisposition to the disease who live in societies that are ambivalent about alcohol use or sanction it as a way to feel good.

Khantzian (1975) and Khantzian and Mack (1983) hypothesize that individuals with alcohol (or other drug) use disorders have deficiencies in a group of ego functions related to self-care (self-esteem and the ability to use affects as signals). Finally, Khantzian and others posit a **self-medication hypothesis**, which proposes that people who abuse substances (whether alcohol or other drugs) choose a drug according to specific sought-after effects (e.g., Khantzian, 1975; Weider & Kaplan, 1969).

Humanistic/experiential: According to this model, people use alcohol to satisfy (temporarily) their need for power. In other words, intoxication is accompanied by thoughts of increased social and personal power.

Behavioral/learning theory: Learning theories reject the assumption that alcoholism is a disease and, instead, view abusive drinking as a learned behavior. They emphasize the rewarding aspects of drinking such as tension reduction, peer approval, and gaining "adult" status. The learned response of excessive drinking is maintained when physical dependence develops, and continued consumption of alcohol allows a person with alcoholism to avoid the negative consequences of abstinence (e.g., withdrawal symptoms).

Conger's (1956) **tension-reduction hypothesis** contends that alcohol reduces anxiety, fear, and other states of tension and that people drink alcohol to reduce tension, which eventually leads to addiction. In other words, addiction is the result of negative reinforcement. An alternative explanation is provided by Marlatt and Gordon (1985) who contend that addictive behaviors, like other behaviors, are acquired and describe addiction as an overlearned, maladaptive habit pattern.

Cognitive theory: Cognitive theorists believe that alcoholism results from the individual's belief that drinking will reduce tension or will act as a euphoriant.

e. **Sociocultural Theories:** Sociocultural theories emphasize the importance of social and cultural factors in determining levels of alcohol consumption. Lawson, Peterson, and Lawson (1982) identified three sociocultural factors that contribute to an individual's consumption of alcohol: (a) the degree to which the individual's culture produces tension in its members (i.e., higher tension is associated with higher levels of drinking); (b) the culture's attitudes toward drinking; and (c) the degree to which the individual's culture provides substitutes for alcohol use (e.g., other activities or drugs). For instance, in the U.S. alcohol use is generally considered a normative and socially acceptable behavior. In cultures with lower rates of alcoholism, drinking is not approved of as a means of coping with personal problems and there is no status associated with intoxication.

f. **Biopsychosocial Models:** Several biopsychosocial models have been proposed that view the initiation, maintenance, and progression of alcohol or other drug addiction as involving an interaction between biophysical, psychological, and sociocultural factors.

2. Etiology of Other Drug Addiction: Investigators have identified specific brain areas that may cause drug effects. For example, Pert and Snyder (1973) demonstrated that certain nerve cells serve as receptor sites for opiates in the brains of rats. In addition, many of the psychological theories used to explain the sources of alcoholism are also used to explain the origins of other drug abuse. For example, learning theorists propose that drug use provides individuals with immediate reinforcement in the form of reduced anxiety or tension, improved mood, and avoidance of withdrawal symptoms.

3. Addiction Risk Factors:

a. Genetic Risk Factors:

- A **family history** of addiction is one of the most influential factors and is associated with a high risk for developing alcohol or other drug addiction.

- A substantial amount of research has suggested that a genetic component influences the likelihood of becoming addicted to alcohol after drinking for the first time.

- Some authorities have concluded that as much as half of an individual's risk of becoming addicted to alcohol (or other drugs) depends on her genes. Environmental factors and genetic-environment interactions are believed to account for the remainder of the risk.

b. Demographic Risk Factors:

- Males have higher rates of drug addiction than females.

- Living in economically, educationally, and occupationally disadvantaged communities (e.g., the "inner city") is associated with an increased likelihood of drug abuse and addiction.

c. Psychiatric Risk Factors:

- Psychiatric problems often play a role in the initiation and maintenance of drug use. For instance, an individual may use alcohol or take drugs to reduce feelings of anxiety.

- While research investigating the relationship between addiction and personality traits has not found evidence of an "addictive personality," there is a group of characteristics that appears to result from addiction, including negative self-image, low stress tolerance, depression, inadequacy, and isolation.

d. Behavioral Risk Factors:

- Some individuals begin to abuse drugs following a period of negative attitudes toward themselves and others, involvement with delinquent peers, and participation in socially unacceptable behaviors (which are usually engaged in to increase self-esteem and achieve gratification).

- Early drug abuse and addiction are associated with childhood and adolescent antisocial or delinquent behavior.

- A higher likelihood of drug abuse is associated with poor academic performance and a low commitment to education.

e. Family Risk Factors:

- Family members, especially parents, can increase the likelihood of drug use and abuse through modeling and example – i.e., children are more likely to grow up to use and abuse drugs when they see their family members condone drug use and use or abuse drugs themselves.

- Parental alcoholism has been found to influence adolescent drug use as a result of stress and negative affect, low levels of parental monitoring, and increased emotionality in the family, which is associated with higher levels of negative affect (Chassin et al., 1993).

- An increased likelihood of early involvement with drugs is also associated with inconsistent parental discipline and a lack of family warmth.

f. Social Risk Factors:

- Children and adolescents are influenced by their peers' use of drugs and attitudes toward drug use.

- Teenagers whose friends have access to drugs are more likely to be exposed to drugs and, therefore, have an increased potential of abusing drugs themselves.

- For adults, peers are more likely to influence the specific drug a person chooses to use.

4. Addiction Risk Factors Specific to Adolescents: Several factors have been linked to problem drug use among adolescents. For example, the results of Shedler and Block's (1990) longitudinal study of youngsters from ages 3 to 18 indicated that adolescents who were frequent users of drugs often exhibited a coherent syndrome that was first evident as early as age 7 and was characterized by a sense of alienation, impulsivity, indecisiveness, and subjective distress. Other studies have identified a number of demographic and environmental factors that are associated with an increased risk for adolescent drug abuse, including male gender, low SES, physical or sexual abuse, and low parental warmth and involvement (e.g., Berk, 2004). Finally, according to the "gateway hypothesis," the abuse of illicit drugs by adolescents often begins with early use of gateway drugs (first tobacco and alcohol and then marijuana), which is followed by the use of cocaine, methamphetamine, and/or other illicit drugs (Pentz & Li, 2002).

C. Consequences of Drug Addiction

Most individuals, once they are addicted to alcohol or another drug, experience a characteristic process that leads to impairment of their physical, psychological, emotional, cognitive, social, and/or spiritual functioning. When these effects are present, they can be used in an informal manner to identify that a person is addicted to a drug (or drugs).

1. Physical Symptoms: Physical symptoms include drug-induced changes in a person's physical health. Many of these changes are gradual, occurring over a period of many years. Physical symptoms that may be warning signs of drug addiction include liver, heart, and stomach problems; injuries; weight loss; exhaustion; blackouts; decreased sex drive; tremors; and an overall deterioration in physical health. For example, **cirrhosis**, a chronic, degenerative disease of the liver, is most often caused by chronic alcohol use.

2. Cognitive Symptoms: Persons addicted to drugs often exhibit short-term and long-term cognitive symptoms that may include intoxication, memory deficits, impaired concentration, periods of amnesia, and various neurological symptoms. **Wernicke-Korsakoff syndrome** is a life-threatening alcohol-related disorder resulting in persistent memory loss and believed to be caused by malnutrition and thiamine (vitamin B1) deficiency. The disease has two stages: (a) *Wernicke encephalopathy* develops suddenly and produces abnormal eye movements, ataxia (loss of coordination), slowness, confusion, and signs of neuropathy (e.g., loss of sensation, impaired reflexes). The level of consciousness progressively falls and, without treatment, may progress to coma and death. (b) *Korsakoff psychosis* may follow Wernicke's encephalopathy if treatment is not initiated early enough. Symptoms include severe amnesia, apathy, and disorientation, with recent long-term memory affected more than remote memory. **Confabulation** (invention of facts or stories) may occur in an effort to compensate for memory gaps.

3. Psychological Symptoms: Severe psychological symptoms of addiction may include suspiciousness, paranoia, and delusions (i.e., addicted persons may misinterpret or distort events in their environment). Milder symptoms may include chronic or episodic depression, frustration, and irritability.

4. Emotional Symptoms: Persons addicted to drugs often experience negative emotions, including anger, resentments, and remorse or guilt. Sometimes, these emotions occur when these individuals sense that they can no longer control their drug use or their reasons for using. People with drug addictions may also be unpredictable in their emotional expression – they may shift rapidly from being affectionate and understanding to being angry and blaming.

5. Social Symptoms: Problematic drug use has negative and often rapid effects on the user's social functioning. For example, individuals who crave drugs often lose interest in social interactions and may neglect old friends in favor of new drug-using peers. Other users may need to take the drug before going out and feel uncomfortable at social events that don't provide alcohol or other drugs. As addiction progresses, problems with family and friends and at work or school usually become progressively worse. The person may also experience legal and financial problems.

6. Spiritual Symptoms: For people addicted to drugs, drugs are the highest priority – their lives center on obtaining and using drugs and on recovering from the effects of drugs. Some individuals will do whatever is necessary to obtain drugs, including, for example, stealing from and manipulating others, including their loved ones. People addicted to drugs may also feel alienated from others and as though their lives have no meaning or higher purpose.

D. Assessment of Substance Use Disorders

1. Screening for Substance Use Disorders: You should ask clients about alcohol and other drug use as a routine part of assessment. When doing so, be forthright in explaining your purposes. Don't ask vague questions because these tend to support a client's inclination to be evasive about this topic and usually yield unproductive responses.

In addition, a variety of **screening instruments** are available to help you determine whether a client may have a substance use disorder (see the review of psychological testing in Section III). Screening instruments tend to elicit more detailed information than interview questions and can be more effective than interviews at overcoming a client's denial that she uses drugs or alcohol at all or reluctance to disclose information related to her drug or alcohol use and its effects.

2. Additional Evaluation of Substance Use Disorders: If the results of screening lead you to suspect that the client may have a substance use disorder, you should then perform additional evaluation in order to document the presence of the disorder and specifically describe it. Important components of this evaluation are described below.

a. Drug-Related History: Eliciting a **drug-related history** involves exploring the following areas: (a) the kind, frequency, and amount of all substances ingested as well as the last time they were taken; (b) signs of tolerance and withdrawal; (c) negative consequences associated with using, including medical, emotional, interpersonal, social, occupational/educational, and legal effects; (d) behaviors engaged in while using alcohol or other drugs; and (e) personality changes associated with using the substance.

Obtaining a reliable history is critical when you believe that a client may abuse alcohol or other drugs, but the client may minimize or deny her alcohol or drug problem. To increase the reliability of the client's report, you should adopt a straightforward, nonjudgmental approach to make self-disclosure feel safer for the client and explain that disclosures and treatment records are confidential. Additionally, you should attempt to obtain information from collateral sources and consider referring the client for blood or urine screening.

b. Medical Evaluation and Lab Tests: Referral for evaluation by a medical doctor is important because people can develop physical problems as a result of long-term or heavy use of alcohol or other drugs. Chronic, heavy alcohol use, for example, can produce a variety of long-term physical effects, including liver cirrhosis, cerebral atrophy, damage to the cardiovascular system, and ulcers. After obtaining permission, also review the client's medical records. Laboratory tests such as urine toxicology testing can assist in both assessment and case management.

c. Mental Status Exam: Both acute and persistent use of alcohol or other drugs can have significant direct effects on a user's mood, thought processes, and personality and cognitive functioning. Therefore, in addition to helping you identify the presence of a co-occurring mental disorder (discussed below), a mental status exam can be useful for detecting the direct effects of a substance use disorder, such as difficulties with cognitive functions, mood and affective symptoms, persistent or transient hallucinations, and suicidal, violent, or paranoid ideation or behavior.

d. Co-Occurring, Independent Psychiatric Disorders: A number of psychological problems and mental disorders occur at a higher-than-average rate among individuals with substance use disorders. Examples include anxiety disorders, depression, suicide, psychoses, antisocial personality, conduct disorder, attention-deficit disorders, marital and sexual problems, and social skills deficits. Therefore, you should screen the client for other psychological problems.

If a client has prominent symptoms of another mental disorder, you should get a complete psychiatric history and perhaps administer (or refer for) psychological tests. On the other hand, because a substance use disorder can exacerbate other psychological problems and because these problems tend to diminish during recovery, some experts recommend that an evaluation of independent mental disorders should occur after the client has been off of all drugs for at least one month.

e. Motivation for Change: In addition to using more standard means of assessing motivation, you can find out about the client's motivation for change by asking her to identify and talk about the negative consequences of her substance use.

f. Factors Maintaining Substance Use: Efforts to identify factors maintaining a client's problematic substance use entail exploring the antecedents and consequences associated with her addictive behavior. For most clients, this should include, in particular, exploring family factors.

g. Collateral Information: Whenever possible, you should collect information from family members, friends, coworkers, supervisors, and other individuals who have frequent contact with the client.

Finally, because abstaining from substance use usually won't solve all of a person's problems, you should monitor and re-evaluate the client's condition after she has started to abstain (for instance, depression may be a cause of or may be caused by persistent substance use). This will help you distinguish between the causes and the consequences of her substance abuse.

E. Addiction and the Family System

Most families with serious alcohol or drug addiction problems are characterized by very rigid boundaries, which isolate the family from the outside community.

1. Roles in an Alcoholic Family System: The "alcoholic family" or "addicted family" is said to be suffering from the diseases of **dependency** and **co-dependency**, and all family members are thought to play specific, dysfunctional roles. The term "co-dependency" describes a relationship in which one person enables the other person to behave in maladaptive ways (see also Enabling, below). Sometimes co-dependency is reinforced by the enabling person's need to be needed.

Wegscheider (1981) labeled roles in an alcoholic family system as follows:

Dependent: The alcoholic family member.

Enabler: Often the spouse who does everything possible to make the alcoholic partner stop drinking except what might work – confronting the alcoholic or leaving the relationship.

Hero: A family member who is aware of what's happening in the family and assumes responsibility for the family's pain by becoming successful and popular. Often, it is the oldest child in the family.

Scapegoat: The member who rejects the family system. Often, it is the second child in the family.

Lost child: The member who quietly withdraws from the family system. Typically, it is the third child in the birth order.

Mascot: Typically the youngest child in the family, the mascot "plays the clown" to relieve her own pain and the family tension and get her parents' attention.

Although the chemically dependent family member's role usually gets most of the attention in treatment, many experts believe that all family members must be taught new roles if permanent change is to occur.

2. Enabling: An **enabler** is a person who, by her actions, makes it easier for a person addicted to alcohol or other drugs to continue his or her self-destructive behavior. As noted above, the enabler in an alcoholic family system is often the spouse who does everything possible to make the alcoholic partner stop drinking except what might work – confronting the alcoholic or leaving the relationship. Examples of typical enabling behaviors include the following: (a) making excuses, providing alibis, or performing tasks for the alcoholic/addict rather than letting her suffer the consequences of her behavior; (b) coming up with reasons why the alcoholic/addict's continued substance use is understandable or acceptable; (c) blaming (e.g., getting angry at the alcoholic/addict for not trying hard enough to control her substance use); (d) controlling (e.g., trying to take responsibility for the alcoholic/addict's substance use by cutting off her supply); and (e) threatening to take action if the alcoholic/addict doesn't control her use but not following through when she continues using.

F. Relapse

The most common **precipitant of relapse** among people recovering from substance-use disorders is the experience of anxiety, frustration, depression, or other negative emotional states.

1. The Abstinence Violation Effect: Marlatt and Gordon (1985) refer to the typical reaction to relapse as an "abstinence violation effect" that involves self-blame, guilt, anxiety, and depression, which lead to an increased susceptibility to further drinking. They propose that the potential for future relapse is reduced when the person views the episode of drinking as a mistake resulting from specific, external, and controllable factors.

2. Gorski's Conceptualization of Relapse: Gorski's conceptualization of relapse is based on the disease model of addiction and emphasizes the physical, psychological, behavioral, and social components of relapse. According to Gorski (1989), relapse is *process* and, therefore, can be interrupted or changed; and this "process" occurs *within a person*, so that appropriate relapse prevention targets include the person's attitudes, values, and behaviors.

a. Post-Acute Withdrawal Syndrome: For Gorski, the major physical correlate of drinking that predisposes a person to relapse is "**post-acute withdrawal syndrome**" (PAW); this syndrome occurs because a chronic drinker's body adapts over time to the effects of alcohol so that drinking ends up having a normalizing effect on her body. PAW can last for up to three months after cessation of drinking and primarily affects higher level cognitive processes, resulting in impaired abstract thinking, concentration, and memory, increased emotionality, and overreaction to stress. Thus, according to Gorski, the cognitive abilities needed for adaptive decision making are compromised at precisely a time when psychological, behavioral, and social factors are also predisposing a newly sober person to drink.

b. Uniform Pattern of Relapse: Gorski defines a "uniform pattern of relapse" that begins long before an individual takes a drink and consists of a sequence of events (**warning signs**) that start with internal change (e.g., old ways of thinking that lead to negative emotional states) and ultimately progress to a loss of control and relapse. According to Gorski, the maladaptive coping behaviors (e.g., denial, defensiveness, isolation, avoidance, lack of planning, compulsive involvement in distracting activities) engaged in during this process, combined with PAW, end up producing confusion, depression, a collapse of social support, a loss of life structure, and withdrawal from treatment. The person then develops feelings of overwhelming frustration, loneliness, anger, etc., and a sense that she has no other option but to drink. Resumption of drinking then produces a loss of control. Gorski suggests that, like PAW, this loss of control may be physiologically induced by the effects of alcohol on the central nervous system. It may also be influenced by a person's belief that she will inevitably keep drinking after taking the first drink.

G. Effects of MDMA and Methamphetamine

1. MDMA: MDMA is considered an hallucinogen. Its effects, however, are actually a combination of those produced by amphetamines and hallucinogens – i.e., people intoxicated on MDMA experience both an increase in motor activity and general arousal and a dream-like state that may include delusions and hallucinations. MDMA is widely known as "ecstasy"; the term "Molly" is used to refer to MDMA that is relatively free of adulterants.

2. Methamphetamine: Methamphetamine is a highly addictive stimulant drug that activates the release of very high levels of the neurotransmitter dopamine, which stimulates brain cells that enhance mood and body movement. Abusers may become addicted quickly, needing higher doses and needing to use more often. Methamphetamine may be taken orally, intranasally (snorting the powder), by needle injection, or by smoking. Street methamphetamine is referred to by many names, such as "speed," "meth," and "chalk." Methamphetamine hydrochloride (clear chunky crystals resembling ice, which can be inhaled by smoking) is referred to as "ice," "crystal," and "glass."

Although methamphetamine is chemically related to amphetamine, at similar doses its effects are much stronger, longer lasting, and more harmful to the central nervous system. Even small doses can result in increased wakefulness, increased physical activity, reduced appetite, increased respiration, rapid heart rate, irregular heartbeat, increased blood pressure, and hyperthermia. Other short-term effects include irritability, anxiety, insomnia, confusion, tremors, convulsions, and cardiovascular collapse and even death. Among the long-term effects are paranoia, aggressiveness, extreme anorexia, memory loss, visual and auditory hallucinations, delusions, severe dental problems, reduced motor speed, and impaired verbal learning. Recent studies of chronic methamphetamine abusers have also revealed severe structural and functional changes in areas of the brain associated with emotion and memory, which may account for many of the emotional and cognitive problems observed in chronic methamphetamine abusers.

Finally, transmission of HIV and hepatitis B and C can be a consequence of methamphetamine abuse. Among abusers who inject the drug, infection is spread mainly through the re-use of contaminated syringes, needles, and other injection equipment by more than one person. In addition, the intoxicating effects of methamphetamine, whether it is injected or taken in other ways, can impair judgment and inhibition and lead people to engage in unsafe behaviors.

H. Blood Alcohol Level

Blood alcohol level (BAL) (a.k.a. blood alcohol content/concentration, or BAC) refers to the amount of alcohol present in the bloodstream. The negative effects of alcohol begin as BAL rises above .05. The typical effects of levels of alcohol in the bloodstream are as follows:

BAL .02: Slight body warmth, less inhibited, slight mood changes, mellow feeling.

BAL .05: Obvious relaxation, lowered inhibitions, the start of coordination impairment, and impaired judgment and decision-making ability.

BAL .08: Obvious impairments in coordination and judgment, deterioration of reaction time and control. BAL .08 is the typical drunk-driving limit.

BAL .15: Obvious intoxication, impaired movement and balance, difficulty walking, standing, and talking.

BAL .30: Diminished reflexes, semiconsciousness.

BAL .40: Limited reflexes, anesthetic effects.

BAL .50: Nerve centers controlling respiration and heartbeat decelerate and death may occur.

After alcohol tolerance has developed, a person must consume more alcohol to achieve the same effects as before tolerance developed. However, heavy alcohol consumption over a period of years can produce "reverse tolerance" due to liver damage: If the damaged liver is less able to metabolize alcohol, even small amounts of alcohol can produce a high BAL and intoxication.

I. Behavioral Addiction

While this section has focused on drug addiction, the term "addiction" can be applied more broadly to any substance, activity, behavior, or object that has become the focus of a person's life to the exclusion of other activities, or that has begun to harm the individual or others physically, psychologically, or socially. Examples other than drugs include gambling, food, sex, pornography, computers, video games, the Internet, work, exercise, watching TV, shopping, and cutting. The term **behavioral addiction** (or "process addiction" or "non-substance-related addiction") is used to refer to a recurring compulsion by an individual to engage in a specific activity, despite harmful consequences, as identified by the person herself, to her physical health, psychological or emotional well-being, and/or social functioning.

IX. Dynamics, Indicators, and Assessment of Abuse and Neglect

A. Child Abuse and Neglect

Although a disproportionate number of known cases of child abuse and neglect (i.e., reported cases, or those that come to the attention of authorities) involve low-income families, child maltreatment occurs in all socioeconomic groups as well as all cultural, racial, ethnic, and religious groups.

Dynamics and Indicators of Child Abuse and Neglect

1. Types of Child Maltreatment:

a. Physical Abuse: Physical abuse involves the nonaccidental physical injury to a child caused by a parent or other caregiver. It may result from an act of commission or an act of omission (e.g., failure to protect the child from injury).

- The perpetrators of child physical abuse are more often female than male; and young, low-income, single mothers with young children are at greatest risk of abusing their children (Goldman et al., 2003; Gelles, 1992).

- Children of all ages are physically abused, but toddlers and adolescents are subjected to the most severe forms of violence.

- In childhood, males are at higher risk and experience more severe forms of abuse (Gelles, 1992); in adolescence, the risk increases for females (Willis et al., 1992).

b. Sexual Abuse: Sexual abuse involves the initiation of an interaction with a child by an adult or older child for the purpose of sexually gratifying or stimulating the adult or older child or another person; sexual abuse may involve genital fondling, molestation, rape, incest, sexual exploitation, exhibitionism, pedophilia, etc. Examples of child **sexual exploitation** include online enticement of children for sexual acts, child prostitution, child sex tourism, and the possession, manufacture, and distribution of child pornography.

- The majority of known victims of sexual abuse are female, but studies suggest that boys are sexually abused much more often than reports have indicated.

- The majority of victims are assaulted by someone they know and trust (e.g., a parent, parent surrogate, other relative, friend).

- Only a small minority of sexual abusers use physical violence; instead, most use bribes, threats, and other forms of coercion and/or the existing relationship with the child to gain the child's cooperation.

- Most known child sexual abusers are men, and most perpetrators report being heterosexual in their adult sexual orientation (this is true even for those who sexually abuse children of their own gender). Female perpetrators are more likely to abuse boys and, compared to male perpetrators, are less likely to use coercion to gain the child's cooperation and more likely to rely on emotional manipulation (Meiselman, 1990).

- Incest occurs in all social classes and is not found disproportionately in any particular ethnic or cultural group and the vast majority of incest victims are female.

- *Father/stepfather-daughter incest:* (a) Stepfathers are more likely than biological fathers to sexually abuse a daughter. (b) Often the victim of father/stepfather-daughter incest is the oldest female child in the household, and her vulnerability may be higher when she has taken on the household duties of her mother or emerged as the central female figure in the family (Meiselman, 1990). (c) Most incestuous relationships are triggered by the abuser's nonsexual needs (e.g., for affection, power, belongingness), and many incest episodes occur when the abuser is under the influence of alcohol. (d) Mothers may or may not be aware of the father/stepfather-daughter incest, and those who are aware may not take action because they fear losing emotional and material support from their husbands. (e) The family environment is often chaotic and emotionally impoverished and there is commonly marital discord and spousal overdependence. Family relationships often are characterized by role reversal, role confusion, and enmeshed boundaries between family members (Trepper & Barrett, 1986), and family isolation is extremely common. In addition, family members may fear abandonment and family disintegration.

c. Emotional Maltreatment: Emotional maltreatment (a.k.a. emotional abuse or neglect, psychological maltreatment) involves a failure to provide for the appropriate emotional development of a child resulting in psychological damage to the child. It may consist of acts of commission or omission. Emotional maltreatment includes verbal or emotional assault (e.g., frequent belittling or other rejection of the child, terrorizing the child); isolation or close confinement (e.g., locking the child in a closet for a long period of time, separating the child from social contact); attempted physical assault; exploiting or corrupting the child; withholding necessities from the child as a form punishment; and withholding emotional responsiveness from the child.

d. Physical Neglect: Any acts of commission or omission that put a child in danger constitute **child endangerment** (e.g., driving without a car seat for one's baby), and physical neglect is the most common type of child endangerment. Physical neglect involves a parent's or other caregiver's persistent lack of attention to the child's basic physical needs (e.g., food, shelter, clothing, supervision, health care). Types of neglect include abandonment/lack of supervision; nutritional neglect; hygiene neglect; medical neglect; shelter neglect (e.g., no heat in the child's room); educational neglect (e.g., parent allows chronic truancy); and some cases of failure to thrive (signs of chronic undernutrition).

2. Factors Consistently Linked With Child Maltreatment:

a. Child Factors: Characteristics of the child that are associated with a high risk for abuse include prematurity and low birth-weight; difficult temperament (e.g., nonresponsivity, irritability, hyperactivity); poor health; and younger age (children under age 3 are at highest risk for physical abuse). Overall, children who are perceived as "different," such as those with a difficult temperament or a disability, are at increased risk for both abuse and neglect (Goldman et al., 2003).

b. Parent Factors:

History of childhood deprivation: (a) The childhood deprivation experienced by the parent may consist of separation, divorce, or death of a parent, an alcohol- or other drug-addicted parent, inappropriate discipline, abuse, neglect, and/or abandonment. (b) Many abusive parents were themselves abused as children. Some experts suggest, however, that psychological, not necessarily physical, abuse during childhood predisposes parents to physically abuse their own children.

Personality and behavioral deficits: (a) Personality and behavioral characteristics frequently found in parents who are physically abusive or neglectful include low self-esteem, an external locus of control (i.e., belief that events are determined by chance or outside forces beyond one's personal control), poor impulse control, depression, anxiety, and antisocial behavior (Goldman et al., 2003). (b) Although some maltreating parents or caregivers experience behavioral and emotional difficulties, most do *not* have severe mental disorders (Goldman et al., 2003). (c) Abusive parents often not only isolate themselves, but also discourage or prevent their children from interacting with people outside the home.

Deficits in knowledge: (a) Abusive parents usually lack adequate knowledge about normal child development and appropriate child-rearing techniques (e.g., they believe a child should be toilet trained by age 12 months, they have an "immature" understanding of what is needed to take care of children and a limited repertoire of parenting skills). (b) Abusive parents usually have a low tolerance for normal infant behaviors and misinterpret their children's behaviors in negative ways. (c) Overall, abusive parents have been found to be less affectionate, supportive, playful, stimulating, and responsive toward their children (Trickett & Susman, 1988) and to be more hostile, controlling, and interfering, even with infants (Crittenden, 1985). (d) While physical punishment is used by both abusive and nonabusive parents, abusive parents are more likely to rely on severe forms of physical punishment, coercion, and threats and less likely to use reasoning and affection to control behavior (Milner & Chilamkurti, 1991).

c. Family Factors: Family factors consistently linked with child maltreatment include abnormalities in family interactions (e.g., absence of appropriate physical contact or eye contact, lack of communication or communication that reflects chronic anger and hostility) and abnormalities in family support (e.g., tendency to emphasize negative characteristics, lack of empathy, lack of concern for the children's safety). In addition, children living with single parents may be at higher risk of experiencing physical and sexual abuse and neglect than children living with two biological parents (Goldman et al., 2003).

d. Environment Factors: Abusive families have been found to experience more stress than nonabusive families, but the nature of the relationship between stress and abuse is unclear. According to some experts, it may be that stress exacerbates existing problems or taxes the family's usual coping resources (National Research Council, 1993b). Other families may have inadequate methods for dealing with stress. Stress may be the result of chronic stressors (e.g., alcoholism, long-term illness, poverty), situational stressors (e.g., job loss), or both. Additionally, there may be unsafe living conditions in the home (inadequate safety, food, heat, light, etc.).

3. Effects of Abuse on the Child: Child abuse has physical, emotional, cognitive, and social consequences for its victims.

- Early maltreatment often results in an insecure attachment to the primary caregiver and subsequent difficulties in developing an autonomous self and self-esteem (e.g., there may be "compulsive compliance").

- Many abused children exhibit abnormalities in behavioral and emotional self-regulation. These may consist of externalizing problems (hyperactivity, aggression, sexualized behaviors, etc.) and/or internalizing problems (depression, anxiety, posttraumatic stress disorder, withdrawal, low self-esteem, suicidality, etc.). Other common consequences include delays in cognitive development; poor school achievement; problems in relationships with peers, teachers, and other adults; pervasive mistrust; learned helplessness; self-destructive behaviors; and drug or alcohol abuse. Victims of sexual abuse may also have low "sexual self-esteem," sexual dysfunction, and psychosomatic illnesses and may participate in prostitution or pornography. Severe child abuse, especially sexual abuse, can result in dissociation both during the abuse and afterwards. **Dissociation** causes a separation of psychological processes (i.e., thoughts, memories, sense of identity) that are normally related. In the context of abuse or other trauma, it may allow the mind to distance itself from an experience that is too painful or frightening to process.

- Certain variables may moderate the effects of abuse or neglect on a child so that not all children are affected in the same way. Important moderator variables include the frequency and duration of the abuse, the child's age and stage of development, the child's basic temperament and premaltreatment adjustment, and the family's and parents' functioning before the maltreatment (Pearce & Pezzot-Pearce, 1997).

- For childhood sexual abuse, the negative effects appear to be less severe when the child is not blamed for the abuse, the child gets protection and support from the family, the child was emotionally stable before the abuse, the family is basically well-functioning, and the consequences of disclosure/discovery for the family are minor (e.g., disclosure doesn't result in incarceration of the abusive family member) (Mayhall & Norgard, 1983). The studies also suggest that the effects of sexual abuse tend to be less severe when the abuse was committed by a stranger rather than by a family member or other familiar person.

4. Infant Abuse: Evidence of abuse of infants includes skull fractures, broken bones, bruising, and burns.

a. Head Trauma: Head trauma is a common injury to babies, and infants most at risk for this kind of injury are those who are difficult to comfort and who cry uncontrollably (Mrazek, 1993). One cause of head trauma is **shaken infant syndrome** (or shaken baby syndrome), which can occur if someone shakes a baby too hard. This form of abuse usually does not produce external signs of injury; instead, the baby usually suffers bleeding of the brain and retinal hemorrhage, which can lead to permanent neurological damage, seizure disorders, blindness, deafness, and, sometimes, death. Symptoms of shaken baby syndrome include lethargy, crying, vomiting, loss of appetite, and seizures.

Parents at risk of physically harming their infants in this way require information on appropriate ways of dealing with a crying baby, education that the baby's behavior is not intentional, and assistance in learning how to appropriately modulate the level of stimulation the baby receives. They may also need assistance in learning how to handle stress in their lives and in finding adequate resources and social support.

b. Munchausen's Syndrome by Proxy: In **Munchausen's syndrome by proxy** (called "factitious disorder imposed on another" in the DSM-5), a caregiver (usually the mother) induces symptoms of illness in the child. For example, apnea (episodes where breathing stops) in a baby may be the result of efforts by the mother to induce the problem by smothering the infant and then seeking help to revive her. Although it's impossible to distinguish SIDS death from death by suffocation through autopsy, abuse is generally suspected when there is a history of apnea in the presence of one particular caregiver, when the death occurred at an age older than 6 months, and when there have been unexplained deaths of one or more of the child's siblings.

5. Indicators of Child Maltreatment: Identifying child abuse and neglect can be difficult for many reasons including the victim's unwillingness or inability to disclose the abuse and the perpetrator's unwillingness to acknowledge it. Thus, social workers need to be familiar with specific physical and behavioral indicators that suggest the possibility of child maltreatment (e.g., Mayhall & Norgard, 1983). These indicators should be used in conjunction with supporting evidence, such as information from family members and medical records (e.g., a suspicious health history, history of poor medical care), to determine whether abuse or neglect has taken place.

a. Indicators of Physical Abuse:

Child's physical condition: (a) Has unexplained bruises, welts, human bite marks, fractures, or lacerations, often in various stages of healing; has burns (i.e., cigarette, cigar, or rope burns; "wet" burns indicating submersion; or "dry" burns with a clearly-defined mark left by the object used). (b) Has unexplained abdominal injuries such as swelling and localized tenderness; frequently vomits. (c) Has unexplained hair loss (due to hair pulling). (d) Has developmental lags in gross or fine motor coordination, language, height, and weight. (e) Wears clothing to hide injuries (e.g., long sleeves in hot weather to hide injuries on arms).

Child's behavior: (a) Is wary of physical contact with parents or other adults; displays a lack of trust in adults (e.g., is apprehensive when an adult approaches a crying child); fears going home. (b) Exhibits extremes in behavior (e.g., extreme aggressiveness, withdrawal, compliance, negativity, hyperactivity, excessive fears, self-destructive behaviors). (c) Is clingy and indiscriminate in her attachments. (d) Displays hypervigilance or "frozen watchfulness" (constant scanning of the environment accompanied by facial immobility and a lack of eye contact). (e) Has a history of acting-out behaviors, school-related problems, running away, alcohol or other drug use, depression, and/or suicidal behavior. (f) Avoids physical activity (usually due to physical soreness). (g) Attributes her injuries to an unlikely cause or states that an injury was inflicted by her parent or other caregiver.

Parent/caregiver behavior: (a) Appears unconcerned about the child's condition. (b) Provides obviously false (or no) explanation for the child's injuries; attempts to conceal the child's injuries or the identity of the responsible person. (c) Has a history of "hospital shopping" (seeking treatment at different facilities to avoid detection). (d) Uses harsh discipline that is inappropriate for the child's age and/or misbehavior. (e) Has a distorted view of the child (e.g., as "bad" or "evil") and/or unrealistic expectations of her (e.g., role-reversal). (f) Is emotionally immature and has poor impulse control. (g) Is socially isolated. (h) Abuses alcohol or other drugs. (i) Describes being abused as a child.

b. *Indicators of Sexual Abuse:*

Child's physical condition: (a) Has genital or perineal trauma and/or venereal disease; is pregnant (especially in early adolescence). (b) Displays sleep disturbances, encopresis or enuresis, abdominal pain, appetite disturbances and corresponding weight change.

Child's behavior: (a) Exhibits a sudden, unexplained change in behavior (e.g., anxiety, depression, hysteria). (b) Displays fear states, night terrors (especially in children under age 5). (c) Displays regressive behaviors, withdraws into a fantasy world; persistently urinates or defecates in her clothes. (d) Engages in antisocial behaviors (e.g., rebelliousness, truancy, running away). (e) Has overly sophisticated knowledge about sex; is promiscuous or overly sexualized; engages in inappropriate sexual play with other children, toys, or herself; engages in excessive masturbation that has a driven quality; has an unusual interest in or preoccupation with sexual matters; gives hints about sexual activity through behaviors or statements that are inappropriate to her age or developmental level; engages in sexually suggestive behavior with adults or older children. (f) Is socially isolated; has poor peer relationships. (g) Is unwilling to participate in physical activities. (h) Has attempted suicide. (i) Has a psychosomatic illness. (j) Abuses alcohol or other drugs. (k) Displays a fear of adults. (l) States that she has been sexually assaulted.

Parent/caregiver behavior: (a) Is extremely jealous, protective, or disinterested in the child. (b) Has a distorted perception of the child's role in the family. (c) Has extremely low self-esteem. (d) Has inadequate coping skills. (e) Describes marital difficulties that cause one parent to seek physical affection from the child. (f) Describes a home situation in which one parent is often at home alone with the child. (g) Lacks social and emotional contacts outside the family. (h) Abuses alcohol or other drugs. (i) Describes being sexually abused as a child.

c. *Indicators of Emotional Maltreatment:*

Child's physical condition: Exhibits abnormalities in motor, speech, social, or intellectual development.

Child's behavior: (a) Has a habit disorder (e.g., thumb-sucking, nail biting, enuresis, rocking). (b) Has a conduct disorder (e.g., antisocial behavior). (c) Displays neurotic traits and/or psychoneurotic reactions. (d) Exhibits extremes in behavior (e.g., extreme aggressiveness, passivity). (e) Displays pseudomaturity or regressive (infantile) behaviors. (f) Consistently makes derogatory remarks about her own behavior (e.g., "I never do anything right"). (g) Is overly concerned about conforming to the instructions of parents or other adults. (h) Has attempted suicide.

Parent/caregiver behavior: (a) Blames, ridicules, and denigrates the child; is cold and rejecting; withholds love from the child. (b) Has inappropriate explanations for the child's behaviors; is disinterested in the child's problems. (c) Treats children in the family unequally. (d) Abuses alcohol or other drugs. (e) Describes being abused or neglected as a child.

d. *Indicators of Physical Neglect:*

Child's physical condition: (a) Is constantly hungry; has signs of malnutrition (e.g., pallor, low weight relative to height, constant fatigue, lack of normal strength). (b) Has unattended physical problems (e.g., untreated wounds). (c) Has poor hygiene.

Child's behavior: (a) Steals or begs for food. (b) Often falls asleep during school, therapy, or other activities; has infrequent attendance at school. (c) Abuses alcohol or other drugs. (d) Has a history of delinquent behaviors (vandalism, theft) and/or suicide attempts. (e) States that there is no one to care for her.

Parent/caregiver behavior: (a) Is disinterested in the child. (b) Has low motivation to make changes in his or her life; expresses futility. (c) Describes chaotic or unsafe conditions at home. (d) Has a long-term chronic illness. (e) Has signs of mental illness or below-average intelligence. (f) Abuses alcohol or other drugs. (g) Describes being neglected as a child.

Assessment of Child Abuse and Neglect

1. Special Assessment Issues: The assessment of suspected child abuse and neglect requires attention to some issues that are not always a significant part of assessment (Kelly, 1983; Lauer et al., 1979). Important examples of these issues are described below.

a. Confidentiality and Reporting: You should inform family members of your legal responsibility with regard to child abuse reporting. In addition, when the family has been referred by an outside agency, you must clarify your relationship with the agency and its effects on the confidentiality of information provided by family members. (A social worker's child abuse reporting obligations are reviewed in Section I of Professional Relationships, Values, and Ethics.)

b. Involuntary Participation: Families with child abuse or neglect problems are frequently involuntary clients – in other words, their assessment is often the result of referral by a child protective services agency or court. As a result, some or all family members may be hostile, defensive, manipulative, and/or unwilling to communicate with you or keep appointments.

c. Characteristics That Interfere With Assessment: Whether they are involuntary or voluntary clients, families with child abuse or neglect problems are likely to have characteristics that diminish their ability to communicate effectively which can interfere with assessment and treatment. These characteristics may include difficulties in forming interpersonal relationships, poor social skills, a distrust of authorities, low self-esteem, difficulties in seeking and accepting help from others, a lack of interest in helping their children, and an inability to recognize that their behaviors are unacceptable.

d. Difficulties in Obtaining Information About Behaviors of Interest: The behaviors of interest in child abuse and neglect cases are both private (usually unobservable in the office or agency setting) and socially undesirable. Because the behaviors are private, you must rely on descriptions provided by family members and other involved parties. Because the behaviors are socially undesirable, family members and other involved parties are often unwilling to accurately describe them.

e. Assessment of Factors of Interest to a Child Protective Services Agency or Court: When you are making an assessment at the request of a child protective services agency or court, you must include an evaluation of those factors of interest to the agency or court. Such factors often include the risk of leaving the child at home and potential negative effects of separating the child from her family.

2. Understanding the Indicators of Child Maltreatment:

a. Physical Abuse: The following questions can facilitate your ability to determine if a child's physical injuries are the result of abuse or, instead, an accident (Reyes, 1979; Lauer et al., 1979): (a) Do the parents respond to your questions about their child with an attitude of cooperation or one of hostility? (b) Are the parents generally concerned about their child's injuries or do they appear unconcerned? (c) Are the injuries consistent with the explanation given by the child and/or the parents? (d) Are there discrepancies in the explanations given by different family members? (e) Are the injuries consistent with the child's age, size, and developmental stage? (f) Is the pattern of injury one that is suggestive of physical abuse (e.g., bruises made by an object such as a belt buckle or coat hanger)? (g) What are the parents' expectations concerning the child's behavior and development? Are their expectations appropriate for the child's age? (h) What are the parents' attitudes toward the use of physical punishment? Do they use excessive or inappropriate forms of punishment? (i) How do the parents ordinarily cope with stress? Do they lose control easily?

b. Emotional Maltreatment: Emotional maltreatment is more difficult to identify than physical abuse or physical neglect because its consequences tend to be more subtle and its symptoms often resemble those of emotional disturbances unrelated to emotional abuse or neglect. Answering the following questions can help you establish whether a child's behaviors are the result of emotional maltreatment: (a) What are the parents' personal capacities? What is the status each parent's physical health, emotional health, and intellectual functioning? (b) What are the parents' beliefs about the parent-child relationship (e.g., about methods of punishment)? (c) Do the parents ignore the child's problems or blame them on the child? (d) Are the parents concerned about the child's problems and finding solutions to them or do they seem unconcerned?

Lauer et al. (1979) suggest that the following criteria can also help you distinguish emotional maltreatment from ineffective parenting or other non-maltreatment: (a) Emotional maltreatment consists of a *pattern* of behavior by the parent(s) that has an adverse effect on the child (i.e., it causes emotional injury); (b) when there is emotional maltreatment, its effects can be clearly observed in the child's behavior or performance; (c) the effects of emotional maltreatment are longstanding; and (d) the effects of emotional maltreatment result in a "handicap" for the child (i.e., they cause significant impairment in her ability to learn, think, enter into relationships with other people, etc.).

c. Physical Neglect: Answering the following questions can help clarify whether physical and behavioral indicators displayed by a child and/or parent reflect physical neglect: (a) What are the prevailing cultural expectations and values with regard to child care and child-rearing techniques? Are the parents' child-rearing practices considered "normal" by the culture to which they belong? (b) Is the lack of care for the child due to poverty or a lack of other resources or is it due to intentional deprivation? (c) Is the lack of care episodic or chronic? Does neglect occur only when a family member is absent or ill or is it consistent over time?

3. Cultural Considerations: To successfully help all clients in need of intervention for child abuse and neglect problems, social workers must be sensitive to diversity issues related to child maltreatment. Although the social norms of most cultures dictate that parents have a duty to care and provide for their children, the actual performance of these duties varies widely along cultural and ethnic lines. For this reason, **ethnocentrism**, or the belief that one's own values and practices are universally accepted as correct, has important implications for the assessment and treatment of families with child abuse and neglect problems. While you must adhere to the requirements of your state's child abuse reporting law, you should also to take into consideration appropriate differences in child-rearing practices, especially when working with families from cultures that differ from your own.

4. A Family in Crisis: For a family with child abuse problems, a crisis could be triggered by an incident of child maltreatment, its discovery, the filing of a suspected child abuse report, the removal of the child from the family home, or the incarceration of the offending parent. If the family is in crisis, your interventions may include the following: (a) Reduce the possibility of future crises by helping family members identify, acquire, and use alternative coping strategies. (b) Build self-esteem. Express appropriate confidence in the parent(s)' ability to act in a responsible way. Make validating statements to reinforce positive behaviors (e.g., "It's good that you told me about what happened"). (c) Use direct influence. Advocate specific actions and mobilize support systems.

5. Interview Techniques: Whenever possible, you should conduct separate assessment interviews with the family, the parent(s), and the maltreated child. Seeing the family together in an interview allows you to observe parent-child interactions.

a. Interviewing the Maltreated Child: Specific techniques that can facilitate interviews with abused or neglected children include the following (Broadhurst et al., 1979; Lauer et al., 1979):

- Provide a comfortable, safe environment.
- Provide the child with structure and orient her to the assessment (e.g., begin with "safe" questions about topics other than the maltreatment and build rapport).
- Gain the child's trust (e.g., display a calm attitude and avoid "overinforming" child).
- Attend carefully to the child's emotional needs (e.g., gauge the child's anxiety about discussing the abuse and adopt a gradual approach).
- Avoid confusing the child (e.g., use language the child can understand; provide stimuli that will help her describe what has happened, such as dolls, crayons, and paper; and avoid suggesting answers to the child).
- Avoid placing the child on the defensive (e.g., avoid conveying value judgments, avoid over- or under-reacting to the child's story, and never encourage the child to "take sides" with any family member).
- Treat the child with respect (e.g., don't "talk down" to the child and respond honestly to her questions).
- Alleviate the child's feelings of guilt (e.g., reassure the child that she is not responsible for the abuse and reinforce her decision to discuss family matters with you and/or to disclose the abuse.

Following the interview, make an effort to validate the child's story. Seek confirming information from other sources. For cases of suspected sexual abuse, establish whether the child's experience conforms to the pattern of most child sexual abuse cases.

b. Assessment for Sexual Abuse: A topic of controversy is the use of **anatomically correct dolls**. Speaking for the Professional Society on the Abuse of Children, Mann (1994) cites five acceptable uses of these dolls: (a) to help initiate discussions with children about sexual matters; (b) as anatomical models to assess a child's knowledge of bodily functions; (c) to help children demonstrate their experiences, which is particularly important when a child's verbal skills are limited or when the child is too embarrassed to describe what happened; (d) as a stimulus for the child's memories; and (e) to provide children with opportunities to spontaneously disclose aspects of the abuse.

Although a number of authorities have criticized the use of anatomically correct dolls on the basis of a lack of reliability and validity, Vizard's (1991) review of the research suggests that children who have been sexually abused are, in fact, more likely than non-abused children to demonstrate sexual activity when presented with the dolls and that their use does not cause young children to act more suggestively than they would with other dolls.

c. Interviewing Maltreating Parents: The following techniques can facilitate information gathering during interviews with parents who are known, or believed, to abuse or neglect their children:

- Gain the parent(s)' trust. For example, be honest, straightforward, and professional, discuss the limits to confidentiality at the start of the interview, be willing to listen to the parents' points of view, and, when appropriate, let the parents know if and when you are going to make a report.

- Use sustainment procedures to alleviate anxiety, guilt, and tension. Express appropriate confidence in the parent(s)' ability to act in a responsible way. Validate positive behaviors. Convey a willingness to help alleviate stress and change the situation.

- Avoid interpretations and accusations. Focus on what has been said and what is directly observable.

- Use open-ended questions to minimize defensiveness and hostility (e.g., "How did your child bruise her arm?" rather than "Did you hit your child?").

- Pay attention to nonverbal signs of anxiety, hostility, withdrawal, etc.

- Maintain a neutral attitude. Avoid words, gestures, and facial expressions that suggest disapproval or shock.

- Avoid condoning abusive behaviors (e.g., say "I see that you were very angry" rather than "Anyone would have felt the same way in that situation").

- Clarify events that precipitated the most recent crisis.

d. Interviewing Non-Perpetrating Parents: When interviewing parents of children who've been abused by someone else, you often need to provide specific information to allay their concerns or fears. The parents may be defensive about their role in their child's difficulties and/or believe that your role is to determine their fitness as parents or perform a legal investigation of the allegation of abuse. You should clear up any misunderstandings the parents have. An important focus of your interview will be on assessing the parents' reactions to the abuse their child experienced, including their responses to the child herself following the abuse. The child should not be present while the parents are discussing these reactions or their own histories.

B. Spousal/Partner Abuse

Because, in heterosexual relationships, the male is more often the perpetrator in cases of spousal/partner abuse (i.e., intimate partner violence), the research has focused on the "battering husband/boyfriend" and the "battered wife/girlfriend," and our review reflects this emphasis.

Dynamics and Indicators of Spousal/Partner Abuse

Types of spousal/partner abuse include (a) physical (e.g., threats of bodily harm, slapping, punching, shoving, stabbing, etc.); (b) sexual (forced sexual activity, often in conjunction with physical and/or psychological abuse); and (c) psychological (e.g., harassment, intimidation, destruction of valued possessions, efforts to control the woman's life).

1. Factors Associated With Spousal/Partner Abuse: The battering of women occurs across all demographic groups, although people in the lower classes are more likely to come to the attention of the authorities. In addition, spousal/partner abuse is more likely to occur when the male's educational and occupational status are lower than those of his partner. Stress factors that commonly precede incidents of abuse include geographical and social isolation, financial difficulties, chronic medical problems, and pregnancy.

2. Characteristics of Batterers: Psychological and behavioral characteristics that are common in husbands/boyfriends who abuse their wives/girlfriends include the following: (a) sexual jealously, emotional dependency on his partner, and extreme possessiveness (e.g., he attempts to control his partner through physical violence when he fears losing her); (b) poor impulse control; (c) higher-than-normal hostility; (d) low self-esteem (although he may act "macho"); (e) severe reactions to stress; (f) adherence to the doctrine of "male supremacy" and to stereotypic masculine and feminine family roles; (g) a tendency to blame others for his actions and to believe that he has done nothing wrong (i.e., he doesn't consider himself to be a "batterer"); and (h) a tendency to resolve emotions and problems through violence.

Also, many batterers have a personality disorder (often antisocial, narcissistic, and/or borderline) and/or substance use disorder (i.e., batterers are more likely than nonbatterers to have alcohol use disorder). Alcohol is only a disinhibitor, however – it does not "cause" abuse. Last, many batterers experienced or witnessed childhood violence (many were abused as children), and some also abuse their own children.

3. The Cycle of Violence: Walker (1984) has identified a three-stage cycle of violence that seems to describe about two-thirds of abusive spousal/partner relationships. As this cycle repeats over time, the frequency and intensity of the violence and psychological manipulation tend to escalate.

Tension building: The tension-building stage begins after a long period during which the batterer has shown unusually loving behavior toward the woman; during this period, the woman commits to a relationship with the man. (If there has been a prior battering incident, the period of loving behavior is shorter, but has a similar effect: The woman decides to stay in the relationship.) At some point after this, the tension begins. Usually, the woman recognizes that something has changed and tries different strategies to reduce the tension (e.g., she may give in to all of her partner's demands). Because these strategies have some effect on the escalation of abuse, they reinforce the woman's efforts to calm her partner, as well as her belief that she can somehow control his violent behaviors for him. These strategies, however, do not prevent an acute battering incident from happening at some time in the future.

Acute battering incident: The acute battering incident can last from a few minutes to a few hours or days, and serves to discharge the batterer's tension. The nature of abuse during a battering incident ranges in intensity from relatively "mild" forms of violence, such as slapping, name calling, and throwing objects, to more serious violence, such as punching and kicking, to extreme violence, such as choking, clubbing, and the use of a weapon.

Loving contrition ("honeymoon"): In the loving contrition stage, there is an absence of tension: The batterer is loving and profusely apologetic (although his apologies often include self-serving excuses and explanations for his behavior) and assures the woman that the abuse will never happen again. This stage can last from a few hours to several months.

4. Why Battered Women Say They Stay in the Relationship: Contrary to what is commonly believed, women who are battered do not, on the average, stay with their partners any longer than nonbattered women (Walker, 1981). Some studies indicate that women are most likely to say that they remain in an abusive relationship because they are afraid of evoking additional violence against themselves or others if they leave (Martin, 1982; Walker, 1984). The accuracy of this belief is supported by data showing that nearly three-quarters of reported battering incidents occur after separation. Other research indicates that women decide to stay with an abusive partner because they are unable to support themselves (economic hardship) and/or because they are committed to the relationship (Strube & Barbour, 1983).

Other reasons why women stay in an abusive relationship include the following: (a) conflicting emotions (e.g., holding on to hope that her partner will change); (b) shame or embarrassment; (c) depression and isolation from friends, relatives, and other supports; (d) cultural or religious pressure to keep the family intact no matter what; (e) custody worries (she fears she may lose custody of her children if she leaves); and (f) fear of being deported (i.e., immigrant women may stay in an abusive relationship because their partners have threatened to have them deported).

5. Indicators of Domestic Violence in the Battered Woman: Because a woman who is abused by her spouse or partner may be reluctant to acknowledge that abuse has occurred, social workers need to be familiar with common indicators of intimate partner violence, including the following:

Physical indicators: (a) Injuries at various stages of healing; (b) obviously false explanations for injuries; (c) making excuses for her injuries, such as being accident prone or clumsy; (d) bruises or injuries that look like they're caused by choking, punching, or being thrown down; and (e) attempting to hide bruises with makeup or clothing. Common injuries in abusive relationships include black eyes, red or purple marks at the neck, and sprained wrists.

Emotional/psychological indicators: (a) Chronic depression, anxiety, insomnia, or nightmares; (b) battered woman syndrome (a syndrome that is similar to PTSD); (c) low self-esteem (e.g., she's extremely apologetic, appears submissive, doesn't make eye contact); and (d) suicidal ideation and/or attempted suicide. In addition, substance abuse is more common in a person enduring domestic violence than in the general adult population. The abuse of alcohol, prescription drugs, and/or illicit drugs may happen as a result of the violent relationship rather than being the cause of the violence.

Other indicators: (a) Has few friends; (b) is isolated from relatives; (c) refers to her partner's temper, jealousy, or possessiveness but doesn't disclose abuse or its extent; (d) seems afraid or anxious to please her partner; (e) frequently misses work, school, or social occasions without explanation; and (f) has limited access to money, credit cards, or the car. In addition, there may be behavioral problems in the couple's children, such as enuresis, truancy, promiscuity, or delinquency (Weissberg, 1981).

6. Domestic Violence in Same-Gender Couples: Studies have found that domestic violence occurs at about the same rate in same-gender couples as it does in heterosexual couples, and that, for both populations, psychological abuse is the most common form of abuse (Rohrbaugh, 2006).

Important ways in which same-gender domestic violence differs from domestic violence in straight couples include the following (Center for American Progress, 2011):

- Victims of same-sex domestic violence may avoid reporting the abuse to police (or otherwise seeking help) because doing so would require them to reveal their sexual orientation or gender identity to strangers.

- Because victims of same-sex domestic violence are more likely to fight back, police and other law enforcement may fail to see the true dynamics of the relationship and attribute blame for the fighting to both partners.

- In same-sex relationships, the batterer may psychologically abuse his or her partner by threatening to expose the partner's sexual orientation to family, friends, and/or coworkers.

- Some victims of same-sex domestic violence worry that revealing the abuse to others might harm the gay community (e.g., some individuals or groups might use the information to support prejudicial beliefs about same-sex relationships). Victims may also be reluctant to take action that others might interpret as showing a lack of solidarity in the gay community.

- Some perpetrators of same-sex domestic violence threaten to take the couple's children if the victim reveals the abuse or leaves the relationship. In states in which same-sex partners can't adopt each other's children, a domestic violence victim without legal standing as a parent may keep the abuse a secret to avoid losing the children.

Assessment of Spousal/Partner Abuse

Important assessment procedures in cases of known or suspected spousal/partner abuse include the following:

- If both partners have come to your agency or office, interview the client and her abusive partner separately, unless you are certain that the likelihood of further abuse is low. Be aware that the batterer may try to prevent his partner from speaking to you outside of his presence.

- Explain confidentiality issues. This is especially important when the client (or couple) has been referred by the legal system (e.g., after arrest of the batterer).

- Identify the current level of danger in the relationship: (a) Evaluate the following types of danger: additional abuse (including the risk of being seriously injured or killed if the client has left her abuser); suicide; homicide (i.e., a client who has left her abuser and is in danger of being killed by him may end up killing him in self-defense); and, when relevant, risk to children living in the client's household. (b) You have *no* legal duty to report spousal/partner abuse to any authority or agency. You do, however, have an ethical duty to do what you can to help your client protect herself from further harm. For instance, if the client is at risk for further abuse, you should tell her about available resources, such as a shelter and the police, and help her develop an escape plan so that she can be safer from harm while making decisions about her life. Note that you should assess danger whether the client is still in an abusive relationship, has just recently left her abuser, or left him months or even years ago.

- Address minimization. Even if the client acknowledges to you that she has been abused, she may continue to minimize the seriousness of her situation. If the client is out of danger, allow her to move past the minimization at her own pace. If the client clearly is in danger, but insists that she isn't, you can label her as "battered" and explain the cycle of violence in an effort to offset her minimization and encourage her to consider taking steps to better protect herself from further abuse.

- Ask specific questions to gather details regarding the most recent battering incident and carefully document the information, including evidence of physical injuries. In gathering this information, be sensitive to each partner's difficulty in describing the acute battering incident.

- Assess the batterer for a substance use disorder.

- The batterer is likely to focus on what his partner did to deserve the abuse. If so, confront his rationalization by emphasizing that, no matter what his partner did, his violent response had severe consequences.

C. Elder Abuse

Elder abuse refers to any maltreatment of an older adult, including intentional or unintentional abuse or neglect, and may take the form of physical, emotional, or financial mistreatment that results in pain, suffering, or loss for the victim. About 90 percent of elder abuse is perpetrated by family members or relatives, usually the spouse or adult child of the victim (Administration on Aging, 2004). Victims are most commonly females and those over age 80 (National Center on Elder Abuse, 2004).

The National Center on Elder Abuse (NCEA), which is directed by the U.S. Administration on Aging, is a useful resource for social workers and families needing information and assistance when dealing with cases of elder abuse. (For information on laws relevant to elder abuse, see Section I of Professional Relationships, Values, and Ethics.)

1. Causes of Elder Abuse: Two common causes of elder abuse are caregiver stress and caregiver impairment (Brownell & Wolden, 2002).

Caregiver stress can result in abuse when a caregiver becomes overwhelmed by the demands of caring for a dependent older person and is then physically abusive in a moment of anger or begins to neglect the older person's needs. Wolf (2000) believes that other risk factors also contribute to most cases of elder abuse caused by caregiver stress: These factors include the relationship between the perpetrator and older person, the perpetrator's mental state, the lack of alternative caregivers, and the inadequacy of available services. **Caregiver impairment** refers to a caregiver's mental illness, personality disorder, or substance abuse, and may be associated with more serious and more frequent episodes of elder abuse.

2. Risk Factors and Signs of Elder Abuse: Key risk factors and signs of elder abuse include the following: (a) mental illness or drug or alcohol abuse in a family member; (b) stressful life events for the family (e.g., financial problems, divorce); (c) cognitive impairment of the older person (she is more likely to be neglected); (d) physical impairment of the older person or her dependency on others for her physical needs (she is more likely to be abused); (e) social isolation of the older person; (f) poor hygiene, malnourishment, and obvious lack of care of the older person; (g) the older person appears hypervigilant or nervous; and (h) the caregiver displays hostility and impatience toward the older person (McInnes-Dittrich, 2005).

3. Self-Neglect: Elder abuse and neglect must be distinguished from self-neglect which may occur when an older adult living alone is incapable of caring for herself and, therefore, is malnourished, dehydrated, unclean, sick, or living in a dirty or unsafe environment. Self-neglect is usually associated with a major neurocognitive disorder (i.e., dementia) or other mental illness and circumstances in which an older person has no family member living nearby who is willing and able to assist in caring for her.

4. Assessment of Elder Abuse: The techniques used to facilitate interviews with parents who abuse or neglect their children (see above) also apply to interviews with families with known or suspected problems with elder abuse or neglect. In summary, you should use sustainment procedures to alleviate anxiety, guilt, and tension; focus on what has been said and what is directly observable; use open-ended questions; pay attention to nonverbal signs of anxiety, hostility, withdrawal, etc.; maintain a neutral attitude; avoid condoning abusive behaviors; and clarify events that precipitated the most recent crisis.

In addition, if the family is not currently involved with an elder protective services agency, you should advocate specific action and mobilize support systems for the family (e.g., self-help groups, hotlines, respite care, social and health care agencies to assist with care of the older person) and, as necessary, obtain medical attention for the abused or neglected elder.

X. Identifying the Needed Level of Care

When a client seeks treatment, you must determine the appropriate therapeutic environment for her based on her present level of functioning. From the most restrictive therapeutic environment to the least restrictive one, the **continuum of care** available for individuals needing mental health services includes inpatient hospitalization, partial hospitalization (a partial or day hospital program), group home or residential program, intensive outpatient program, home health care, and outpatient therapy.

The same problem may be managed and treated in any of these environments, but, in each setting, there is a different focus and intensity of treatment. For example, the commitment criteria for **inpatient hospitalization** require that a person exhibit a need for medical and/or mental health intervention in a safe environment 24 hours a day for a specified period of time. Generally, the person must be a danger to herself or others or be gravely disabled. A person is considered to be gravely disabled when she is unable to carry out basic activities of daily living (see below).

In contrast, with **partial hospitalization**, a client continues to live at home but commutes to a treatment facility up to seven days a week, where she receives individual therapy, group therapy, and/or medication monitoring. Partial hospitalization focuses on overall treatment of the client rather than on only safety and, therefore, is not appropriate for clients who are acutely suicidal or dangerous to others. Finally, in a typical **intensive outpatient program**, a client attends group therapy two to five times a week. She may also receive individual therapy, but treatment takes places primarily in the therapeutic group setting.

As a client improves, she may be moved from a more restrictive environment to a less restrictive one. Or, if a client's behavior or condition worsens, she may be moved to a more structured and intensive treatment setting. Throughout the course of intervention, a client has the right to as much freedom in treatment as her condition allows.

1. Functional Status and ADLs: Social workers and others refer to the ability or inability to perform **activities of daily living (ADLs)** as a measurement of a person's functional status. ADL criteria are particularly useful for clients who have physical disabilities, chronic diseases, or certain mental disorders (e.g., schizophrenia), and those who are very old.

Basic activities of daily living are those skills needed in typical daily self-care (e.g., bathing, dressing, feeding, toileting). **Instrumental activities of daily living** refer to skills beyond basic self-care that evaluate how individuals function in their homes, workplaces, and social environments. Examples of instrumental ADLs include typical domestic tasks such as cleaning, cooking, driving, and shopping, as well as other less physically demanding tasks such as operating electronic appliances and handling budgets. In the work environment, an ADL evaluation assesses the qualities necessary to perform one's job, such as strength, endurance, manual dexterity, and pain management.

A number of ADL indexes are available, including the Katz Index of Independence in Activities of Daily Living, the Revised Kenny Self-Care Evaluation, and the Barthel Index of Activities of Daily Living. These indexes typically evaluate an individual on her self-care skills and rate her according to how functional she is. Scoring is based on how independently the person can perform a task and whether she needs supervision or assistance in performing the task.

If a client is having difficulty performing ADLs, particularly basic ADLs, you should explore questions such as the following: What is the client's living situation and level of support needed? Are ADLs performed by the client or by a spouse, family member, or other caregiver? Is the client safe? Are others (such as children in the home) endangered? Does the client use community support services? Does she need additional support or residential services?

2. Treatment Settings for Different Levels of Functioning: The following guidelines are useful when selecting the treatment setting for your client based on her present level of functioning (Johnson, 1997).

a. Acute Psychiatric Symptoms and Difficulty Stabilizing: The initial goals of treatment are to provide a safe environment and protect the client and others.

> *Possible treatment settings/modalities:* Usually, inpatient treatment; sometimes, partial hospitalization or intensive outpatient care. At the selected level of care, treatment approaches may include individual therapy, group therapy, medication evaluation and monitoring, and case management.
>
> *Focus of treatment:* Monitoring of the patient, stabilization, and medication evaluation and monitoring.

b. Acute Psychiatric Symptoms: The initial goals of treatment are to provide a safe environment and rapid stabilization.

> *Possible treatment settings/modalities:* Partial hospitalization, intensive outpatient care, or increased outpatient therapy contact. At the selected level of care, treatment approaches may include individual therapy, group therapy, medication evaluation and monitoring, case management, and/or a support group.
>
> *Focus of treatment:* Stabilization, decreased symptomatology, and medication evaluation and monitoring.

c. Severe Psychiatric Symptoms: In the initial level of care, the client needs to be monitored and provided a safe environment.

> *Possible treatment settings/modalities:* Inpatient treatment if the client poses a danger to herself or others or is gravely disabled; otherwise, partial hospitalization, intensive outpatient care, or home health care may be appropriate. Conventional outpatient individual therapy can be initiated or reinitiated when the client is adequately stabilized.
>
> *Focus of treatment:* Stabilization, decreased symptomatology, medication evaluation and monitoring, and improved judgment, insight, and impulse control. All areas of the client's life and environment should be attended to.

d. Moderate Psychiatric Symptoms That Interfere With Adaptive Functioning and the Client Requires a Higher Level of Care Than Conventional Outpatient Therapy: The treatment goals in the initial level of care are to improve daily functioning and self-management.

> *Possible treatment settings/modalities:* Intensive outpatient individual therapy (i.e., more frequent contact with the client) plus case management, a therapeutic or educational group, and/or medication evaluation and monitoring.

Focus of treatment: Stabilization, symptom management, development of coping skills, and development and utilization of social supports.

e. *Mild to Moderate Psychiatric Symptoms That Interfere With Adaptive Functioning:*

Possible treatment settings/modalities: Outpatient treatment such as individual therapy, couples therapy, family therapy, and/or group therapy dealing with specific issues and/or long-term support.

Focus of treatment: Decrease symptomatology, increase self-care, and improve coping, problem solving, and management of life stressors.

f. *Adaptive Functioning With Minimal or No Psychiatric Symptoms:*

Possible treatment settings/modalities: Outpatient, such as an educational group, community support group, therapeutic group or class focused on developmental issues, and/or recommended reading.

Focus of treatment: Education, prevention, and increased self-efficacy, knowledge, understanding, problem solving, awareness of choices and alternatives, etc.

3. Discharge Planning: While most patients improve in controlled, intensive therapeutic settings where medical and mental health professionals are available around the clock to meet their needs, once discharged from such settings, many patients relapse, often because of noncompliance with the aftercare program. In many cases, these patients have chronic mental illnesses that diminish their capacity to cope with the pressures of daily life outside of a protected environment. Thus, proper discharge planning is critical for increasing the chances that these patients will be able to function once they are outside of the initial, intensive level of care.

The two main purposes of discharge planning are to (a) provide information to the treatment professionals who will be continuing the patient's care in the next level on the continuum of care and (b) develop a plan of follow-up care or aftercare that maximizes the patient's chances for treatment success.

According to the Centers for Medicare and Medicaid Services (CMS), a **discharge summary** should include the following information (Johnson & Johnson, 2003):

- The extent to which goals established in the patient's treatment plan have been met.
- A summary description ("recapitulation") of the patient's hospitalization.
- A summary of the circumstances and grounds for admission.
- A baseline of the patient's psychiatric, physical, and social functioning at the time of discharge.
- Evidence of the patient's/family's response to the treatment interventions.

Providing the treatment professionals at the new level of care with understanding and insight into what worked therapeutically for the patient at the prior level of care helps maintain continuity in the patient's care and contributes to a more favorable treatment outcome.

The discharge summary should also provide recommendations concerning **follow-up** or **aftercare**. The following information should be included (Johnson & Johnson, 2003):

- The services and supports that are appropriate to the patient's needs and that will be available and effective on the day of discharge.

- A complete description of arrangements with treatment providers and other community resources for the provision of follow-up services or aftercare (including information about prior written and verbal communications and other exchanges of information).

- A outline of the planned psychiatric and medical/physical treatments and any medication regimen.

- Specific appointment dates and names and addresses of service providers.

- A description of community housing/living arrangements.

- Economic/financial status or plan (e.g., SSI benefits).

- Recreational and leisure resources.

- A complete description of the involvement of family and significant others with the patient after discharge.

Finally, a discharge plan should also include a brief summary of the patient's status on discharge, including her psychiatric, physical, and functional condition, and a description of anticipated problems following discharge and suggested means for intervention to address these problems.

XI. Organizing Assessment Data and Formulating the Problem

Ideally assessment results in an understanding of a client's problem, motivation for change, inner strengths, and environmental resources, as well as a realistic assessment of her adaptive capabilities. Based on this understanding, you and the client then reach a mutually agreed on definition of the problem that represents both your thinking and the client's and is acceptable to both of you. The client's problem may include difficulties within the biophysical, psychological, and/or social dimensions of her life. When identifying the problem(s) to be worked on, you and the client must consider what is actually doable given the constraints of the case, setting, and any other limiting factors. For example, treatment must focus on behaviors and/or situations that can, in fact, be changed, and avoid including issues that are beyond anyone's control.

1. Organizing Assessment Data: Sheafor and Horejsi (2003) suggest that social workers use the "**4 Ps**" (Perlman, 1957), "**4 Rs**" (Doremus, 1976), or "**4 Ms**" as a tool for organizing available data about a client, assessing her behavior and functioning within a social context, and beginning to formulate a treatment plan.

a. The 4 Ps:

Problem: The nature of the problem or concern and its cause, intensity, frequency, and duration; how the client defines or describes it; how others who know the client define it; how you define it; whether the problem or situation can be changed; what aspects of the problem can feasibly be addressed; the nature and helpfulness of prior efforts by you/your agency and the client to deal with the problem; whether the problem or situation is an emergency that requires a rapid response; what the consequences would be if you or your agency did nothing for or with the client.

Person: How various dimensions of the client (e.g., physical, emotional, social, economic, spiritual) are related to or affected by the problem or situation; client strengths that can be used as a foundation on which to build an effective treatment plan; how the client's usual ways of thinking and behaving have become barriers to dealing effectively with the problem.

Place: What meaning the client assigns to her involvement with you or your agency (e.g., hopefulness, stigma, fear, humiliation); whether you or your agency can provide the services needed by the client (and if not, whether referral to another agency is likely to be effective); whether your agency's procedures, policies, or methods are contributing to the client's problem.

Process: The type of helping approach, method, or technique that the client is likely to find acceptable; the approach, method, or technique that is likely to be effective; how the requirements of the helping process (time, fees, scheduling, etc.) will affect the client's current roles and responsibilities.

b. *The 4 Rs:*

Roles: The roles and responsibilities the client has in her life (e.g., parent, spouse, employee); what others (e.g., family, employers) expect of the client; how satisfied the client is with her role performance.

Reactions: The client's reactions (e.g., physical, behavioral, emotional) to her problem and situation; how these reactions compare to her usual patterns; whether the client is in a state of crisis.

Relationships: What people are significant and meaningful parts of the client's life (e.g., family, peers, friends); how they are being affected by the client's problem or situation; how the behavior of significant others is contributing to the client's current problem.

Resources: Community resources (including informal resources) the client has used in the past to cope with similar problems; whether these resources are available now; new or additional resources needed by the client and whether they are available and the client is willing to use them; whether the client is eligible for or able to pay for needed services and programs.

c. *The 4 Ms:*

Motivation: What the client wants to do about her problem or situation; the extent to which discomfort, pressure from others, or other aversive factors are pushing the client toward action; the extent to which hope is pulling the client toward action; steps that can be taken to enhance the client's motivation.

Meanings: The meaning the client assigns to her problem and situation; ethnic, cultural, and religious beliefs and values that are important to the client and relevant to her current problem or situation.

Management: How you can best use your limited time, energy, and resources to help the client overcome her problem or change her situation; the overall plan or strategy that will guide your activity with the client; how work with the client will affect your other responsibilities.

Monitoring: How you will monitor your impact on the client and evaluate the effectiveness of the intervention; how peers, supervisors, or consultants can help to monitor and evaluate the intervention.

2. Formulating Problem Statements: Your formulation of the client's problem – the **problem statement** – will usually incorporate as many of the components on the following list as are relevant to the client's concerns and situation (Zuckerman, 1995):

- Presentation of the problem, including its nature, severity, history, and course, and (where relevant) the diagnosis. You will typically describe the following: (a) The presenting problem (what the client has described as her reason for coming in). (b) A list of the primary problems or concerns you have identified within the biophysical, psychological, and social domains of the client's life. These problems can be divided in the following way, as relevant to your findings: acute, short-term, and noncharacterological problems in one or more of those domains; chronic symptoms, behaviors, and issues, and characterological deficits and skills affecting one or more of those domains; and/or DSM-5 diagnosis. (c) A prognosis derived from an evaluation of multiple factors, such as symptom severity, social supports, compliance with past mental health and medical treatment, defensive style, psychological-mindedness, and motivation for treatment.

- Physical, psychological, and social factors that predispose the client to the problem (or disorder) or contribute to it.
- Stressors affecting the client (precipitants).
- The client's current level of physical, psychological, and social functioning.
- Client factors and factors in the environment (other individuals, organizations, and agencies) reinforcing and maintaining the problem.

3. Setting Priorities for Attention: Although many clients seen by social workers have multiple problems, it is usually ineffective to address more than three problems at one time (task-centered practitioners call this principle "the rule of three"). One reason for this is that treatment plans that attempt to address too many problems at once tend to lose focus and direction. Therefore, you and the client must identify the most significant problems on which to focus intervention before you can begin formulating the treatment plan. In many cases, a primary problem will emerge, and a few secondary problems may also be evident. Some other problems may also be present, but may have to be set aside if they are not urgent enough to require intervention right away.

The following criteria can be used to determine the priorities for attention from among a client's various problems and needs (Fine & Glasser, 1996; Sheafor & Horejsi, 2003). Problems and needs meeting one or more of these criteria tend to be the ones you should work on first, while all other problems can be left for later in the treatment process:

- The most immediate concern expressed by the client. In other words, what the client considers to be her most distressing problem or greatest or most urgent need.
- Problems that have the greatest impact on the client's situation (e.g., problems that cause the most worry or anxiety).
- Problems that, if not resolved, will have the most negative and extensive consequences for the client, significant others, or society.
- Problems that, if resolved, would have the most positive impact on the client.
- Problems that, if resolved, would make it easier to resolve other problems. In some cases, there may even be problems that must be dealt with before other problems can be handled (e.g., a truant teenager who is failing in school must go back to school before her performance can improve).
- Problems that are of greatest interest to the client. The client may be more motivated at this time to work on some problems and less motivated to work on others.
- Problems that can be worked on with only a moderate investment of time, energy, and other resources. By contrast, problems that would require an unusually significant investment of time, energy, or resources or that appear relatively unchangeable should usually be set aside until later.
- With an involuntary client, the most immediate concern expressed by the referral source.

The following is a typical process used to set priorities for attention with a client (Sheafor & Horejsi, 2003):

- Step 1 – you ask the client to list what she sees as her problems or concerns (i.e., what she wants to change).

- Step 2 – you offer your own recommendations, if any, and explain why these problems also need to be considered. Make sure to include any mandated problems (i.e., ones imposed on the client by a court, probation officer, child protection agency, or other legitimate authority).

- Step 3 – you and the client sort the problems identified by steps 1 and 2 into meaningful categories or combinations. It's a good idea to create groupings that allow you and the client to see how various problems are interrelated.

- Step 4 – the client reviews the resulting list of problems and selects the two or three problems that are of highest priority to her.

- Step 5 – you select the two or three problems you consider to be of highest priority.

- Step 6 – you and the client examine the problems identified by steps 4 and 5 according to the criteria for determining priorities for attention that we listed above.

- Step 7 – after examining each problem against these criteria, you and the client select the three problems of highest priority.

Remember that the principle of **self-determination** dictates that a client has the right to choose which of her problems will be addressed by the intervention. You can make recommendations, as mentioned above, but should allow the client to make the final decision, unless a problem is mandated. Additionally, a client's motivation to participate and cooperate in the treatment process and commit to personal change is likely to depend, in part, on the degree to which the treatment plan addresses what she considers to be her greatest needs. Even an involuntary client who has been mandated to see you should be given as much choice as possible. You or your agency might mandate one problem (i.e., the problem mandated by the court or other legitimate authority), but allow the client to choose the second or third.

Also keep in mind that a client's problems will almost always affect or involve her significant others (e.g., spouse, children, employer). If these individuals are overlooked when you and the client select the problems to be worked on or plan the intervention, they may unknowingly or even deliberately become obstacles to the client's efforts to change.

Assessment in Practice with Client Systems

Practice with Client Systems includes social work activities undertaken to improve the effectiveness and efficiency of service provision and bring about changes in policies, programs, or budgets. Most of the content related to these activities (e.g., policy management, implementing macro change, administration, community organizing) is reviewed in your chapter on Interventions with Clients/Client Systems. In the remaining section of this chapter, however, we describe the first steps of macro level intervention, which focus on evaluating a community or organizational problem and developing a working hypothesis of etiology about that problem. We've divided our review of indirect practice in this way in order to be consistent with the ASWB's examination content outline.

The Macro Change Process – A Brief Introduction

Macro-level intervention is intended to improve either the quality of life for clients or communities or the quality of work-life for employees at an organization to help them provide the best possible services to clients or communities.

1. Systems Involved in Macro Change: The major systems involved in the macro change process are described in detail in your chapter on Interventions with Clients/Client Systems, in Section XIX. In summary, these systems are the following:

- *Initiator system* – the person or group who first recognizes the existence of a community or organizational problem and calls attention to it.

- *Change agent system* – the *change agent* is the individual (i.e., social worker) who initiates the change process; and the *change agent system* includes the change agent and a core planning committee or task force that initially analyzes the problem, the population, and the "arena" (community or organization) where the change will take place.

- *Client system* – the individuals who will become either direct or indirect beneficiaries of the change (i.e., either a group of clients with similar characteristics or qualifications for receiving services or resources, or an organizational or community segment that will benefit from the macro-level intervention).

- *Support system* – other individuals and groups who may be willing to support a change effort if they are needed.

- *Controlling system* – the individual or group with the formally delegated authority and power to approve a proposed change and require its implementation.

- *Host and implementing systems* – a *host system* is the organization or unit with formally assigned responsibility for the area to be addressed by a proposed change; and the *implementing system* includes employees and/or volunteers within the host system who will have day-to-day responsibility for implementing the change.

- *Target system* – the individual, group, structure, policy, or practice that needs to be changed so that the primary beneficiaries of the change effort can receive its intended benefits (i.e., the system that is the target of intervention efforts).

- *Action system* – individuals from any or all of the other systems who have an active role in planning and implementing the intervention and seeing it through to completion.

2. Steps Involved in a Macro Change Episode: The major steps involved in an episode of macro change include the following:

Step 1: Analyze the problem, population, and arena.

Step 2: Develop a working hypothesis of etiology about the problem.

Step 3: Develop a working hypothesis of intervention based on relevant findings from the earlier steps and the working hypothesis of etiology.

Step 4: Select an approach to change (policy, program, project, practice, or personnel).

Step 5: Build support for the change.

Step 6: Estimate the probability of success.

Step 7: Decide whether to pursue the change effort.

Step 8: Select strategies and related tactics to get the change approved by relevant decision-makers and others.

Step 9: Plan the intervention.

Step 10: Prepare to implement the intervention.

Step 11: Monitor the intervention.

Step 12: Evaluate the effectiveness of the intervention.

In this chapter (Section XII), we review steps 1 and 2. Steps 3 through 12 – in which the intervention is planned, implemented, monitored, and evaluated – are discussed in the chapter on Interventions with Clients/Client Systems.

XII. Initiating Macro Change – Understanding the Problem, Population, and Arena

The focus when initiating an episode of community or organizational change is on analyzing and attempting to understand the problem, population, and arena that will be affected by the change. The following major activities are performed:

- organize the activities of the change agent system;
- analyze the problem, population, and arena; and
- develop a working hypothesis of etiology (Netting et al., 2004).

Note that, when undertaking an episode of community change, change agents select a target population and then seek to understand the community from the perspective of that population's concerns and needs; in other words, change agents don't attempt to understand the community as a whole. The **target population** consists of those who are experiencing the problem and for whose benefit the change is being considered.

Organize Activities of the Change Agent System

Organizing the change agent system requires effectively planning and coordinating the activities of those who are undertaking the initial analyses, including the change agent and a core planning team. Tasks include (a) assigning roles and responsibilities based on abilities, (b) monitoring progress, and (c) managing interpersonal, intergroup, and political dynamics.

Analyze the Problem, Population, and Arena

An episode of macro change may target an identified problem, need, or opportunity. For the sake of simplicity, we will usually refer to this phenomenon as a "problem."

1. Identify and Interview Those Affected By the Problem: Change agents interview individuals in the community or organization in order to (a) understand the development of the problem at the local level, (b) identify major participants and systems, (c) identify personal perspectives, (d) understand personal experiences in relation to the problem and efforts to deal with it, (e) understand how the problem is perceived by different groups within the community or organization, (f) establish boundaries for the proposed change, (g) identify key decision-makers and funding sources, and (h) understand different perspectives on the etiology of the problem.

a. Learn About the Problem: Change agents interview individuals in the community or organization who are knowledgeable about the problem. These informants may be individuals who (a) first identified the problem, (b) participated in prior efforts to resolve the problem, (c) support the change, (d) oppose the change (opponents should be encouraged to express their opinions), and/or (e) have the power to approve or reject the change. In an organization, the latter is usually the CEO or someone on the board of directors; in a community, the identity of decision-makers with this power depends on the domain targeted by the change effort.

Change agents use these interviews to learn about people's perspectives and experiences related to the problem, gather a history of significant events related to the problem, and explore what can be learned from past efforts to address it. Having historical information is important because the history of a problem affects the way individuals currently perceive it. Change agents also explore the extent to which different problems are interconnected and whether some problems need to be resolved before others can be addressed.

b. Learn About the Population: Change agents also interview members of the target population – people in the community or organization who have experienced the problem firsthand – to learn their perspectives and past experiences, including how target population members perceive their primary needs (i.e., they may perceive their primary needs as a need for resources or services, access to opportunity, empowerment, freedom from oppression, removal of barriers, or protection). When the target population includes diverse groups, change agents seek credible information from relevant people reflecting different perspectives.

2. Create a Condition (Problem) Statement: Based on information gathered from individuals in the community or organization, change agents identify what the community or organization views as its priority problem(s) and then develop a preliminary condition statement describing a target population, a geographical boundary, and the nature, size, and scope of the difficulty. This statement is refined later as new information emerges.

A "condition" is a harmful situation in a community or organization that has yet to be formally or publicly identified as a "problem." If a target condition is not formally recognized as a problem, then change agents must take steps to obtain this formal recognition because decision-makers won't allocate resources to resolving a problem if they don't recognize it.

3. Explore Relevant Literature and Collect Data: Interviewing informants and members of the target population allows change agents to initially frame the problem and formulate an initial condition (problem) statement. After this, change agents study the problem and the population more closely by exploring relevant theoretical and research literature (texts and journal articles). Change agents review this literature in order to (a) conceptualize the problem, (b) identify relevant theory related to the causes and consequences of the problem, (c) locate relevant quantitative data and other forms of information concerning the problem, (d) learn as much as possible about the population affected by the problem, (e) understand gender issues and cultures and ethnic groups affected by the problem, (f) locate demographic and other data about the community or organization, (g) create relevant maps of the community, and (h) locate data on how the problem has been addressed by the community or organization.

a. Study the Problem More Closely: Change agents read reports on empirical testing of theoretical and practice-related questions and evaluations of existing social services programs and examine frameworks that may be useful for understanding the problem. Gaining an understanding by conducting this research prepares change agents to collect supporting data.

b. Collect Supporting Data: Change agents collect statistical data and other supporting information to document the existence of the problem and clarify factors such as its size, scope, trends, etc. Their objective is to reach the point where the quantity and quality of their supportive data is sufficient to demonstrate why resources should be allocated to their cause. Supporting data may be obtained from census data, needs assessments, levels of demand for service as reported by agencies, rates of service, or data from hospitals, schools, police departments, etc. Obtaining data on the same problem at the county, state, or national level can provide a basis of comparison for the local data.

c. Study the Target Population More Closely: Change agents review available literature on the target population, study texts on human growth and development and human behavior in the social environment, and examine relevant racial, ethnic, and gender considerations. They weigh different theoretical perspectives carefully and choose the ones that best fit the population and setting, seem to have the most utility for explaining the relevant variables, and offer the widest range of testable hypotheses (possible interventions). Change agents evaluate each theory for potential biases and the extent to which it has been tested especially in relation to the problem and population being examined.

d. Study the Arena More Closely – Communities (Netting et al., 2004): In analyzing a community, change agents explore the following questions: What are the major social problems affecting the target population as perceived by its members; are there subgroups of the target population experiencing significant social problems; what priority is given to the needs of the target population; how do members of the target population perceive their community and its responsiveness to their needs; how many persons comprise the target population and what are their relevant characteristics (e.g., what percentage are people of color, ethnic group members, women, gay men or lesbians, older persons, or persons with disabilities); and what does available information show about quality-of-life factors as they affect the members of these groups?

Other specific considerations explored by change agents include the following:

Community values: In many modern communities, members don't share a single value system, and, in some communities, certain populations are valued more than others. Change agents examine the degree of fit between target population values and dominant community values and whether target population values are taken into consideration when decisions are made that affect them.

Community differences: Potential differences between the target population and other groups and within the target population include those based on culture, race, ethnicity, gender, age, social class, etc. Depending on the target population, certain "isms" – e.g., racism, sexism, ageism, ethnocentrism – may be relevant. Indicators of sensitivity to "differences" in a community include the level of involvement of people from different groups in decision-making and the availability of services and resources to these people.

Community structure: The specific structural domains (e.g., a school district, a mental health catchment area) analyzed by change agents depend on the problem and the needs of the target population. Aspects of community structure include the following:

Power: Change agents identify formal and informal leaders within the community and examine their effectiveness in achieving their goals. They also assess the political climate by determining what issues are competing for funding.

Resources available to the target population: Change agents consider both concrete (money, goods, services) and symbolic resources (support, status, information). King and Mayers (1984) recommend that change agents study each resource domain separately (health, welfare, education, housing, recreation, employment, business, religion, etc.), examining questions of policy, practice, eligibility, participation, and location to determine how available each resource is to the target population and assessing how programs within each domain relate to one another.

Service provision and service-delivery units: Change agents assess informal units (household units, neighborhood groups), what some authors call "mediating units" (self-help groups, grassroots associations, voluntary associations), and formal units (voluntary nonprofit agencies, for-profit agencies, public agencies).

Patterns of resource control and service delivery: Most communities will have horizontal relationships that connect informal and formal groups and organizations within the community, as well as vertical relationships that go beyond geographical boundaries. Forces outside the local community may have a substantial impact on decision-making and local conditions, including service distribution patterns.

Linkages between units: There may be competition and conflict between organizations within the community or, alternatively, organizations may relate to one another in constructive ways (i.e., communication, cooperation, coordination, collaboration, or consolidation).

Patterns and levels of citizen participation: Evaluating citizen participation is important because the power of controlling (decision-making) entities in a community often depends on the extent of citizen participation. Change agents should be aware, however, that citizen participation often involves groups who disagree with one another.

e. *Study the Arena More Closely – Organizations* (Netting et al., 2004): Organizations are linked to the external environment – they are in constant interaction with other systems in their social environment (task environment), including individuals, groups, other organizations, and communities. Change agents attempt to understand these external elements affecting the organization as well as the organization's internal structure and functioning. They approach each element in terms of its relationship to the identified problem, attempting to understand how interactions among the elements influence continuation of the problem.

Change agents usually seek information from board members (if the agency is private) or the person to whom the organization's CEO is accountable (if the agency is public), as well as from other organizational personnel.

Specific areas explored by change agents include the following:

Funding and other resources: An organization's decisions on how to spend funds may rest primarily with its funding sources. A governmental agency that depends solely on direct appropriations usually will have most of its activities rigidly specified by public policy. A nonprofit agency may have greater flexibility because it tends to receive funds from a wider variety of sources, but even donated funds usually come with conditions attached. A for-profit agency that depends on paying clients will have more flexibility than a public agency, but its decision-making is heavily guided by the need to make a profit for its investors. An organization's behaviors may also be influenced by its efforts to acquire noncash resources, such as volunteers, in-kind contributions (donations of food, clothing, facilities, vehicles, office equipment, etc.), and tax benefits.

Relationships with clients: Change agents compare demographics of the organization's clients with those of the target population and examine whether the organization's clients are generally full-pay or non-full-pay.

Relationships with referral sources: Change agents assess the organization's formal and informal referral arrangements with other agencies for exchanging clients.

Relationships with other service providers: Change agents assess how the organization relates to other agencies in its task environment. They recognize that relationships among organizations in the same task environment can be competitive, cooperative, or both. For instance, competitive relationships may occur when the organization is competing with other agencies for the same resources from the same sources. Productive relationships with other agencies may take the form of communication, cooperation, coordination, collaboration, or consolidation.

Relationships with other elements in the task environment: Agencies providing social services interact with clients, funding sources, legislative and regulatory agencies, politicians, community leaders, and other social service agencies. Change agents are concerned with all external elements that establish the context in which the organization operates and the regulatory boundaries for its practices. These elements may include government contracting agencies that require a provider organization to follow procedural guidelines in order to be reimbursed for services, regulatory bodies, professional associations, accrediting bodies, state licensing agencies, labor unions, and the general public. Public opinion is shaped and conveyed through elected officials, interest groups, civic organizations, and the media. Change agents assess how the organization is perceived by these elements (e.g., is the organization considered a valued member of the community service network or is it seen as self-serving?).

Mission statement: A lack of clarity in the organization's mission statement or differences between its mission and its activities may be indicators of a problem.

Program structure: Relevant questions include whether the structure is rigid or flexible, whether it is appropriate to the needs of the organization or program, whether communication comes primarily from higher levels of the organization or flows in all directions, whether staff are competent to do the jobs expected of them, and whether supervision is sufficient.

Administration, management, and leadership style: Relevant questions to explore include how organizational goals are established, where program-level decisions are made, how information flows through the organization, and who provides feedback about performance.

Programs and services: Ideally the organization will have a written plan that provides explicit guidelines for its programs and services and is used as a standard against which its programs are evaluated. Relevant questions to explore include whether services are consistent with the goals and objectives of the program; whether staffing patterns are appropriate to the services provided; whether workload expectations are reasonable; whether management and line staff understand in the same way the problems to be addressed, the populations to be served, the services to be provided, and the client outcomes to be achieved; and whether there are established standards for the quality of services.

Personnel policies, procedures, and practices: Information about an organization's effectiveness in these areas can be found by examining its manual of personnel policies and procedures, human resource plan, statistics on absenteeism and turnover, and grievances and complaints filed with the human resource department.

Budgeting, facilities, and equipment: Relevant issues to explore include the organization's approach to budgeting and accountability; whether program staff are allowed to provide input concerning budgeting; whether resources appear to be adequate to achieve program goals and objectives; whether staff get useful feedback about spending and unit costs during the year; the quantity of space, physical maintenance of facilities, and geographical location of the organization; and the availability of computers, Internet access, and management information systems.

4. Prepare Collected Data for Presentation: To build support for the change, change agents will need to present the data they've accumulated to decision-makers, and, ideally, their presentation will succinctly demonstrate the need for change and be easily understood by their audience.

Techniques available for collecting and displaying data include cross-sectional analysis, time-series comparisons, comparison with relevant data from databases maintained by federal, state, and local agencies, epidemiological analysis, and standard comparisons. Comparative data are generally more useful than a single statistic. **Cross-sectional analysis** provides several perspectives on a single population at a specific point in time; it does not reveal changes over time. The data collection may sometimes be **retrospective**, which involves asking people to reflect back on their past experiences and attitudes. A **time-series comparison** provides data from repeated observations over time. It displays trends in the variable(s) of interest which can help predict future needs and cost based on assumptions about these trends. **Standard comparisons** are used when other comparative data are not available. A "standard" is a measure or criterion accepted by recognized authorities that is regularly used and has a permanent status.

Develop a Working Hypothesis of Etiology About the Problem

Etiology refers to "the underlying causes of a problem or disorder" (Barker, 2003, p. 149). Therefore, speculating about etiology is an effort to understand cause-and-effect relationships.

1. Review the Analyses and Select Key Factors Explaining the Problem: Change agents identify the major concepts, issues, and perspectives found in their analyses of the problem, population, and arena and look for patterns of events, behaviors, or factors that appear to be associated. They then develop statements listing the key contributing factors and speculate about effects or results arising from each factor. This process helps focus the change effort on a manageable number of factors and identifies which factors seem, at this point, to be the most sensible ones to address in the intervention.

Usually change agents find multiple contributing factors for a community or organizational problem, as well as multiple perspectives about what is relevant to the current situation. For example, while several different explanations of cause and effect may be "correct," they might apply to different groups within the population. Rather than trying to select one "correct" point of view on etiology, change agents would instead choose a subgroup to address (e.g., they would elect to focus on adolescents at risk for dropping out of high school because of bullying; and they would not include adolescents facing this risk because of other factors such as discord at home).

Although resource deficits are usually a factor, change agents also consider fundamental causal or contributing factors – ones that explain why the problem emerged, why it has persisted, and what has prevented progress toward solutions.

2. Prepare a Hypothesis of Etiology Based on the Above Review: Only information relevant to the change effort is retained at this point. Change agents identify the most significant contributing factors that have resulted in the need for change and distill these into a final working hypothesis of etiology. The result is a working statement that expresses an acceptable degree of consensus concerning what participants see as the cause-and-effect relationships and how they apply to the need for change.

Appendix I: Descriptions of Common Medical Disorders and Diseases

Psychophysiological Disorders

The psychophysiological disorders are characterized by physical symptoms that are caused, maintained, or exacerbated by emotional factors.

1. Hypertension: There are two types of hypertension. Primary (essential) hypertension is diagnosed when high blood pressure is not due to a known physiological cause, while secondary hypertension is diagnosed when elevated blood pressure is related to a known disease. Untreated essential hypertension can lead to cardiovascular disease and is a major cause of heart failure, kidney failure, and stroke. Factors linked with an increased risk for essential hypertension include obesity, cigarette smoking, excessive use of table salt, stress, and older age. Essential hypertension tends to run in families and is more common in men than women and in African-Americans than whites.

2. Fibromyalgia: Fibromyalgia involves general muscle aches, tenderness, and stiffness, fatigue, and sleep disturbances. The condition is more common in women than men and occurs most often in middle-age. Although fibromyalgia may have a physical cause, psychological factors also play a role, and symptoms are often alleviated to some degree by psychological (especially cognitive-behavioral) treatments.

3. Migraine Headaches: Migraine headaches are severe, recurrent throbbing headaches that are usually limited to one side of the head and often accompanied by nausea, vomiting, diarrhea or constipation, and sensitivity to light, noise, and odors. Migraines are precipitated or aggravated by a broad range of factors including menstruation, stress and relaxation after stress, changes in barometric pressure, alcohol, decongestant and analgesic overuse, and certain foods (especially those containing tyramine, phenylethylamine, or nitrates). The etiology of migraine headache is not entirely understood, but it is believed to be related to the constriction and dilation of blood vessels in the brain. In addition, recent research links it to low serotonin levels (e.g., Johnson et al., 1998). Treatments include nonsteroidal anti-inflammatory drugs (a combination of acetaminophen, aspirin, and caffeine is particularly effective), drugs that act on certain serotonin receptors (e.g., SSRIs), and beta-blockers.

4. Bronchial Asthma: Bronchial asthma is caused by a narrowing of the airways leading to the lungs and is characterized by attacks of wheezing, coughing, and gasping. This response is triggered by the parasympathetic nervous system. The cause of asthma varies from person to person but often involves both physical and psychological factors. Allergens (e.g., pollen, dairy products, shellfish) and infections are the most common physical causes; psychological factors include anxiety, anger, and other strong emotional reactions.

Neurological Disorders

1. Traumatic Brain Injury: Traumatic brain injury (TBI) refers to an injury to the brain that is caused by an external force and involves temporary or permanent impairments in cognitive, emotional, behavioral, and/or physical functioning. It can be due to an open-head or closed-head injury. Open-head injuries occur when the skull is penetrated (e.g., by gunshot). In contrast to closed-head injuries, open-head injuries do not usually cause a loss of consciousness, and they produce highly specific symptoms that often have a rapid, spontaneous recovery. Closed-head injuries result from a blow to the head and usually cause an alteration or loss of consciousness followed by anterograde and retrograde amnesia. Anterograde amnesia is referred to as post-traumatic amnesia, and its duration is a good predictor of recovery. Retrograde amnesia affects recent memories more than remote memories and, when long-term memories begin to return, the more remote memories return first.

2. Broca's Aphasia and Wernicke's Aphasia: Damage or injury to certain parts of the cerebral cortex may result in language difficulties. The frontal lobe contains Broca's area, which is involved in speech production; damage produces Broca's (expressive) aphasia, which is characterized by difficulties in producing spoken and written language. The temporal lobe contains Wernicke's area, which is involved in the comprehension of language; lesions produce Wernicke's (receptive) aphasia, which is characterized by severe deficits in language comprehension and abnormalities in language production.

3. Cerebral Stroke: The term "stroke" is used to describe a sudden or gradual onset of neurological symptoms resulting from disruption in the blood supply to the brain. The major risk factors for stroke are hypertension and atherosclerosis (thickening of the lining of the arterial walls). Other factors that increase the risk include atrial fibrillation, myocardial infarction, diabetes mellitus, cigarette smoking, and increasing age (risk increases rapidly after age 60). Symptoms of stroke depend on the location and extent of the damage.

4. Injury to the Spinal Cord: The consequences of injury to the spinal cord depend on its location and extent. Damage at the cervical level ordinarily results in quadriplegia (loss of sensory and voluntary motor functioning in the arms and legs), while damage at the thoracic level causes paraplegia (loss of functioning in the legs). Injury can also be either complete or incomplete. A complete transection of the spinal cord produces a lack of sensation and voluntary movement below the level of injury. When the injury is incomplete, some sensory and motor functions below the level of injury are maintained.

5. Huntington's Disease and Parkinson's Disease: Huntington's disease and Parkinson's disease both result from damage to the motor areas of the brain. In **Huntington's disease**, emotional and cognitive symptoms often appear first (e.g., depression, anxiety, forgetfulness); early motor symptoms include fidgeting and clumsiness; later motor symptoms include slow, writhing movements and involuntary rapid, jerky movements (chorea); over time, cognitive impairments progress to deficits in planning, problem-solving, and decision-making, and, eventually, to dementia. Symptoms of **Parkinson's disease** include tremor at rest, muscle rigidity, akathisia ("cruel restlessness"), postural disturbances, slowed movement, speech difficulties, and a mask-like facial expression. Up to half of people with Parkinson's also experience prominent symptoms of depression at some time during their illness (Cummings, 1992).

6. Seizure Disorders (Epilepsy): A seizure is due to abnormal electrical activity in the brain that causes one or more of the following symptoms: an aura that signals the onset of the seizure (e.g., a "feeling," odor, or noise); a loss of consciousness; and some type of abnormal movement. Tonic-clonic (grand mal) seizures include a tonic stage in which the muscles contract and the body stiffens; a clonic stage that involves rhythmic shaking of the limbs; and postictal (postseizure) depression or confusion with amnesia for the seizure event. Absence (petit mal) seizures are brief attacks involving a loss of consciousness without prominent motor symptoms.

Disorders of the Endocrine System

The endocrine system consists of glands that produce hormones. A number of disorders are associated with abnormalities in hormonal output, and many have both physical and psychological symptoms. (Too little output of a hormone is termed hyposecretion, and too much output is termed hypersecretion.)

1. Pituitary Gland: The pituitary gland secretes antidiuretic hormone (ADH) and somatotropic (growth) hormone. Hyposecretion of ADH produces **diabetes insipidus** (excessive water loss). Hyposecretion of somatotropic hormone in childhood produces dwarfism, while hypersecretion results in giantism. Hypersecretion in adulthood causes acromegaly, which is characterized by grossly enlarged hands, feet, and facial features.

2. Thyroid Gland: The primary secretion of the thyroid gland is thyroxine, which regulates general metabolism. Hyposecretion produces **hypothyroidism**, which involves slowed metabolism, reduced appetite with weight gain, slowed heart rate, lowered body temperature, lethargy, depression, decreased libido, apathy, confusion, and impaired concentration and memory. Hypersecretion produces **hyperthyroidism** (**Grave's Disease**), a disorder characterized by speeded-up metabolism, elevated body temperature, heat intolerance, increased appetite with weight loss, accelerated heart rate, nervousness, agitation, emotional lability, fatigue, insomnia, and reduced attention span.

3. Pancreas: The pancreas releases insulin which is involved in the uptake and use of glucose and amino acids. Hyperinsulinism causes **hypoglycemia** (low blood sugar), a disorder involving hunger, dizziness, headaches, blurred vision, palpitations, anxiety, depression, and confusion.

Hypoinsulinism produces **diabetes mellitus** (excessive blood glucose). Diabetes mellitus is often referred to as simply "diabetes." Forms of diabetes include type 1 diabetes, type 2 diabetes, and gestational diabetes.

a. Type 1 Diabetes: **Type 1 diabetes** is an autoimmune disorder which is a type of disease that develops when the body's immune system turns against a part of the body. In the case of type 1 diabetes, the immune system attacks and destroys the insulin-producing beta cells in the pancreas, so that the pancreas then produces little or no insulin. Symptoms of type 1 diabetes usually develop quickly and may include increased thirst and urination, constant hunger, weight loss, blurred vision, extreme fatigue, apathy, confusion, and mental dullness.

People with type 1 diabetes must take insulin every day in order to avoid a life-threatening diabetic coma ("diabetic ketoacidosis"). Taking too much insulin, however, as well as not eating enough food or exercising more than usual, can cause a person's blood sugar level to drop rapidly, resulting in low blood sugar (hypoglycemia). Type 1 diabetes occurs most often in children and young adults, but can develop at any age.

b. Type 2 Diabetes: **Type 2 diabetes** is the most common form of diabetes – 90 to 95 percent of people with diabetes have type 2. When type 2 diabetes is first diagnosed, the pancreas is usually producing sufficient insulin, but the body is unable to use the insulin effectively ("insulin resistance"). After several years, insulin production decreases, and the result is the same as for type 1 diabetes – glucose builds up in the blood and the body can't make efficient use of its primary source of energy.

The symptoms of type 2 diabetes develop gradually and may include fatigue, nausea, frequent urination, increased thirst, weight loss, blurred vision, frequent infections, slow healing of wounds, and cognitive symptoms similar to those found in type 1 diabetes. Some people, however, have no symptoms.

Type 2 diabetes is associated with older age (but it is increasingly being diagnosed in children and adolescents), obesity (about 80 percent of people with type 2 diabetes are overweight), family history of diabetes (particularly women with this history), previous history of gestational diabetes, and low levels of physical activity. In addition, type 2 diabetes occurs more often in African-Americans, American Indians, and Hispanic Americans.

c. Gestational Diabetes: Women who are diagnosed with diabetes before they become pregnant have a higher risk of complications and usually require close medical management before, during, and after pregnancy. Most cases of diabetes during pregnancy involve gestational diabetes, however, a form of diabetes that begins or is first diagnosed during pregnancy. Women with gestational diabetes must monitor and manage their blood glucose levels and run the risk of developing diabetes after pregnancy. Uncontrolled diabetes can result in miscarriage, fetal death, and birth defects.

HIV/AIDS

Human immunodeficiency virus (HIV) is the causative agent of AIDS (acquired immune deficiency syndrome). HIV is a sexually transmitted disease (STD). It can also be spread by contact with infected blood or from a mother to her child during pregnancy, childbirth, or breast-feeding. The risk to the baby is significantly reduced if the mother receives treatment for HIV infection during pregnancy.

1. HIV Risk Factors: Anyone of any age, gender, or sexual orientation can become infected with HIV, but individuals with one or more of the following risk factors are at a much higher risk:

Having unprotected sex: Unprotected sex means having sex without using a new latex or polyurethane condom. Anal sex is more risky than vaginal sex. The risk increases for individuals who have multiple sexual partners.

Having another STD: Many sexually transmitted diseases produce open sores on the genitals. These sores act as doorways for HIV to enter the body.

Using intravenous drugs: People who use intravenous drugs often share needles and syringes, which exposes them to other people's blood.

2. HIV's Effects on the Body: HIV infects immune system cells needed to fight disease. Several cell types can become infected by HIV, but the most important ones belong to the immune system. HIV belongs to a group of viruses known as retroviruses. Like other viruses, retroviruses enter, infect, and take over host cells, but they do so in a different way, a way that makes them more difficult to understand and treat.

Over time HIV disables the body's immune system, which places the infected person at high risk for a variety of **opportunistic infections**, including Kaposi's sarcoma (a form of cancer), lymphoma, pneumonia, and a number of serious fungal, viral, and bacterial infections. HIV can also affect the central nervous system and cause neurological symptoms such as confusion, forgetfulness, depression, anxiety, and trouble walking. One of the most common neurological complications of HIV disease is **AIDS dementia complex**, which results in behavioral changes and diminished mental functioning (in the DSM-5, this is called neurocognitive disorder due to HIV disease). People with HIV are also susceptible to **wasting syndrome**, which is defined as a loss of at least 10 percent of body weight and is often accompanied by diarrhea, chronic weakness, and fever.

Although there are a few reported cases of remission in people who have tested HIV-positive, so far, the majority of individuals infected with the human immunodeficiency virus have eventually developed AIDS.

3. Stages of HIV Disease: Most adults infected by HIV pass through four stages of infection, which are described below.

a. Acute Infection: HIV disease begins when the virus enters the body and begins to establish itself inside immune system cells, forcing them to make viral copies. Just after infection, the body reacts with an acute HIV symptom illness ("primary HIV infection") and/or with an immune response against the virus. The appearance of HIV antibodies signals seroconversion; after seroconversion, HIV antibodies are detectable in a person's blood or saliva. A common way of diagnosing HIV is an HIV antibody test, in which a sample of blood or saliva is tested for the presence of HIV antibodies. It usually takes up to 12 weeks for the body to develop HIV antibodies after exposure to the virus, and, in rare cases, it can take up to six months for an HIV antibody test to become positive. A newer type of test checks for HIV antigen, a protein produced by the virus immediately after infection. This test can confirm a diagnosis within days of infection.

b. Asymptomatic Infection: This period may last from six months to 10 years or longer (especially with advances in medical treatments for HIV disease). The infected person has no symptoms and can carry on with her life as usual, but the virus is still damaging her immune system.

c. Chronic or Symptomatic Phase: It is in this phase that illness symptoms begin to appear. HIV-associated symptoms in this phase (called "early symptoms of HIV disease") may include fever, unintentional weight loss, chronic fatigue, chronic diarrhea, skin conditions, and thrush (infection of the mouth and throat). Since these symptoms appear after the immune system has been impaired, they may be accompanied by infections caused by bacteria, fungi, or parasites. If these infections are not progressive, however, they are not considered part of an AIDS diagnosis.

d. AIDS: Although the majority of HIV-infected people progress to AIDS, advances in medical treatments against HIV and in medications to fight opportunistic infections have made it possible for many people to live much longer without acquiring AIDS and for those who already have AIDS to survive longer.

Generally, AIDS begins when the immune system has degenerated to a point where the body can no longer protect itself from disease: When the immune system has been sufficiently impaired by HIV, certain viruses, bacteria, fungi, and protozoa that do not endanger a healthy body become capable of causing serious illnesses. These diseases are known as **opportunistic infections** because they take advantage of a compromised immune system that is no longer able to fight them off. Signs and symptoms of common opportunistic infections include soaking night sweats, shaking chills or fever higher than 100F for several weeks, cough and shortness of breath, chronic diarrhea, persistent white spots or unusual lesions on the tongue or in the mouth, headaches, persistent and unexplained fatigue, blurred and distorted vision, weight loss, and skin rashes or bumps.

To be actually diagnosed with AIDS, a person must either experience an AIDS-defining illness or infection (e.g., pneumocystis jiroveci pneumonia, cytomegalovirus, tuberculosis, toxoplasmosis, cryptosporidiosis) *or* have a CD4 count under 200.

Finally, the last stage of AIDS (near death) generally occurs when the immune system cannot fight a persistent and progressive illness or infection that is no longer responding to available medical treatments.

4. Viral Load Tests and CD4 Counts: For people with HIV disease, viral load tests and CD4 counts are two important ways of monitoring their disease, guiding medical treatment, and predicting how their disease may progress.

- The HIV **viral load** is the number of copies of the human immunodeficiency virus in a person's blood and other parts of her body. Keeping the viral load *low* can reduce complications of HIV disease and extend a person's life.

- CD4 cells (also called T-helper cells) are a type of white blood cell that fights infection. The **CD4 count** measures the number of CD4 cells in a sample of blood and is a good indicator of how strong a person's immune system is. The CD4 count is also useful for identifying the stage of a person's HIV disease. Keeping the CD4 count *high* can reduce complications of HIV disease and extend a person's life.

5. Medication Taken By People With HIV Disease: A client with HIV disease may be taking many different medications including anti-HIV drugs ("HIV drugs") that treat the HIV infection, drugs that treat side-effects of the disease itself or side-effects of anti-HIV drugs, and/or drugs that treat opportunistic infections that have resulted from a weakened immune system.

So far, the FDA has approved dozens of anti-HIV medications to treat HIV infection. These medications, called **antiretroviral drugs**, help by both lowering a person's viral load and fighting infections. Patients must take all of their anti-HIV medication exactly as directed; if not, they may develop resistant strains (mutations) of HIV, which can cause the medication to stop working. Even when anti-HIV medications are effective, however, a person can still transmit HIV to others. These medications are not a cure for HIV disease.

a. Combination Therapies: Anti-HIV medications are developed to control the growth of the virus, improve overall immune system function and status, and suppress symptoms. To maximize their effectiveness at achieving these goals, doctors usually recommend that patients with HIV take a combination of anti-HIV drugs from at least two of the main classes (reverse transcriptase inhibitors, protease inhibitors, etc.). This combination is called **highly active antiretroviral therapy** (**HAART**). HAART helps combat new resistant strains of the virus that emerge as HIV makes copies of itself and also decreases the rate of opportunistic infections.

b. Antiretroviral Drug Side-Effects: Drugs used to treat HIV often have side-effects, especially when a person first starts using them. Examples include the following: (a) nausea and vomiting; (b) diarrhea (which needs to be managed by a medical professional if it lasts more than three days); (c) a rash (this may be a sign of an allergic reaction and should always be reported to a doctor immediately); (d) sleep disturbances; (e) pain, numbness, or tingling in the hands and feet (which is called peripheral neuropathy and needs to be reported to a doctor); (f) accumulation of fat on various parts of the body (called lipodystrophy syndrome); and (g) cholesterol and blood sugar changes (blood tests are required to monitor these). If a client with HIV disease reports troubling medication side-effects, you should encourage her to see her medical doctor. And, as indicated, certain side-effects would require the client to see her doctor as soon as she can.

Appendix II: Psychoactive Drugs and Their Uses and Side-Effects

Psychoactive (psychotropic) drugs are those agents that interact with the central nervous system in a way that produces changes in mood, consciousness, perception, and/or behavior. The psychoactive drugs exert their effects in various ways but all have one of two basic effects: They either increase or decrease the effectiveness of transmission at nerve synapses. Psychoactive drugs also have side-effects that may interfere with a person's physical, psychological, and/or social functioning or well-being. Uses of and potential side-effects of many of these drugs are reviewed below.

Antipsychotic Drugs

The antipsychotic drugs are also known as major tranquilizers and neuroleptics.

1. First Generation Antipsychotics: First generation antipsychotics include thiothixene (Narvane); **haloperidol** (**Haldol**); and fluphenazine (Permitil and **Prolixin**) and chlorpromazine (**Thorazine**), which are phenothiazines. The first generation antipsychotics are also known as "typical," "traditional," or "conventional" antipsychotics.

a. Uses: The first generation antipsychotics are effective for alleviating psychotic symptoms and are most often prescribed as a treatment for schizophrenia. They are also used to treat acute mania, delusions and hallucinations associated with major depressive disorder, and organic psychoses. These drugs alleviate the positive symptoms of schizophrenia (hallucinations, delusions, agitation, etc.), but are much less effective for its negative symptoms (i.e., apathy, blunted affect, autism, and social withdrawal).

Generally, as a treatment for schizophrenia, first generation antipsychotics induce a **"neuroleptic state"** characterized by the following (Buelow & Hebert, 1995): psychomotor slowing (reduced agitation, impulsivity, and aggressiveness); emotional quieting (decreased hallucinations and delusions); and affective indifference (decreased arousability and lack of concern with the external environment).

b. Side-Effects: The first generation antipsychotic drugs are associated with a number of undesirable side-effects.

- **Anticholinergic** side-effects include dry mouth, blurred vision, tachycardia, urinary retention, constipation, and delayed ejaculation. These effects appear early, and tolerance ordinarily develops within a few weeks or months.

- The most common **extrapyramidal** side-effects are Parkinsonism, akathisia (extreme motor restlessness), and acute dystonia (muscle spasms in the mouth, face, and neck). **Tardive dyskinesia**, the most serious extrapyramidal effect, is late occurring and more common in females and older adults. Its symptoms include involuntary rhythmic movements of the jaw, lips, tongue, and extremities. Although tardive dyskinesia has traditionally been viewed as irreversible, more recent studies indicate that this is not true for all people. For many people, symptoms eventually improve when the drug is gradually withdrawn (although there may be an initial worsening of symptoms). In addition, tardive dyskinesia may be alleviated to some degree by administering a **benzodiazepine** or other GABA agonist.

- A rare, but potentially fatal side-effect is **neuroleptic malignant syndrome** (NMS). NMS is characterized by a rapid onset of motor, mental, and autonomic symptoms including muscle rigidity, tachycardia, hyperthermia, and altered consciousness. To avoid a potentially fatal outcome, the drug must be stopped as soon as symptoms of NMS develop.

- Seizures are a rare but dangerous side-effect associated with Prolixin (fluphenazine). Physicians advise individuals taking Prolixin to stop taking the medication and seek medical attention immediately if they experience a seizure. In general, Prolixin is less sedating than many other antipsychotics, but has more movement side-effects.

2. Second Generation Antipsychotics: Examples of second generation (a.k.a. "atypical" or "novel") antipsychotics include **clozapine**/trade name **Clozaril**; **resperidone**/trade name **Risperdal**; olanzapine/trade name Zyprexa; quetiapine/trade name Seroquel; and aripiprazole/trade name **Abilify**.

a. Uses: A disadvantage of the second generation antipsychotics is that they may have a slower onset of therapeutic effects than the traditional antipsychotics do.

- The second generation antipsychotics are used to treat schizophrenia and other disorders with psychotic symptoms. An advantage of the second generation antipsychotics is that they alleviate both the positive and negative symptoms of schizophrenia. In addition, they can be effective in cases in which first generation antipsychotics have failed. **Clozaril/clozapine**, for example, can be used when a severely ill person with schizophrenia hasn't responded adequately to conventional drug treatment for the disorder due to insufficient effectiveness or inability to achieve an effective dose because of intolerable side-effects. Due to the high risk of agranulocytosis (a blood disorder) and seizure associated with its use, however, Clozaril should be used only in individuals who have failed to respond adequately to conventional drug treatments.

- Clozaril/clozapine has also been found useful for treating alcohol and drug addictions, as well as bipolar disorder that hasn't responded to a mood stabilizer. It is also used to treat the motor symptoms of movement disorders such as Parkinson's disease.

- Risperdal/resperidone is approved by the FDA for the symptomatic treatment of irritability (e.g., sudden mood changes, tantrums, aggression, self-injury) in adolescents with autism and children over age 5 with autism.

- Abilify/aripiprazole may be used as an add-on treatment for depression when antidepressants have been ineffective by themselves.

b. Side-Effects:

- Common side-effects include anticholinergic effects (e.g., blurred vision, dry eyes, constipation, and urinary retention), lowered seizure threshold, and sedation.

- Compared to first generation antipsychotics, extrapyramidal side-effects (except for akathisia) are less common. In fact, an important advantage of the second generation drugs is that they are less likely to cause tardive dyskinesia.

- These drugs can produce **agranulocytosis** (loss of the white blood cells that fight infection) and other **blood dyscrasias**, and, consequently, their use requires careful blood monitoring.

- Like the traditional antipsychotics, they may cause **neuroleptic malignant syndrome**.

Antidepressant Drugs

The antidepressant drugs include the tricyclics, the SSRIs, the MAOIs, and several other types that have been introduced more recently and are also described below.

With children and adolescents, antidepressants (SSRIs, TCAs, MAOIs) must be used with extreme caution due to concerns about behavioral side-effects (particularly increased risk of suicide) in young people who take these medications. If antidepressant medications are necessary to treat a severely depressed child or adolescent, the risk of suicide should be frequently monitored.

1. Tricyclics: The tricyclics (TCAs) include amitriptyline (Elavil, Endep), doxepin (Sinequan, Adapin), imipramine (Tofranil), and clomipramine (Anafranil).

a. Uses: It takes two to four weeks for TCAs to exert their therapeutic effects.

- The TCAs are most effective for depressions that involve decreased appetite and weight loss, early morning awakening and other sleep disturbances, psychomotor retardation, and anhedonia. They are particularly useful for alleviating the vegetative, somatic symptoms of depression.

- The TCAs are also used for panic disorder, agoraphobia, bulimia, and obsessive-compulsive disorder, especially clomipramine (Anafranil); and for enuresis in children and adolescents, especially imipramine (Tofranil).

b. Side-Effects: Many of the adverse effects of the TCAs are more common in older adults, and most can be alleviated by lowering the dosage level.

- The primary side-effects are cardiovascular symptoms (see below), anticholinergic effects (e.g., dry mouth, blurred vision, urinary retention, constipation, sexual dysfunction), confusion, drowsiness, fatigue, weight gain, fine tremor, paresthesia, and blood dyscrasia.

- The TCAs are **cardiotoxic**, producing such cardiovascular symptoms as tachycardia, palpitations, hypertension, severe hypotension (drop in blood pressure), and cardiac arrhythmia. For this reason, they must be used with caution with people suffering from heart disease.

- Symptoms of tricyclic overdose include ataxia (loss of muscle control during voluntary movements such as walking), impaired concentration, agitation, severe hypotension, fever, cardiac arrhythmia, delirium, seizures, and coma. Because an overdose can be lethal, the tricyclics should be prescribed in small quantities for individuals at high risk for suicide.

2. SSRIs: Examples of SSRIs (selective serotonin reuptake inhibitors) include fluoxetine (Prozac), citalopram (Celexa), fluvoxamine (Floxyfral), paroxetine (Paxil, Pexeva), sertraline

(Zoloft), and escitalopram (Lexapro). The SSRIs are the most commonly prescribed antidepressants and exert their effects by blocking the reuptake of serotonin.

a. *Uses:*

- The SSRIs are used to treat moderate to severe depression.

- Several of the SSRIs are also prescribed for obsessive-compulsive disorder, bulimia, panic disorder, and posttraumatic stress disorder (PTSD), and escitalopram (Lexapro) is effective for treating symptoms of generalized anxiety disorder.

- Citalopram (Celexa) is also effective for relieving symptoms of anxiety.

- Studies have found that, for people with autism, certain antidepressants – including **fluoxetine** (**Prozac**) and the TCA clomipramine (Anafranil) – may reduce the frequency and intensity of repetitive behaviors and decrease irritability, tantrums, and aggressive behavior. In some children with autism, these medications may also improve eye contact and responsiveness to others.

b. *Side-Effects:*

- Side-effects include gastrointestinal disturbances (e.g., nausea, appetite loss, constipation or diarrhea), insomnia, anxiety, headache, dizziness, anorexia, tremor, frequent urination, and **sexual dysfunction**. People taking escitalopram (Lexapro) may experience somnolence (prolonged drowsiness or sleepiness).

- Compared to tricyclic antidepressants, SSRIs are associated with several advantages: They are less cardiotoxic, safer in overdose, less likely to produce cognitive impairment, and have a more rapid onset (Gelder et al., 1996).

- Use of an SSRI in conjunction with an MAOI or other serotonergic agent may result in a serious condition called **serotonin syndrome**. Symptoms include neurological effects (headache, nystagmus [involuntary eye movement], tremor, dizziness, unsteady gait), changes in mental state (irritability, confusion, delirium), and cardiac arrhythmia and can progress to coma and death.

3. MAOIs: Examples of MAOIs (monoamine oxidase inhibitors) include isocarboxazid (Marplan), phenelzine (Nardil), and tranylcypromine (Parnate).

a. *Uses:* The MAOIs are most effective for treating nonendogenous and atypical depressions that involve anxiety, reversed vegetative symptoms (e.g., hypersomnia), and interpersonal sensitivity.

b. *Side-Effects:*

- Side-effects of MAOIs include anticholinergic effects (e.g., dry mouth, blurred vision, nausea, constipation, sexual dysfunction), insomnia, agitation, confusion, skin rash, weight gain, edema, headache, dizziness, tremor, blood dyscrasia, and hypertensive crisis.

- The most dangerous side-effect is **hypertensive crisis**, which can occur when an MAOI is taken in conjunction with barbiturates, amphetamines, antihistamines, or certain other drugs or with foods containing the amino acid tyramine (e.g., aged cheeses and meats, beer, red wine, chicken liver, avocados, bananas, fava beans).

4. Newer Antidepressants: There is evidence that the newer antidepressants are comparable to the TCAs and SSRIs in terms of effectiveness but differ in terms of some side-effects (AHRQ, 2007; APA, 2000): (a) Venlafaxine (Effexor), desvenlafaxine (Pristiq), and duloxetine (Cymbalta), are serotonin norepinephrine reuptake inhibitors (SNRIs) that increase the levels of both norepinephrine and serotonin. (b) **Bupropion** (**Wellbutrin**) is a norepinephrine dopamine reuptake inhibitor (NDRI) used to treat major depression and the depressive phase of bipolar disorder. Under the name Zyban, this medication is used to facilitate smoking cessation.

Mood Stabilizing Drugs

The mood stabilizing drugs include lithium and carbamazepine.

1. Lithium:

a. Uses: Lithium has long been considered the drug-of-choice for the treatment of bipolar disorder. It not only reduces or eliminates manic symptoms but also suppresses mood swings.

b. Side-Effects:

- Early side-effects of lithium include nausea, fine hand tremor, polyuria, and polydipsia. These effects usually subside within a few weeks.

- The major danger of lithium use is **toxicity**, which results when the dose is too high. Initial signs of toxicity are diarrhea, nausea, vomiting, sedation, slurred speech, confusion, coarse tremor, and loss of coordination. Because severe toxicity can result in seizures, coma, and death, serum levels of lithium must be regularly monitored.

- The retention of lithium is affected by the body's sodium levels, and people taking this drug must be careful to avoid fluctuations in their salt intake and avoid caffeine, alcohol, and other diuretics.

- Lithium is contraindicated for people with cardiovascular, kidney, liver, thyroid, or gastrointestinal problems.

2. Carbamazepine: Carbamazepine (Tegretol) was initially used as an anticonvulsant drug but has also been found effective for mania. Other anticonvulsant drugs that are useful as mood stabilizers include valproic acid (Depakote), **clonazepam** (**Klonopin**), and lamotrigine (Lamictal).

a. Uses: Carbamazepine is an effective treatment for bipolar disorder, especially for people who have not responded to lithium. There is some evidence that it is more beneficial than lithium for those who experience frequent mood swings ("rapid cyclers") and those with dysphoric mania.

b. Side-Effects:

- Side-effects of carbamazepine include dizziness, ataxia, visual disturbances, anorexia, nausea, and skin rash, but tolerance for many of these symptoms develops fairly quickly.

- Because of its potential effects on cardiovascular functioning, carbamazepine is contraindicated for people with abnormalities in cardiac conduction.

- There is a slight risk for agranulocytosis and aplastic anemia, and careful blood monitoring is required.

Sedative-Hypnotics

The sedative-hypnotics include the barbiturates, anxiolytics, and alcohol. These drugs are generalized CNS depressants, and their effects, for the most part, are dose dependent: At low doses, these drugs reduce arousal and motor activity; at moderate doses, they induce sedation and sleep; and at high doses, they can produce anesthesia, coma, and death. Chronic use of a sedative-hypnotic produces tolerance and psychological and physical dependence, and abrupt cessation causes a **withdrawal syndrome** that is characterized by tremors, anxiety, nausea, vomiting, paranoia, and, in extreme cases, hallucinations, delirium, and life-threatening convulsive seizures. The effects of the sedative-hypnotics are synergistic: combining an anxiolytic with a barbiturate or alcohol can have lethal consequences because of the superadditive nature of their actions on the brain structures that control respiration.

1. Barbiturates: The barbiturates include amobarbital (Amytal), pentobarbital (Nembutal), secobarbital (Seconal), and phenobarbital (Luminal).

a. Uses: In the past, barbiturates were frequently used as sedatives and anesthetic agents, but due to recognition of their potentially lethal effects and the development of safer and more effective drugs, they are now infrequently prescribed. In young children, older adults, and people experiencing pain, the barbiturates sometimes produce paradoxical excitement.

b. Side-Effects: The barbiturates are a much abused class of drugs, and they are frequently involved in suicides and accidental deaths.

- Side-effects include slurred speech, nystagmus (involuntary eye movement), dizziness, irritability, and impaired motor and cognitive performance.

- Increasing the dose of a barbiturate to maintain its soporific (sleep-inducing) effects can have lethal results. An overdose can produce ataxia, confusion, agitation, respiratory depression, and death.

- When used to alleviate insomnia, the soporific effects of the barbiturates generally last for only a few weeks; after that, total sleep time may actually fall below the pre-drug level. Barbiturate use causes a decrease in REM sleep, and abrupt cessation can produce an REM rebound and nightmares.

- Withdrawal symptoms are generally severe and, without medical supervision, can be life threatening.

2. Anxiolytics: The anxiolytics (a.k.a. "minor tranquilizers" or "antianxiety drugs") are the most widely used psychiatric medication. Of the anxiolytics, the **benzodiazepines** are the most commonly prescribed. The benzodiazepines include diazepam (Valium), alprazolam (Xanax), oxazepam (Serax), triazolam (Halcion), chlordiazepoxide (Librium), lorazepam (Ativan), and temazepam (Restoril). The anticonvulsant (anti-seizure) medication clonazepam (Klonopin) is also a benzodiazepine. These medications exert their effects by stimulating the inhibitory action of the neurotransmitter GABA.

a. Uses: The benzodiazepines are prescribed primarily to relieve anxiety but are also used to treat sleep disturbances, seizures, cerebral palsy and other disorders involving muscle spasms, and alcohol withdrawal. For instance, temazepam (Restoril) and triazolam (Halcion) are frequently used for insomnia; and chlordiazepoxide (**Librium**) is often used for **alcohol withdrawal**.

The various benzodiazepines differ in how quickly they work –e.g., diazepam (Valium) has a rapid onset of action (within 15 minutes); oxazepam (Serax) has a slow onset (30 to 60 minutes); and lorazepam (Ativan), alprazolam (Xanax), and clonazepam (Klonopin) have intermediate onsets of action (15 to 30 minutes).

b. Side-Effects: The less severe side-effects of benzodiazepines are often alleviated by lowering the dosage level.

- The most common side-effects are drowsiness, lethargy, slurred speech, ataxia, and impaired psychomotor ability.

- Other effects include irritability, hostility, paradoxical excitation, increased appetite and weight gain, skin rash, blood dyscrasias, **impaired sexual functioning**, disorientation and confusion, sleep disturbances (e.g., reduced REM sleep), anterograde amnesia, and depression.

- The relaxation, euphoria, and sense of well-being produced by the benzodiazepines promote psychological dependence, and chronic use results in tolerance and physical dependence. Withdrawal symptoms can be severe, and abrupt cessation may induce rebound hyperexcitability, which can be accompanied by seizures, depersonalization, panic, and stroke.

- Certain benzodiazepines (e.g., Valium, Xanax) are associated with a significant overdose risk, and benzodiazepines are the most frequently used drug in overdoses.

Finally, when a benzodiazepine is taken daily, the amount of time it takes to achieve "steady state" ranges from one day to about three weeks. "**Steady state**" is the point at which the amount of a drug going into the body is the same as the amount being eliminated from the body – when a drug reaches steady state, its side-effects are diminished or completely absent.

3. Azapirone: Azapirone (buspirone, **Buspar**) is the first anxiolytic that reduces anxiety without sedation. It appears to be nonaddictive, not habit forming, and not subject to abuse. Unlike the benzodiazepines and similar anxiolytics, which can have immediate therapeutic effects, buspirone must be taken for several weeks before it is effective.

Beta-Blockers

Included in this category is **propranolol** (Inderal). Beta-blockers are used to treat high blood pressure, angina, and other cardiovascular disorders, tremors, migraine headache, and glaucoma. They have also been found useful for reducing the palpitations, tremor, excessive sweating, and other physical symptoms associated with anxiety.

Side-effects of propranolol include bradycardia, shortness of breath, arterial insufficiency (usually of the Raynaud's type), nausea, depression, and dizziness. Propranolol is potentially lethal for people with certain respiratory problems and should not be prescribed for those with obstructive pulmonary disease. In addition, propranolol and other beta-blockers should not be discontinued abruptly because doing so can cause sweating, palpitations, headache, tremulousness, and cardiac arrhythmias.

Narcotic-Analgesics

Narcotic-analgesics (**opioids**) have both sedative and analgesic properties. Examples of narcotic-analgesics include opium, morphine, codeine, fentanyl, hydrocodone, hydromorphone (Dilaudid), oxycodone (OxyContin, Percocet), Demerol, Vicodin, Norco, and Percodan.

Medically, narcotic-analgesics are commonly used as analgesics to treat moderate to severe pain; they may also be prescribed as treatments for diarrhea and cough suppressants. Their immediate effect is a short-lived "rush" or sense of euphoria. This effect is usually followed by a feeling of tranquility, drowsiness, apathy, decreased physical activity, and impaired attention and memory.

Common physical signs of narcotic-analgesic use include constricted pupils, increased perspiration, constipation, nausea, vomiting, and respiratory depression. **Overdose** (toxicity) can produce slow and shallow breathing, muscle rigidity, clammy skin, decreased blood pressure and pulse rate, convulsions, coma, and death.

Chronic use of a narcotic-analgesic results in tolerance and psychological and physical dependence. Users of these drugs often develop psychological dependence first as a result of the euphoria produced by the drug. By the time this effect has diminished, physical dependence has developed, and users continue taking the drug to avoid withdrawal. Withdrawal symptoms resemble those associated with a bad case of the flu and include stomach cramps, nausea, vomiting, weakness, fever, muscle and joint pain, sweating, and insomnia.

Psychostimulants

Included in this category are the amphetamines and methylphenidate. Amphetamines are used to treat narcolepsy and attention-deficit/hyperactivity disorder (ADHD); and **methylphenidate** (**Ritalin**, Concerta) is used to treat ADHD in both children and adults. Other specific medications used to treat ADHD include the amphetamines Dexedrine and **Adderall** and methamphetamine (Desoxyn). The apparent paradoxical effects of central nervous system stimulants on children with hyperactivity was once used as evidence that hyperactivity is due to certain physiological factors but studies have shown that people without ADHD have similar reactions to the low doses prescribed for the disorder.

Common side-effects of amphetamines include restlessness, insomnia, poor appetite, tremor, palpitations, and cardiac arrhythmia. Repeated use produces tolerance and dependence and can also result in sensitization, which is basically the opposite of tolerance and involves a greater behavioral response to the drug than occurs when it is used intermittently. Prolonged use of an amphetamine can lead to a psychotic state that resembles schizophrenia.

Side-effects of **methylphenidate** include dysphoria (anxiety, irritability, depression, euphoria, sadness), nausea and abdominal pain, decreased appetite, and insomnia. Higher doses of the drug may cause growth suppression, although the research has found that this effect is temporary and adult height and weight are usually unaffected (Taylor, 1994). Occasional "drug holidays" (e.g., during school vacations) can be used to minimize growth suppression and other adverse side-effects and confirm that the drug is still needed. An important limitation of methylphenidate is that symptoms quickly return when the drug is discontinued. In addition, methylphenidate is contraindicated for individuals with anxiety and tension, anorexia, severe hypertension or angina pectoris, a history of functional psychosis, a recent history of drug or alcohol abuse or pre-existing motor tics, or a family history of Tourette's syndrome.

Finally, the stimulant drug pemoline/**Cylert** was once used to treat ADHD but was taken off the U.S. market in 2005 because it can result in rare but serious side-effects, including liver (hepatic) failure.

Strattera

Atomoxetine hydrochloride (**Strattera**), a norepinephrine reuptake inhibitor, is a *nonstimulant* medication approved by the FDA for the treatment of attention-deficit/hyperactivity disorder (ADHD) in children, adolescents, and adults. Common side-effects in children and teenagers include mood swings, tiredness, dizziness, nausea or vomiting, and deceased appetite. Additionally, there is an increased risk of suicidal thinking in children and adolescents taking Strattera, and youth taking this drug must be monitored closely. Side-effects in adults include sexual dysfunction, constipation, dry mouth, nausea, decreased appetite, dizziness, insomnia, and problems passing urine.